NAPOLEON'S
WATERLOO CAMPAIGN:
AN ALTERNATE HISTORY

NAPOLEON'S WATERLOO CAMPAIGN: AN ALTERNATE HISTORY

Volume II

Steven Marthinsen

To order additional copies of this book, contact:
Xlibris Corporation
1-888-795-4274
www.Xlibris.com
Orders@Xlibris.com
16283

CONTENTS

To Colonel John R. Elting, US Army (ret.),
for his encouragement, knowledge and ready wit.

CHAPTER 12

OHAIN PRELIMINARIES

HAUPTMANN von Bergmann, an officer on the staff of Lieutenant General von Hacke's 13th Infantry Brigade of Bulow's IV Corps, gives an impression of the morning's battle at Ohain.

When day broke on the nineteenth, we found that the enemy had slipped into the woods and was very near our position. Our orders, so recently changed from being defensive to offensive, designated the IV Corps of Graf von Bulow to spearhead the attack through the trees and at the enemy line. Proudly, we formed up to attack and waited. Finally, when everything was ready, the first word of command was heard, "Brigade, march!" All along the line the men took their first steps and soon singing could be heard as we approached the French position. Some men had taken up the folk song Heil dir im Siegerkrantz *and it spread quickly along all the regiments which most certainly disconcerted the enemy.*

There lay a light mist across the ground that morning and our countrymen made the most of it, overthrowing the enemy's first position and chasing him back to his supports. The fighting here was confused and very slow; you could easily lose your comrades amidst the undergrowth, the mist and the heavy smoke made by our muskets. Once we engaged an enemy line with fire and kept on firing without realizing that the enemy had in fact fallen back and all we were doing was wasting ammunition! Our advance continued until an enemy counterattack forced us back but this was just momentary as we gathered ourselves again and put them back on their heels. Casualties were constant and I only later saw just how many men, both French and Prussian, were lying at out feet. These poor souls were a terrible sight, each face with the mark of death upon his brow, beseeching us to not walk upon them and increase their dreadful agony. I entreated the men to watch their step.

Ahead of us lay more trees upon which we advanced. The enemy had flown in a westerly direction and out into the morning sun we appeared. I remember being almost blinded by the dawn, having fought in the trees this whole time. Here we were stopped by General Hacke who rode up to reform us before moving on. It was only then that we realized that we had broken through the enemy's line and were positioned behind another of their divisions which was at the moment unaware of its peril. The enemy was still moving men up to the front and General Hacke sent me back to ask for reinforcements from General Pirch, the commander of our II Corps, as he felt that we were not strong enough to secure the success. I rode like the devil to this general but was to be disappointed by his curt reply to my request. He refused me without a second thought, pleading he had no orders from Blucher, and sent me on my way.

The morning of the nineteenth of June was to prove one of those sleepless times that generals often are forced to take when the action moves faster than there are hours available to fight. Napoleon had only gone to bed at just past twelve, taking refuge in the ironically named inn La Belle Alliance, after having toured part of the battlefield, established aid stations and posted gendarmes up and down the ridge to prevent the dead and wounded from being tormented by the crueler elements in the armies and civilian populations and, finally, issuing preliminary orders for the next day's movements. That done, he had gone to bed like a rock, enjoying a short but remarkably calm sleep for almost four hours. At half past three in the morning he rose; a relatively late hour for him to get up during a campaign, Napoleon probably was physically drained and needed every moment to recover. That he succeeded was obvious when his groggy staff was welcomed by sharp retorts and crisp orders. Napoleon was once more the Napoleon of old.

The Emperor went over all of the dispatches from his field commanders, especially Lobau's men who had penetrated into the Bois de Paris late on the eighteenth and had reconnoitered Blucher's position in a brief and spastic little firefight in the darkness. A clearer picture of the Prussian position gradually began to take shape as he read the reports and he turned to look at his situation map. Colonel Bonne, the director of the Topographic Service of the Imperial Staff, was busy shifting pins whose heads bore different colors to differentiate the various enemy units on the field. As the Emperor commented on the placements to Bonne, yet another courier arrived from Gerard who now was keeping in constant communication with headquarters. Reporting with a sharp click of the heels, the courier brought the same message that had been checked in some ten minutes previously by another aide and that, too, was commented on favorably by the Emperor. A groggy Soult, having not slept really since the night previous, stepped over to Napoleon's side as another staff officer handed the courier a receipt for his report and sent him on his way. The Emperor was silent for a moment as he considered Blucher's position and the options available to him. Soult waited, notebook and pen at the ready.

Napoleon had stared at his situation map for some time before the aide had arrived and he felt, based on the reports from his subordinates, that Blucher had formed a line stretching from the Bois de Paris near Couture to the town of Ohain in the north. Into this area was the bulk of three enemy corps, estimated at about 60,000 to 70,000 men, none of which had really fought a pitched battle since Ligny on the sixteenth. The Prussians were obviously fresh then and, knowing that they were about to engage in battle in the morning, probably ready to put up a fair fight. Based on this knowledge, Napoleon calculated that Blucher had three options available to him come daybreak, more options, incidentally, than the French had.

The first option was a direct withdrawal from the Ohain position in the direction of Thielemann and, distantly, Kleist which would once more reunite the Prussian army and give them strength enough to take the offensive when the Austrians and Russians arrived to help out. The Emperor didn't like this possibility at all as it would only give him a partial victory in Belgium and possibly not win him the all important war; in 1814 the allies had managed to take Paris without direct British help and likely they might do that again, especially with all of their other forces, including the Spanish, attacking from all sides. Clearly this would be a prudent choice but that left out Blucher's impatient lust for battle against the French and the leader who he considered little better than a brigand. Napoleon was almost counting on the old field marshal's personality to make itself felt and hold the Prussian army in place for a final cataclysmic battle in Belgium. If they held, he could defeat them. If they flew, things could get dicey. Uniting against the forces of Grouchy, the Prussians just might be able to inflict some serious casualties on them before he could arrive to relieve the pressure. This line of thinking did not include Gerard; the Emperor had already noted that this corps commander could take care of himself in the best way possible. However, scouts from Gerard suggested that, aside from a few stragglers, the enemy had not moved at all from any position from Lasne all the way up to Chapelle St. Lambert.

Blucher's second option was to stand defensively in the position chosen and, fighting in their normal mode against the French from strong positions, they could then inflict heavy losses on Napoleon's men and indirectly win the campaign by causing the Army of the North to be too weak to contest the French countryside properly against the other invading allied armies. The position occupied by the Prussians was not a great one, as it was suspiciously like the previous one at Ligny but, given the circumstances under which it was occupied, it was the best then available. If handled correctly, the Prussians could hold for as long as they needed before retiring to the east while preventing Napoleon from winning his desperate campaign.

Napoleon knew that three Prussian corps were on the field and, not wishing to underestimate his foe, he formulated his thoughts around the supposition that they were at least at two thirds of their original strengths. This in mind, the army opposing him numbered upwards of 70,000 men under a leader who, even if not a brilliant general, could raise his troops to the very height of tenacity and thus prove to be a dangerous enemy. The three corps that had been identified from prisoners taken belonged to Bulow, Zieten and Pirch which also meant that, by process of elimination, Grouchy was therefore facing Thielemann's lone corps at Wavre. However, no significant movement of troops had been noticed during the night and, judging by the campfires in the distance, the enemy had bivouacked in the places he had last occupied. This judgment placed Pirch at Lasne, Bulow in the Bois de Paris and Zieten stretched out from Bulow's flank to the town of Ohain in the north. The fighting, should there be any on the nineteenth, would then be focused in the area between the brooks of Lasne and the Smohain which could actually give an advantage to the French army as it would restrict the superiority of numbers that the Prussian enjoyed and allow him to pick where he wanted the battle to be fought. However, as we shall see, Napoleon was planning much more than a simple defeat of the Prussian army.

Judging from the temperament of the Prussian commander, Napoleon doubted that the second option was viable for them. Blucher wanted to fight and another battle like Ligny would not exactly be his idea of a favorable engagement. The third option available to the Prussians thus reared its head. This option, taking into account the overly aggressive nature of the Prussian leader, envisioned the enemy going over to the offensive, something he had not been able to do on the eighteenth because of the fortuitous intervention of Gerard. Given the strung out situation of the French army, Blucher could very well attack the weaker French forces now that he knew his own corps were all massed together; limited attacks at Ligny had produced good results though the Prussians didn't realize that d'Erlon's corps had been more the reason for the French faltering than anything they had done. Still, it was in Blucher's mind to deal against the French, perhaps catching them strung out as at Lutzen in 1813, rather than waiting passively in

Wellingtonian fashion to reap possibly greater rewards by simply defending in place. This option appealed to Napoleon's well groomed sixth sense and he seriously gave it some thought should it become a reality. That he was embarrassed for a moment by his current dispositions only strengthened his resolve to fix them as quickly as he could. The more he thought about it, the more the third option carried the day. If the cautious Gneisenau did not convince him to retreat, Blucher would attack in the morning.

As can be imagined, the French emperor's main plan always involved striking Blucher in place and handing him a crushing defeat; nothing less than total victory would suffice now, especially since Wellington's army had been practically destroyed. The opportunity presented to him by that fickle lady Fortune was too tempting to turn down and all the military maxims he had studied over the years told him what he already knew: go on the offensive. For Napoleon to do otherwise in this position would have been a huge mistake and no repeat of the seventeenth by Ney was going to happen here. Having previously formulated a plan in his head, he now began to visualize it on the map spread before him. Lobau's corps would form the temporary pivot on which the army would maneuver as he was already partly in the Bois de Paris and his force should be able to hold there with the help of the light cavalry divisions on the flanks until the corps of d'Erlon and Reille reached the field. By well intentioned design, the divisions of the I Corps would be reversed in action with Durutte's men, who would reach the field first, forming the left flank forces along the Smohain brook followed by the other units of the corps filling in the center of the line. Napoleon, impressed by this commander's grasp of the tactical situation at Mont St. Jean, wished him to once more prove his expertise by taking up the French left flank position following the Smohain brook. Reille's II Corps, having the longest distance to cover would be sent north of the Smohain to strike at the town of Ohain itself, the capture of which would prove a boon to the French and possibly seal Blucher's fate. Posted as it was north of the possible battlefield, the seizure of the town would place French troops practically on Blucher's line of retreat which at the very least would force him out of his current position. Of course, given the anticipated attacks all along the line, Napoleon knew that any withdrawal by the Prussian would be very difficult if not impossible.

One of the more important roles in the coming battle would be played by a corps that would barely be engaged at all. Gerard's IV Corps, safely ensconced across the Lasne brook, was to be assigned a very important task that would change the whole complexion of the battle of Ohain. Gerard's assignment was twofold; first, he was to march his fast stepping corps from its current position south of Lasne to the town of Chapelle St. Lambert where they would act, much like Reille's II Corps, as another force located along the line of retreat of Blucher's army (Napoleon was, as usual, quite certain that the Prussians would be defeated). Secondly, Gerard was to leave a force at Lasne itself to include a detachment of engineers, a few guns and some infantry. This last force was a typically Napoleonic stratagem of the same type used on many previous occasions as the French army was always ready to make a good bluff. Probably the best example was the ruse made by Napoleon during the retreat from Moscow in 1812 as the wreck of the Grande Armee reached the Beresina river to find the main crossing at Borisov burned and the opposite bank controlled by the Russians under Tshitshagov. Napoleon, in probably one of the most dangerous moments of his life, laid a trap for the Russian admiral which was unwittingly helped along by Kutusov, the overall Russian commander. Marshal Oudinot, the often wounded French commander on the scene, was ordered to make demonstrations at repairing the Borisov bridge while the bulk of the engineers moved slightly north to force the crossing at Studenka instead. Tshitshagov, confused by these apparently real bridging attempts and notified of various best guesses by both Kutusov and Wittgenstein that Napoleon would try to cross further south, shifted his men away from the actual French crossing. When Napoleon arrived at the river, he immediately pushed his men over to the other side, secured his courageously built bridges and thereby saved the army from imminent destruction. While Gerard's small group of engineers might not be trying to save the Grande Armee from a Russian anvil, their activities would rivet the attentions of at least some Prussians and thus drag them away from the main fight to the west.

Napoleon, in his element and very much taken by the roll of pride and satisfaction following his great victory the day before, appeared to his staff a bit jumpy and even nervous at times. This, they all knew, was very normal for him. The night before any battle he was always like that, fretting like a pregnant woman, but this time, since they had not seen him act that way all campaign, it seemed to act like oil being squirted into a rusty machine. The gears of the French army, for too long allowed to rust, were at last beginning to sound a little closer to normal, closer at any rate to the machine that had carried the imperial eagles from Madrid to Moscow. For his part, the Emperor was full of energy, only rubbing his eyes every now and again, and his thoughts, when spoken, were focused and clear. The first great part of the campaign had been achieved with spectacular results and now the chance at a knockout blow to finish the second part was in their grasp. At this point, one might recognize in the Emperor's feverish activity the pulsating excitement that was moving between the men of the French staff. Recently, in 1813 at the battle of Bautzen, Napoleon and his commanders had been poised with a similar opportunity, one that Ney squandered by an attack in the wrong direction at the critical moment. Given the chance, Napoleon was planning for an all out movement by his army to envelop and then annihilate Blucher's army.

Before anything offensive could happen, however, the French army had to be moved into position and that was a task that would take several hours to complete. The soldiers, having camped on the battlefield, had thrown their fires together in quick time and gotten themselves something to fill their ravenous stomachs and parchment dry throats; typically, this involved a company marauder who scoured the area and always seemed to find food even where two armies had foraged before him. Sleeping in place by the late hours of the eighteenth, they had to be roused by their sergeants, organized back into battalions and regiments and finally marched off to their new posts to the east. Napoleon recognized the need for speed and his final battle plan took this into consideration as it was both simple and decisive. Reille's men would march to and take Ohain before turning south into Blucher's rear. D'Erlon would form with Lobau the main line between the brooks and together they would pressure the main Prussian line while Gerard made loud noises to the south of Lasne as a distraction. As the battle ripened, massed guns would rip open the center of the Prussian position followed by a charge by Milhaud's and Kellermann's cavalry to be backed up with Marcognet's and Quiot's infantry divisions which would be kept as the I Corps mass of decision. Napoleon being Napoleon, he was convinced that the enemy would not be able to withstand the attacks of his victorious army and would be beaten a good deal quicker than Wellington had been the day before. However, being the complete commander that he was, the Emperor also planned quietly for defeat by ordering Girard's former division from its recuperating position at Ligny to a new position at Genappe along the Brussels highway.

"The Prussians are lost," Soult said as he passed a finger across the map.

Napoleon nodded. "Yes, but only if they do not attack us before our troops are formed up." He turned to Count Lobau. "Hold them, Lobau, and they are ours."

"Yes sire," the commander of the VI Corps said as he stared at the pins in the map marking the position of his men. "My men are in the forest already."

"Good," the Emperor commented before handing Soult's first written order to Count de la Bedoyere. "Take this to d'Erlon and tell him to leave his camp fires burning."

"Sire?" questioned the aide de camp.

Soult smiled conspiratorially at the aide. "It will double our numbers, sir, a very useful stratagem."

Shaking his head in clear wonderment, la Bedoyere took the order and tucked it into the cuff of his riding glove. He saluted smartly and mounted his horse.

The imperial staff didn't watch his departure. Such was the

urgency of the moment that Soult and his small staff were soon engulfed in writing intelligible orders for all the units involved. So important did Napoleon feel this work to be that he drafted some of the orders himself although these last, being unreadable, were quietly reworked by another of Soult's men before being sent out.

*   *   *

The scene was anything but calm at Prussian headquarters. Blucher and Gneisenau had set up their army headquarters at an isolated farmhouse three hundred yards west of Lasne and it was here that the Prussian field marshal and his commanders met to discuss the situation of the army and to decide what to do in the morning. Count Gneisenau, pessimistic about their chances in battle against Napoleon's victorious army, stood quietly at one end of the dining table with his clenched fist under his chin and his eyes wandering between the present corps commanders and the seated Blucher. He wasn't pleased with the position they now occupied and had only one thought on his mind: retreat, a movement he had already begun preparing for. The other commanders stood around waiting for a chance to speak but no one said anything until Blucher himself began.

"We failed Wellington this day," Blucher said as much to the wall as anyone in the room. His voice, a near even mixture of anger and sorrow, announced a certain disgust to the men around him and it was obvious that he was a very frustrated man. Determined to get at the French any way he could, he had grasped at the beast's tail and come up empty on two separate occasions.

"We could no other, sir," Gneisenau said without moving his fist. Standing at the head of the table, his imposing figure cast a large shadow on the wall behind him. "But now we are in a critical position and must fall back. I have sent instructions to be ready to withdraw."

Bulow found his moment. Famous for his insubordination, he deliberately wished to go against Gneisenau's authority and lack of aggressiveness. "Sir, the French are spread from the far end of the Waterloo field to the Bois de Paris!" He took a step towards the small window on the opposite end of the table from the chief of staff. Waving his arm, he added, "We've seen their campfires in the distance. They are not ready to continue the battle. We must regroup and attack them!"

Gneisenau shook his head. "Sir, it is too dangerous. Grouchy's men could come over at any moment . . . ."

Bulow cut in. "The Frenchman is held by Thielemann at Wavre. Where can he go?"

"Gerard's corps is still on the loose," Pirch threw into the general conversation as if he was trying to justify his earlier debacle. "He may attempt to storm across the river into our flank while we are on the offensive."

"That isn't very likely," Bulow retorted, "the brook is still too high to be forded. They would have to build a bridge."

Blucher sat, taking in the facts. Normally, Gneisenau's plan would have been adopted, like after Ligny, but he felt the force of what Bulow was suggesting. The French were strung out and would take several hours to concentrate for a decisive battle that would favor them in any way. If the already concentrated Prussian army could strike first from the forest, they could catch the extended corps and rout it before any help could arrive. Such a victory could seal the doom of Napoleon's French army. But what about afterwards? What about Grouchy and Gerard? Could they march into the Prussian rear and cut them off? Would the French emperor rally his troops in time? Thinking quietly, he remained silent.

The commander of the IV Corps pointed at their map. "We are together and strong, the troops will be fresh and full of spirit in the morning. We needn't fear any foe. Napoleon's army has been in heavy battle since noon yesterday and they must have suffered heavily against the British. Our course is obvious, sir, we must attack."

"It could work," said Gneisenau, warming to the idea that he knew his chief was considering though he loathed sending out orders for many of the service troops to redeploy to the front again. "But what about Thielemann? He will be cut off."

"The devil to Thielemann," Blucher declared suddenly before

really noting that he had insulted his corps commander. "He will be able to take care of himself."

"Well then, sir?" asked Gneisenau cautiously. He knew that the field marshal wanted to attack Napoleon again and they could very well have a substantial superiority in men against the French. By the same token, they were potentially caught between two enemy forces which could prove equally disastrous.

Blucher stood knowing full well that his decision would decide the issue. Both sides spoke reason but one side, Bulow's, spoke to his imagination as well and that would prove the winning point. What would happen if they retreated? Would not the French launch their vaunted cavalry into an immediate pursuit? Would they be able to stand anywhere? Could the retreat become another debacle like after Jena? The field marshal hated everything French, especially Napoleon, and, having participated in the disaster of 1806, he did not want to risk having the army hounded and destroyed without ever having fought its decisive battle. He stared each man in the eye, perhaps hoping to instill the same spirit he carried into their hearts. "We attack!"

Gneisenau was a little taken aback by Blucher's abrupt choice but, being the fine soldier that he was, he simply nodded and began to plan in his mind what they would do. French divisions would be marching all the way from Merbe Braine and that would give them the advantage of position in the early hours. Attacking swiftly along Bulow's front could potentially shatter the exhausted French army and drive it from the field. Then again, maybe it wouldn't. He decided on a preliminary plan. Having Bulow attack in the morning with all of his troops, they could "test the waters" as it were to see if the French were buckling or not. If they were, Pirch's men would be used as reinforcements to add weight to the attack in the forest. If no real advance were forthcoming, honor and opportunism would have been served and then they could retreat from the field in good order to rejoin Thielemann, if he was still in one piece by then, and Kleist who was many leagues away. Knowing his post and duty, Gneisenau was prepared to do whatever it took to assure his army had the best chance possible to win or escape.

"We must not fail again," Blucher declared loudly to the group. "We must destroy the enemy here, tomorrow."

Bulow pulled out his watch. "Today, sir."

While Blucher's aide Nostitz left to get some beer and the corps commanders retired to their respective units, Gneisenau sat himself down at the table to do his job. He had to go over the noted terrain, issue the movement orders and in general make the whole look as if it had been a real plan. Unfortunately, some of the work he had done previously had to be undone and that was a frustrating point. Nevertheless, he did those orders first as they involved artillery and supply troops. Finishing those, he peered through the flickering candlelight at the position they were in and rubbed his tired eyes. Here, in the early hours of the morning, the preliminary plan he had thought at the meeting became a detailed one. Bulow's corps, the strongest of all, would lead the attack at dawn through the woods to catch Lobau's men unawares and chase them off the field. Zieten, positioned to the north of Bulow, would initially hold his position near Ohain until it was clear that Bulow was making headway and then he would add his weight to the French flank to help break it. That done, Pirch would move forward as well with the intent of giving Bulow as much support as he could handle. The target would once more be the Brussels highway and the shattered Plancenoit, the town that, if captured, would sever Napoleon from his lines of communication and effectively cut him off from his other forces. Like the Austro-Russian plan at Austerlitz, the Prussians presupposed that they had the advantage in position; Gneisenau would probably have thought differently if he knew that even at that very moment cursing French columns were on the march to the next day's field of battle.

*　　*　　*

The men of Napoleon's army were all "grumblers" even though only the veterans of the Imperial Guard ever really officially received that title. Every man in the French army thought himself a general on the day of battle and many a conversation could be heard between the men as the loudest of the group announced how he would turn an enemy position and win the battle in less than an hour. In addition, others cursed the roads, the weather, the food they hadn't been able to eat, the enemy and practically anything else that came to mind. It had always been like that in the Grande Armee and the year 1815 was no different. Marching slowly through the early hours of the morning, the long columns of mumbling soldiers wound their way across the position occupied the previous day and towards the dark mass of trees in the distance which, for many, would be their whole battlefield in a few short hours. The men knew that the Prussians were positioned here, somewhere, but beyond that they had no idea what Napoleon had planned for the day though the older veterans assured the younger men that the Emperor would not miss a chance to twist old Blucher's mustache if it could be gotten a hold of. Like most of the men, the soldiers did not understand much beyond their narrow little regimental world and could not know that their moonlight marching would save many a life when the dawn broke in a few hours. Indeed, even if a victory was won on the nineteenth, most everybody would have to wait for one of the famous Bulletins to actually figure out what the success meant for France. Nonetheless, the trust placed in the Emperor by his ever talkative soldiers was total as the endless marching to battle was almost always accompanied by glorious victory somewhere down the line.

Marshal Soult, having had his real baptism of fire as chief of staff of the army on the eighteenth, was now a more sober and concerned man than he had been before. With certain disaster staring them in the face against Wellington the day before, he had finally begun to realize how truly important and timely his position was and that it required a constant hands-on approach in order to be run successfully. Too many things had gone wrong at Mont St. Jean from the misunderstanding of orders to the loss of couriers in transit and it completely sank in just how difficult the chief of staff's job was. Determined to do better against Blucher and his Prussian army on the following day, Soult was a busy man looking over every written order for errors and ambiguities, anything in fact that might possibly lead to a serious misunderstanding between he and Grouchy at Wavre. His opinion of the new marshal remained low, however, and he decided then and there that the cavalry commander would need special attention if events were to be guided in their direction that day.

Taking advantage of the momentary lull, Napoleon took a nap for an hour at La Belle Alliance before getting up and looking over the most recent dispatches from the field. Gerard seemed to be in good shape and safe behind the broken bridge and so it would be easy for him to do what was expected of him in regards to the short march north. Every corps commander had reported in, stating that their troops were on the march and currently at various points on the map. Making some quick judgments, Napoleon knew that his men would not be in position much before half past six and Reille's corps, which had the farthest to go, would arrive a good deal after that time. Nevertheless, the French Emperor was confident and pleased with events, especially when he looked over to a corner in the room and spied the piled enemy colors from the previous day. Costly though it had been, the battle of Mont St. Jean had been another Marengo which clearly meant that his star just might be rising again.

Soult, asleep with his note pad in his hand, woke with a start and rubbed his burning eyes. Seeing the Emperor by the map table, he stood up wobbly and stepped over to him. "Did you sleep well, sire?"

Napoleon nodded. "Yes, Soult, but I will sleep even better once the Prussians have been crushed."

"You think they will attack us?"

"It is the only thing they could be planning," the Emperor said as he swept his hand across the map over the Bois de Paris. "They would have withdrawn already from their position but none of the reports from Gerard at Lasne or Lobau have noted a large scale withdrawal. Blucher wants to fight and if he feels he is in a good position, he will."

"If he strikes soon," Soult said, concern in his voice, "Lobau will be in trouble. The sun is up already and we are not ready."

"Don't be deceived, Soult," Napoleon replied as he stared at the rays of light filtering through the window of the inn. "Lobau can handle them. Besides, it will take the Prussians as long or longer to form their men up to attack us . . . ."

A rider raced up and entered the dimly lit inn. The usual clashing of spur and saber made a racket in the Imperial headquarters but all could tell that the man was clearly agitated. Napoleon approached to receive the report, a circumstance that did nothing to help the aide.

"Capitaine Madelin, sire, of VI Corps staff," the aide announced with a stammer.

"What news have you?" said Napoleon, almost knowing what the man was going to say.

"Count Lobau gives his regards and states that the Prussians opposite his position in the forest are forming to attack. Scouts north of us report massing cannon."

"How many guns?"

"Over forty, sire."

"How much infantry?"

"There was too much mist to tell."

The Emperor considered. "Too much mist? Lobau says they are concentrating around him? They are in earnest."

Napoleon passed a glance at Marshal Soult and then began an abbreviated version of his usually thorough interrogation. In his head he felt that there was not a moment to lose for what he feared would soon become reality. Finishing the round, he dismissed the aide and reached for his hat. "Soult, it is time to ride the enemy position. I want to see what Blucher is up to. Drouot, get those guns up!"

Rushing out, the Emperor mounted a different horse this time, a dark bay, and swept from the inn to inspect the lines. On his route, followed as he was by his escort squadron of Guard Chasseurs, he passed march columns of every type from overcoat clad line infantry to artillery supply trains moving east to what would be the new battlefield. A horse artillery company rattled by, the mounted gunners not realizing in their haste that they had just passed the commander in chief and one even cursed him for getting in the way; the soldier probably thought that Napoleon was a veterinarian or some such due to his unadorned uniform (the man, a veteran of many years service, would never live down the day he swore at the Emperor). Nevertheless, despite being rebuked by his own troops, Napoleon was satisfied as to their ardor; the animation of the men left nothing at all to be desired and his own confidence swelled in his breast.

"We can do this," he was heard to mumble as the group rode on.

*   *   *

As the sun began to realize its full potential on the morning of the nineteenth, one commander was getting quite nervous as to what it was going to bring on his position, pretty much the same position, in fact, that he occupied at the beginning of the battle of Mont St. Jean. This man was, of course, General Mouton, Count of Lobau and the commander of the VI Corps of the Army of the North. Late on the eighteenth, he had cautiously pushed forward his men right to the Bois de Paris in accordance to Napoleon's orders to develop Bulow's final line for the night. After some energetic skirmishing that produced shattered bark and falling branches, both sides seemed to satisfy this inquiry and the troops settled down for the night amidst the trees of the forest. Things were quiet for some time after that and Lobau took the opportunity to catch up on the sleep that everyone in the army needed so badly by propping his large body up against a sympathetic tree. Unfortunately for him, being a veteran commander, he slept with the proverbial one eye open and never really relaxed as much as he should have. By the time the sky began to turn pink, he was up and around again, certainly being the first man in either army to enjoy a cold shave in the twilight hours. That done, he wrapped his cape around his wide shoulders and stalked out to the north to inspect the lines, incidentally without his bicorne hat which had suffered far more than he in the fighting on the previous day.

Touring the lines and discovering for himself where his own troops had ended up, he examined what he could of the Prussians, an exercise that rewarded him with the knowledge of some activity in the enemy camp. At first it was difficult to tell whether or not the enemy was preparing to retreat or attack but the telltale signs soon came into view. Instructing one aide de camp to climb a nearby tree, the man reported seeing not only moving infantry and artillery but also additional ammunition caissons which clinched it for Lobau that the Prussians were getting prepared to go over to the offensive. Reasoning that the heavy caissons would not be brought up unless some prolonged firing was intended, Lobau sent off his aide to tell the Emperor that Blucher was going to launch an attack, a correct assumption as it turned out.

Lobau, a thorough and brave soldier, was quick in getting his divisional commanders, Simmer and Jeanin, their orders to get the men roused and into battle formations. His own instructions had been very clear and precise from Napoleon (a definite change in style he noted from the day before though he, like most of the generals, blamed the ambiguities in the orders on Soult and not Napoleon) and he knew that his men would be playing a critical role in the morning before the rest of the army came up to bolster his position. Relatively isolated as he was, he had to hold his position so as to prevent Bulow from escaping the confines of the forest and thus more easily being able to use his greater numbers. This made sense to the man and he reflected how, if more had been known and they had been fighting only one opponent, this same strategy could have worked the day before. But, war never is the same battle twice and thus it would be here too. Like Lannes at Friedland, it was his job to hold the enemy and keep him busy for the Emperor who would administer the coup de grace.

The position of the French VI Corps could be likened to a cork in a wine bottle that if it falls out, the contents will spill all over the ground. Lobau's men were heavily outnumbered by the enemy but could count on at least two great advantages that would help them in the fight. First, they were defending in a fairly thick wood where their loose order tactics, always better than their continental opponents, could be put to good use in slowing the Prussian attack. Second, they had just won a critical battle on the previous day and so were riding a crest of solid confidence in themselves and their leaders. The Prussians, on the other hand, enjoyed no such distinctions. Having lost one major battle and then played the marching game for two days, their morale was no longer at the fever pitch it had been though it must be said that it was still quite good and could be improved significantly with an early success in their attack. Lastly, he had as a reserve Duhesme's division of the Young Guard which he jealously held as his only second line unit.

One of Napoleon's primary concerns during the march up to the battle was the necessity of getting his artillery moving as fast as possible to their new positions. To this end, Intendant General Daru had collected as many horses as he could find from those captured on the battlefield (which included a good many team horses from captured caissons and limbers) and had these distributed to the companies of guns that had lost some during the fighting. Working in the twilight hours, the process went extremely well, each company collecting the horses it needed from a central "depot" and then racing away to the east ahead of their mother divisions. General Lallemand, the artillery general who had taken over from the killed St. Maurice, was instructed to build a battery to the north of Lobau's position in the woods to cover what would be the French center and block any advance of the Prussians in this area. First securing horse artillery companies by express consent of the Emperor, he sent these ahead to hold the line while the bulk of the foot artillery followed behind to replace the lighter horse guns as they arrived at the front. The artillery that had brushed past the Emperor had been amongst the last of the companies assigned to this task and Lobau was able to note with satisfaction the strengthening of his flank as more and more guns wheeled into position beyond the confines of the forest. Every minute now counted as the Army of the North continued its inexorable march to Ohain.

Lobau's two infantry divisions stretched from the high banked

Lasne brook to the edge of the Bois de Paris. Nearest to the brook was Simmer's 19th Infantry Division backed up by Subervie's 5th Cavalry Division from the I Cavalry Corps which posted itself in the rolling plains to the southeast. Jeanin's 20th Infantry Division, completely gobbled up by the forest, would spend most of the day fighting amongst the trees and barely see any sunlight before the afternoon. Backing him up was Domon's 3rd Cavalry Division, attached from Vandamme's III Corps, which initially sat loosely in the gap north of the forest but gradually withdrew as more and more horse guns arrived to take their place. The Young Guard was posted well back of the trees to be used strictly to counter any enemy breakthrough. When General Domon felt that sufficient cannon had arrived, he withdrew his two brigades out of enemy gun range yet well within supporting distance of the "petite" grand battery.

General Lallemand had arrived amongst the horse artillery companies in the meantime and from the gun line he watched the advancing Prussian teams as they began to arrive within range of his men. Whether they liked it or not, the action would have to begin now.

The 4th Company of the 2nd Horse Artillery Regiment under Captain Dumont would have the honor of firing the first shots of the battle of Ohain. Watching the dust cloud thrown up by the advancing vehicles, a six pounder cannon loosed its iron ball at them, narrowly missing an artillery caisson but in general waking up the Prussians on the other side. The already deployed batteries of the Prussian IV Corps abruptly returned the favor and the fight was clearly on.

*   *   *

Bulow's IV Corps was full of spirit that morning and they formed up as best they could amongst the trees of the Bois de Paris, ready to once more advance on Plancenoit. A light mist clung precariously to the ground giving the scene a surreal look but the troops, preceded by the jagers, were eager to get to grips with the French who hid themselves somewhere deep in the trees ahead.

General Bulow had been assured of the support of Pirch's II Corps, which was to be represented by Krafft's and Tippelskirch's brigades who were deployed more or less in the center of the Prussian line. Knowing this, he deployed his four brigades from the Lasne brook to the tip of the forest just south of the assembling Prussian gun line. In the south was Hiller's 16th and Losthin's 15th Infantry Brigades residing in the order they had ended up at that previous night after recrossing the brook. North of them was Hacke's 13th Infantry Brigade, the unit destined to do the best in the attack. Kept as a reserve to the rear of the forest was the 14th Infantry Brigade temporarily commanded by Colonel Funck as its actual commander was not present at the battle.

Just before six in the morning, the Prussian attack commenced. The rifle armed jagers led the way though the mist and the trees took away any advantage that they had in terms of range and actually put them at a disadvantage as the French could load and fire their less accurate weapons faster. The troops behind took to song after the first musket shots echoed across the forest and what would be several hours of fighting under the canopy of the trees began. The jagers loosed their shots and then quickly fell back to begin the laborious task of reloading while the French pickets sent up the alarm to their brethren in the rear that the enemy was coming. Word arrived to General Simmer's headquarters and he immediately ordered his elite voltigeur companies to advance to harass the enemy troops while he kept the bulk of his men hidden behind the rolling hills to the west. Simmer had the more difficult job of the two division commanders on this flank as his command not only occupied part of the forest but it also had to cover the fields leading down to the brook, an area that promised to attract large numbers of Prussian troops looking to outflank the French position. Shots were soon flying in all directions.

As so often happens in war, despite all indications to the contrary, some units always seem to be surprised when the enemy attacks. Such was the case with one of the regiments in Jeanin's division. The 107th Ligne, defending in the forest, collapsed at first sight of the Prussians and retreated west as fast as it could carry itself. Perhaps the Prussians seemed larger than life in the midst or some such thing but this left a nice hole in the French line that the local enemy did not hesitate to take advantage of. Pushing ahead, a serious rupture of the French line appeared imminent. Fortunately for the French, the 107th had run directly into the path of General Lobau who commented dryly on their successful out running of the enemy. That done, he rallied them in place and sent them back into the fray while he himself positioned a pair of reserve grenadier companies in the areas that marked the boundaries between his brigades. The shamed 107th, embarrassed and angry, was further humiliated by their own officers when the latter advanced against the Prussians with nothing but swords and pistols. That did it. The regiment, with unloaded muskets, charged directly into the advancing Prussians and stopped them cold before fiercely pushing them back about one hundred yards. Taking up a position in the under growth, a firefight began that quickly eliminated all visibility in the forest due to the dense and clinging smoke that choked the air.

Ignoring his injuries, Field Marshal Blucher had ridden the lines before the attack had begun and had told his men, "No prisoners!" which had raised their morale to a fever pitch. Attacking all along the line with that certain fanatic flair in their eyes, they surged forward along Bulow's front and struck the local French positions very hard. Greeted with success from the outset, they pushed Lobau's men steadily back everywhere except on Simmer's far right flank where that general ambushed the first attack and drove Hiller's men back into the trees. However, the success of the attack also became its temporary undoing. As the troops moved ahead in the dim light of the forest, the units began to lose their cohesion and get intermixed amongst one another. In one case, a Prussian unit in Hacke's brigade began an imaginary firefight with a French unit that had already retreated simply because it couldn't see through the smoke. These factors helped the retreating French recover from the early shock of the attack and gave Lobau the time he needed to organize local counterattacks and retake some of the positions that had been lost. This was especially important when it is remembered that one of the great advantages Bulow had was that he still had strong reserves whereas Lobau, heavily outnumbered, had far fewer.

The fighting was a confused affair made worse by the floating smoke from fired muskets which hung suspended in place before slowly dissipating. The shouts of command mingled with the screams of agony from wounded soldiers coupled with the crack of the muskets produced a bizarre scene and was a far cry from the more tidy affairs on the plains. More than once, units on both sides shot at their own troops until, at least on one occasion, a thundering swear word rose over the firing and made the men realize they were engaging a friendly regiment. Lieutenant colonel von Thile, commander of the 3rd Silesian Landwehr, found himself giving orders to troops who seemingly couldn't hear him until they both realized that he was speaking another language and he had no choice but to surrender on the spot (he later escaped during the same confused fighting and was grazed with a musket ball by one of his own men). The confusion necessarily slowed the Prussian attack but their weight of numbers gradually told, especially in the center of the line. Hacke's and Losthin's men forced the fighting French regiments back though they became ever more intermixed as the advance continued. Halting to redress, they were struck by the reserve grenadier companies of Jeanin and forced to relinquish what they had just gained. The French in turn lost their way and cohesion and were forced to retreat when the Prussian line reformed to attack again. The red plumed grenadiers were veterans, though, and they did what they knew would buy them some time. Firing all at once, they formed an effective smoke screen and fell back while the Prussians, thinking that they had found the French main line, stopped to return the fire. The bizarre fight went on.

Lobau's line was under tremendous pressure and may well have broken if it was not for General Simmer's counterattack along the French right. Simmer, holding the line along the southern edge of the forest and the bank of the brook, had been attacked by Hiller's brigade but he displayed his skill again in holding their assault and stubbornly resisting the latter's attempt to turn his flank. When the Prussians fell back to regroup for another strike, he prepared an ambuscade for them by deploying two companies of voltigeurs along the riverbank with orders to not to show themselves until the Prussian attack had developed fully; he also requested Subervie to be prepared in case things got ugly. His men ready, once more hidden from the view of the enemy, he waited for the inevitable. The Prussians were quick in reforming, animated as they were by visions of victory, and they swept forward again, their lead unit being the battered fusilier battalion of Infantry Regiment #15 which had been one of the prominent forces the previous day against Gerard.

Captain Laurent, in charge of the two companies of voltigeurs from the 27th Ligne hidden along the steep bank of the brook, watched the Prussian attack as it emerged from the trees with jagers deployed and immediately being fired upon by the other light companies of the division. As planned, the loosely deployed voltigeurs fell back past the hidden men and returned to their own firing line as the jubilant Prussians took up the chase again. At sixty yards, the French line fired and staggered the enemy advance for a moment but the Prussians shook it off and returned the favor while attempting to deploy a Landwehr battalion around the flank of the French line. Laurent, a winner of the Legion of Honor, was up to the task assigned to him. Contrary to normal practice, Simmer had given the eagle of the 27th to the voltigeurs along with a handful of extra drummers complete with drums. Laurent used these to create what his leader expected of him: one terrible racket. Choosing the right moment, he led his men over the crest of the embankment in a solid line, two deep, with drummers beating an awful noise and the eagle proudly soaring above the smoke. Pausing at thirty yards from the unfortunate Prussian Landwehr, they fired a savage volley into the rear of the militia and in an instant had broken them. The ruse quickly had its intended effect. Believing that another French regiment was about to strike them in the flank, Hiller ordered a hasty retreat of his brigade before the situation became a disaster. Now the scenario developed on its own. As so often happened in the Napoleonic Wars and indeed in war in general, the withdrawal of the Prussian brigade stimulated a French counterattack by Simmer's division which advanced close on the heels of the enemy brigade. Hiller's command, up until then retreating in good order considering the nasty surprise they had just taken, broke apart in the face of the disciplined attack of the French and ran pell-mell for the safety of the woods.

Simmer had no intention of losing control of his men but the opportunity offered to him was just too great to let get past. Quickly dashing an order to Laurent to become the divisional reserve, he pushed forward with his men right after the retreating foe. The 27th Ligne, a veteran regiment in every way, shook out a fusilier company into open order ahead of the French advance and, without flag flying, occupied the position left by the Prussians. Hiller's men, rallied at last well beyond the trees, were able to watch the French take their start line and begin to turn the Prussian flank. This was all too much for the watching Bulow as he failed to believe what had happened and desperately sought to save his reputation. Ordering the nearby and fresh brigade of Colonel Funck into the attack, he told Hiller to form behind them and thereby become the IV Corps reserve brigade while the other patched up the line. Other instructions quickly followed. Artillery batteries from Pirch's corps limbered and hurried to the scene and Bulow's own cavalry redeployed from their central position to also stop the French drive. Simmer's division of 3,200 men had indeed stirred up a hornet's nest as it attracted almost 15,000 scrambling Prussians coming from all directions. As Funck's men advanced toward their opponents, the French raked them with a blinding volley but it was clear that they were up against a very numerous foe. A firefight began between the two sides and Colonel Aubree was killed while exhorting his men to hold their positions. As more and more Prussian troops joined the fight, it became clear to the commander of the French 19th Infantry Division that nothing more could be done here. Carefully redressing their lines, Simmer's men began a grudging withdrawal in the face of the heavy enemy pressure that was only hastened when some of Pirch's guns began to fire in support of the Prussian reaction. Nevertheless, Simmer pulled his men back behind another roll in the landscape and occupied part of the nearby woods to enfilade the Prussians as they marched up and throw them into as much confusion as he could in order to buy some time.

Funck's brigade, the 14th, was full of fight and it showed in their attack. Struck front and flank by enemy musketry, the brigade troops weren't thrown into any sort of panic and instead engaged each foe in turn. Throwing a regiment at the company in the woods proved too much for the French and they fell back hurriedly while the rest of the Prussian mass, notwithstanding heavy casualties, brought their superior numbers to bear on the main French line and gradually forced them back as well. Simmer, his troops under enormous pressure and in danger of being overwhelmed, ordered up his reserve companies of voltigeurs, minus the eagle, to slow the enemy troops and complete his withdrawal from the Prussian flank. Baron Subervie, watching the infantry marching back, posted a squadron of the 1st Lanciers along the crest of the embankment with fluttering lances upright to give an impression of numbers and to stimulate second thoughts in the Prussians. The latter, spotting the potentially dangerous cavalry, responded to the threat by pausing in their march and redressing their tattered ranks. Simmer, now unmolested by the halted enemy, continued to pull his men back until they had arrived at their start point again. The relief they all felt was profound but they were also secure in the knowledge that they had defeated superior numbers and stopped the enemy attacks along the vulnerable French right.

The counterattack of Simmer's division was to have a greater effect on the fighting in the early hours of the nineteenth all out of proportion to its real force. By breaking Hiller's brigade, Simmer's men had punched a hole in Blucher's line that would require immediate repair. Bulow had thus been forced to commit his vital reserves to hold their attack thus taking away his immediate reinforcement for his own attacking brigades, one of which had just achieved an unexpected success. Additionally, reinforcements of all types had converged against Simmer's division and now found themselves out of place and in need of reorganization. Prussian staff officers had their work cut out for them.

*   *   *

The morning of the nineteenth was far quieter for another commander but no less active. General of Division Gerard, the youngest of the French corps commanders in the campaign, was an early riser though he was careful to make sure that this trait was not inflicted on anyone who didn't need it as yet. Making sure that his tired troops were left alone while he read his orders from the Emperor, Gerard worked by candlelight and planned his important route march to Chapelle St. Lambert. He smiled when he read the part about the engineers and the phony bridge as it stirred his imagination and, in a more disturbing memory, reminded him about the campaign in Russia. Pausing for just a moment to think about it, he then summoned his engineer commander, General of Brigade DuFriche de Valaze, to come to his small headquarters building outside one of the farms and help him plan the sham attack. De Valaze reported far quicker than Gerard ever expected and the irritated look of the former's red eyes suggested that the he had anticipated an assault crossing order for the morning.

Gerard pushed his hair back from his face as he looked at the tall, dark blue uniformed engineer enter the room with his chief of staff Colonel Marion. "You couldn't sleep either, eh?"

De Valaze shook his head. "I've been at the crossing sight most of the evening, sir, and I was just . . . ."

The commander of the IV Corps heard his engineer's voice trail away before he finished the sentence himself. "Just waiting for my orders to be ready for a crossing sometime this morning?"

"Yes, sir," the other replied, nodding his head.

Gerard could tell instinctively that de Valaze, a plucky engineer if there had ever been one, was reluctant to throw his men away in a blaze of dangerous glory against a very strong foe. The Prussian position, lined with cannon and guarded by at least one corps, was made even more formidable by the steep banks of the brook which would put any French attack under plunging fire from the guns. He could understand the man's sentiment but, feeling suddenly mischievous, he decided to carry the conversation a little further.

"Well, I have received orders from the Emperor to just that affect." He picked up the written papers for added drama. "He wishes me to deploy my companies of engineers, your men, along the brook as soon as light permits."

De Valaze's head sagged for a moment before he snapped to attention and removed any pretense towards emotion. "I will have artillery support? The Prussians oppose us with a great many cannon and my men will not be able to work under a hail of shells from the opposite bank. They have an excellent field of fire."

"Indeed," Gerard agreed, a little worn smile appearing on his face. "And that's why I don't want your men to spend too much time actually building a bridge."

The engineers, both of them, stared in bewilderment. "What, sir?"

Gerard finally let the deception end. "The Emperor wants you to mount a phony crossing attempt of the river, sir, only made to convince the enemy that we might cross. The bulk of the corps will be marching north, to Chapelle St. Lambert to cut off the anticipated Prussian retreat."

De Valaze removed his hat and gave a bow to the IV Corps commander, a wry smile on his leathery face. "Well done, sir, and our performance shall be at least as good at the riverbank. Colonel Marion? Strip all the houses around here of wood and have it carried down to the water, we must be convincing."

As the somberly clad engineers left, Gerard was joined by his chief of staff, Loriere, and together they poured over the remainder of the orders from the Emperor. It was clear that their chief was planning a knock out blow against Blucher but quickly calculated mathematics revealed the chance he was taking. The main army, given the length and ferocity of the battle on the eighteenth, was probably a good deal weaker than it had been while three of Blucher's four corps were massed together north of the brook. Certainly, the Emperor was gambling on his army working efficiently for once in the campaign (or in their case, perhaps twice) and was preparing to end the war in an afternoon.

"We need more cavalry," Loriere announced while Gerard measured the distance to Chapelle St. Lambert.

Gerard, remembering Vandamme's debacle at Kulm two years before, stopped for a moment and nodded. Advancing out of the mountains south of Dresden after the great victory, Vandamme and his corps had come across an allied force that they had attacked with the intention of driving off the field. Unexpectedly, another allied force, retreating from Dresden as well, appeared in the French rear and resulted in a largely accidental but very important victory for the allies. "If Blucher withdraws and Thielemann slips away from Maréchal Grouchy, it might get unpleasant for us. Looks like we'll have to have scouts along every road leading to the town because I'll be damned to be caught like that, not after yesterday."

Loriere grinned. Gerard was referring to the battle of Lasne which he was convinced would win him his marshal's baton from the Emperor for saving the flank of the army. The last thing he wanted was to risk that baton in a blatant action without doing his best to elude any enemy trap. "As you ordered, our scouts have been sent out already. Pajol's cavalry corps is at Limale. They would be a nice gift for us."

"Agreed," Gerard said as he worked out the distance between his forces and those of Pajol. "But only if the marshal doesn't want to use him against Thielemann."

"Our last dispatch from Grouchy placed everyone to the east of Limale," Loriere said as he ritually picked up the report sent to them. "He really needs to write these better because I can't tell you with any certainty exactly where he is. Is Vandamme at Wavre still and is Exelmans protecting his right? I don't know."

Gerard frowned. Having Grouchy as a commander had been difficult at best but perhaps more than any other reason why Gerard and Grouchy had such limited communication was the former's fear that his nominal commander would even now recall him to fight Thielemann at Wavre. Consequently, the commander of the IV Corps, enjoying his new found freedom and recent glory, was extremely hesitant to give Grouchy the chance to undo any of the privileges he had acquired. "I'm not going to ask him to clarify it," the general said, "but we will ask for Pajol's corps to be sent to support us in our struggle against the Prussians."

"Our struggle sir?" Loriere questioned. "But we aren't engaged."

Gerard smiled. "You and I know that but I dare say he does not."

The request by Gerard to Grouchy for the support of Pajol's corps is a clear indication that communication between the two forces was not at its best. Grouchy had received Napoleon's order from the previous evening around ten thirty but had failed to inform his subordinate of the coming help. Pajol, on the other hand, had been informed and he was the one who would eventually send a dispatch to a surprised Gerard announcing his approach to the latter's position. The one bright spot in all this fumbling was something few of the commanders quite realized yet: given Gerard's position, information running between the three wings of the army was now almost safe and, in the case of Napoleon's staff at least, fairly constant. However, the overall lack of coordination in the French army was Napoleon's great bane during the campaign and until everything was once more under his total control he was to suffer the consequences.

*   *   *

Grouchy's position on the morning of the nineteenth was a bit better and more relaxed for the new marshal than the previous day had been though this is not to say that he did not have important work to complete. Having thoroughly fouled up during the day of the eighteenth from his late start to his lack of overall control of his forces, Grouchy felt truly Machiavellian in that someone else's success had completely erased his many mistakes. Knowing that people are rarely given second chances to prove themselves, the commander of the now smaller French right was determined to not let his opportunity slip away.

From incoming dispatches from the Emperor's headquarters, Grouchy knew that first he was in the proverbial doghouse with his chief for not maneuvering towards Waterloo like he was supposed to the previous day and that three of Blucher's corps now faced the Emperor at Ohain. This last news burst a bubble with the marshal as it proved that the force he had caught was nothing more than a single corps rearguard. Reading on, pointed instructions from Napoleon carefully mapped out everything he had to do that day with a reiteration to release Pajol's corps to support Gerard and maintain a link between the two forces. Determined to get things right this time, Grouchy moved with uncharacteristic speed to get out his orders for the day. Starting with Count Exelmans and his dragoon corps, he instructed him to move towards Limale in support of Teste's infantry which he had already decided to hang onto (Lobau still wished that division was with him!). Vandamme's corps would necessarily have to be split in half by leaving one division at Wavre, Berthezene's, to maintain appearances and moving the other two down the road to the bridgehead at Limale. Grouchy's clear intention here was to interpose himself between Thielemann and the rest of the Prussian army just like he was supposed to do the day before.

On the other side of the Dyle, General Thielemann was also having his own problems. Having been told of the crushing defeat of Wellington, he had been ordered by Gneisenau to hold his position at Wavre or, if this became untenable, then to maneuver towards the main Prussian army massed at Ohain. Unfortunately, Thielemann no longer felt that he had the strength to do either.

During the early morning hours, the commander of the Prussian III Corps had received requests from two of his units to march and rejoin their respective commands. As Gneisenau had implied in his dispatch, a battle could be in the offing for the morning of the nineteenth and so he had approved the requests with the proviso that they not march before six in the morning; Thielemann wanted to be sure that Grouchy was quiet before he sent off a chunk of his forces. Events were quiet and the morning very still at six when the detachments marched off but the situation had changed by seven when masses of French infantry were reported heading towards Limale by a pair of his more courageous scouts. This demanded a quick decision and his was to order Colonel

Stulpnagel and his 12th Brigade to direct another assault against the French bridgehead in the hopes of pinching it out before the reinforcements came to expand it. The counterattack got off in good time, the Prussian brigade having been mostly in place since the previous night, but, even though they struck from another angle, they could make no headway against the tenacious French at Limale as Teste skillfully shot down their attacks with cool precision and took precious few casualties in doing so.

"It is a cauldron!" the handsome Prussian colonel was heard to yell to an aide as his men staggered back to their start line. "We need support!"

Hearing of the setback, Thielemann was forced to shift more of his forces to his sagging left flank. Any sizeable French unit at Limale would effectively isolate him from any chance of rejoining the main army and so he was fairly energetic in reinforcing the area before the earlier French troops shifts made themselves felt. However, given his situation over the past two days and lack of reinforcements from Blucher, Thielemann at best felt discouragement and definitely operated under a cloud of imminent defeat; he had no concrete way of knowing that Grouchy, as well, had lost strength and that the forces were in fact fairly well matched. What was more to the Prussian commander, however, was that Stengel's men had already marched off to the west and so his strength had dwindled further. Intelligence was also lukewarm. Recent reports from another officer deserter and, apparently, a planted French spy (Vandamme's trick?) told different stories and only served to confuse the situation more. One version had it that Pajol's whole cavalry corps had marched off in the morning to join Gerard at Lasne while the other suggested that Pajol's corps was intending to meet Gerard's marching troops as they returned to their parent unit and crushed Thielemann, thus situating themselves along Blucher's direct line of retreat. Thielemann had no idea which one to believe and while it bolstered him to think that Gerard was not with Grouchy it scared him thoroughly to think that he might yet be marching back to outflank the position and take Wavre from the west. After much deliberation and some precious time, Thielemann reverted to his original plan of reinforcing his positions, retaking Limale and finally destroying the dangerous bridge over the Dyle; this was a logical first step to any defensive plan so it seemed the easiest to invoke.

The Prussians reduced their garrison along the river bank at Wavre to a bare minimum, leaving the 3rd Kurmarck Landwehr of Luck's brigade and a handful of cavalry, but they also left a large portion of their guns to keep the French honest on the other side. The remainder of Luck's brigade and many of the walking wounded he rounded up and sent to join Stulpnagel's brigade outside of Limale.

As the men of the Prussian III Corps marched so did their counterparts in the French III Corps. Vandamme, eager to grab some of the fast fading glory, acted with spirit and energy to Grouchy's order to move and his men, with a resounding sigh of relief, swept out of the Wavre cauldron and headed southwest towards Teste's bridgehead at Limale. By this time, Pajol's horsemen had left for Chapelle St. Lambert. Being a conscientious commander, he left one regiment to cover the flank until Exelmans' dragoons arrived to take over the duty. Teste, therefore, was understandably concerned for the arrival of Vandamme's men as his position was quite vulnerable to the mass of Prussians arriving in the area. Surveying his troops, he told them that reinforcements were on their way and that they were the flank of the army: Limale must be held.

Thielemann's troops, moving on interior lines, arrived first outside Limale and the Prussian III Corps commander lost no time in getting them ready to attack the town again. If the French intrusion could be kept to an absolute minimum and then pinched off, they might yet have a chance at holding the place. Aides galloped back and forth to the brigades designated for the attack and for once it seemed that the confusion in the Prussian ranks would be kept to an absolute minimum during an open field attack. Checked by the watch of Thielemann himself, the advance against the bridgehead began at precisely ten minutes past eight in the morning. The weather was clear and splendid, the ground dry and firm and the objective tantalizingly close to the Prussians. Little did they know how tough a nut Teste's entrenched men would be to crack.

As stated earlier, the men of the French 21st Infantry Division were every bit as eager to fight as their veteran commander. General of Division Teste, an active participant in many battles including the intense fights at Wagram and Borodino, the latter where he was severely wounded, had shown his skill to the Emperor in war's harsh classroom and for that reason had secured rapid promotion, especially after the Russian campaign though his career was cut short by his capture, along with Vandamme, at Kulm in 1813. Recommended by arguably the best of Napoleon's marshals, Davout, for the command of the 21st before the 1815 campaign began clearly showed the esteem and trust which he had earned from his superiors. If there ever was a man perfectly designed for a difficult mission like holding a critical town on a river, it was Baron Teste.

Like their commander, the regiments holding the bridgehead were as ready as they were ever going to get. Based on their level of experience, Teste sought to organize his defense around the cornerstone of the 75th Ligne, his most veteran regiment, and the 2nd Brigade to which it belonged. These men would hold the eastern section of Limale while the single regiment first brigade, supported by the 5th Hussars left by Pajol, held the west. Stretched fairly thin, Teste resorted to loop holing certain buildings, barricading the exit streets and strictly forbidding any unauthorized counterattacks out of the safety of the town. The general was everywhere during the lull in the fighting. He regarded the first Prussian attack as merely a test of his defenses and the resulting knowledge led him to make modifications in his battle line that resulted in a few strong points held by his elite troops and the remainder of his forces held back to launch a counterattack. Watching the Prussians form up in the distance, he wondered who would arrive first. A veteran of Kulm, he wryly figured it would be the Prussians.

Thielemann had deployed thirty two of his forty eight corps

guns to support the grand attack on Limale and these opened up a loud and smoky barrage on the French position. Firing for about twenty minutes, the incoming shells and balls punched holes in walls, rolled down the streets and set fire to a handful of buildings one of which was hastily abandoned by the 75th's regimental band in a mad scramble of drums, brass and Chinese hats. Teste's eight divisional guns, manhandled back behind buildings on the outskirts of town, for the most part escaped damaged but they too were under strict orders not to do anything until the Prussian infantry advanced; until then, the artillerists would have to hug the same dirty ground as the infantry which actually only seemed degrading to them for a few moments.

The Prussian III Corps advance was spearheaded by two brigades with one in reserve. Luck's 11th, being that it still held part of Wavre, was chosen for this latter task while simple colonels would bear the responsibility for the attack. Colonel von Kampfen, commanding the 10th in place of Major General von Krauseneck, and the indefatigable Colonel von Stulpnagel, commanding the 12th in the absence of Major General von Lossau, carried the brunt of the assault. Like most of the fighting between the French and the Prussians, the action was both savage and without quarter.

The Prussians advanced over the open sloping ground in their standard order as their jagers engaged the few French voltigeurs who had deployed in front of the town. Brushing these aside, the attacking troops came into clear view of Limale and here is where the fighting began in earnest. Upon Teste's own order, the artillerists of his single company of guns dragged their own cannon from around the buildings they had been hidden behind and, since they were already loaded with double canister, the experienced gunners picked their large enemy target and let fly with a savage blast. Firing from no more than two hundred yards, groups of Prussian infantry crumbled but the others bravely closed their ranks and kept pushing ahead. The French artillerists raced to load more shot.

Teste had been forced to deploy his eight guns in a strictly supporting fashion all along the threatened front. Consequently, while the effect of these weapons was most savage, it was also isolated and this helped the two Prussian brigades to sustain their advance in the face of the guns. Prussian jagers, crawling up to near one hundred yards, began to pick off the gunners who then seemed to choose their direction for the next blast thus spreading the death around the attackers. The French general, mounted on horseback behind one of the primary barricades, knew that his guns alone would not hold them and that the enemy would soon be amongst the buildings. Realizing he would need his reserves at the quickest possible moments, he placed aides in various sectors across the front to report any enemy breakthroughs to him personally. If he deemed the situation dangerous enough, two line center companies stood ready to surround and throw the enemy back in confusion.

"For the Fatherland!" yelled Stulpnagel over the heads of his men as he ordered them to carry the town.

The Prussian infantry broke into a run over the final few yards to the buildings, taking a final canister blast that swept away the front troopers but could not stop the rest. Cheering at the top of their lungs, the Prussian overran the cannon and came up to the first barricade. A blinding sheet of smoke and flame erupted from the makeshift roadblock and again knocked over more than a few of the attackers. However, to the French there were simply too many of them. Pushing on regardless of casualties, the gallant Germans scaled the barricade or began to tear it down from the other side. Bayonets and musket butts struck out across the barrels and overturned wagons as a desperate fight ensued over the tiny position along the street. Some Prussian troops vaulted over the obstacle and carried on down the road where they were met by French service troops and a scratch force made up of French wounded from the previous day. These men, fighting for their lives, again, made a stand in the town center around an ornate fountain and the small church where they caused just enough casualties amongst the enemy that the latter fell back in haste to take the French at the initial barricade in the rear. Along this one road, smoke rose dry and thick. French soldiers fired from loop holed buildings down on the enemy, bayonet fights were going back and forth and bodies lined the streets. The Prussian surged again over the barricade and this time carried it completely only slowing to regain their bearings and attempt to fire back at the enemy. Prussian officers exhorted their men to keep moving.

There was no need to inform Teste of what had happened already. Racing to the scene of the fighting, the grim situation was not lost on him. Ordering up his reserve center companies, he personally organized the retreating fugitives and the wounded into another holding force around the town church, using the structure to act as a rallying point and a defensive redoubt; being a smart and practical man, he quickly dismounted and pulled out a pair of loaded pistols.

"Move! Get next to him! Load your weapons!" he yelled to the disorganized men as the defenders of the barricade attempted to amalgamate into the line of the walking wounded. In such situations, men are emotionally charged and it takes a strong hand to keep them under control and prevent them from either running away completely or trying to take the enemy on by themselves. Teste, one pistol stuffed in his sash and the other in his left hand, pointed with his sword where he wanted his men to go. Soon, and it was necessarily just that, he had made a solid two deep line across the small town center plaza of men with loaded and primed muskets though one man had to be reminded not to shoot his ramrod at the enemy, yet.

Thankfully for Teste, aside from the one breakthrough, no other Prussian troops had been able to breach the barriers along the perimeter of the town. The 5th Hussars, the regiment left behind by Count Pajol, was enough of a deterrent for Kampfen's men, who had the longest distance to march, to not press the western approaches despite the fact that some of their corps cavalry, certainly more than one regiment, was in the area. Clearly, the Prussians trusted their men less to carry the field against fierce French hussars than the latter to ride roughshod over their whole force. Nevertheless, the fighting along the perimeter was quite fierce and on more than one occasion a breach seemed inevitable before casualties or a local counterattack once more swept the area of the enemy. For the moment, the French were holding.

Stulpnagel had watched the breakthrough with fascination and he was not slow in reinforcing success. More troops followed the first ones in but the village acted like a tightening vice since the French still held the outermost buildings and were thus making the Prussians fight in a salient. Ordering his artillery forward, the Prussian colonel sought to break the stalemate on the perimeter and rupture the French front.

"Fire!"

Teste cut the air with his sword as he gave the word of command and instantly the line vanished in a sudden haze that obscured everything and everyone. Isolated shots retorted through the cloud giving the French general an idea of what had happened and he signaled the center companies to charge the staggered Prussians.

"Now men! Now!"

The excited infantrymen, held in reserve this long, had felt like their counterparts in the Imperial Guard except without the pay and privileges. Making up for lost time, they swarmed forward, bayonets leveled, and passed the French line to get at the shattered Prussian front. Yelling or crying "Vive la France!" the soldiers came upon the Prussian troops withering in agony on the ground while others behind them endeavored to come up to the front and carry on the fight. As before, it was a brutal moment. The soldiers bayoneted everything in sight and threw the rest of the troops into a panic along the street as they desperately tried to get away from the menace only there seemed to be nowhere to go. Pressed from behind to go forward and crushed in front by a wall of bloody bayonets, Stulpnagel's troops were in a terrible situation made worse by the human tendency to return by the same route approached. Other French infantry, closing off the exit streets of the town, fired mercilessly down on the panicked Prussians who at last finally managed to spill down another road and flee to the safety of their own lines leaving behind more than one hundred prisoners. The attack, so close to success as it had been, had been defeated and routed in the nick of time.

Teste, mounted again on his own horse, recalled the center companies and directed them to the mini town plaza, an actually easy task as everyone knew the standing orders not to leave the confines of the perimeter. Left with a sizeable number of both trampled and actually wounded enemy prisoners, the French general ordered them taken to beyond the bridge for their own safety; at least there they should be out of harm's way unless the enemy began to bombard the French position again. It is interesting here to note that while the two sides cruelly dealt with each other in the actual fighting, when it came to the aftermath of an action they did all they could to succor the wounded and attend to their needs.

As Stulpnagel's troops fell back in confusion along one part of the front, the French reoccupied the ground as best they could but not all the Prussians had been chased away and some had taken over perimeter buildings and turned them into good footholds in the town. One such buildings was where one French cannon, a six pounder, had been abandoned and Captain Duverrey, hidden amongst the buildings occupied by his own side, burned with anger at having lost one of his guns. For him, watching was bad enough but things really got out of hand when some Landwehr tried to attach pull ropes to it and take it with them as a trophy. Demanding every loaded musket in rotation that could used, he had his own men load while he kept up a very accurate and deadly fire on anyone who neared the gun. After three men had fallen to the captain in succession, the rest of the Prussians decided against the idea and slipped back into their own building.

The Prussian seizure of various buildings on the perimeter of the French position made their next attack that much easier. Stulpnagel's men, resuscitated and rallied, had their doubts about carrying on the attack but nonetheless were formed back up and pushed ahead once more against the French defenses. As might be expected, the attack was not pressed with any ardor and Teste's men were able to throw them back well before they reached the barricades. The men on Kampfen's front were a good deal different. Initially paralyzed by the small but potent threat of the French hussars, they now responded to the cursing of their officers and attacked the town while a third Prussian cavalry regiment arrived to cover their flank. Now, the French had their hands full as the enemy infantry swarmed up to the barricades, received their blasts of cannon fire and pressed ahead regardless. The center cracked. Teste threw in his reserves to stem the attack but the Prussians had managed to break through on a wide front and had isolated the buildings where the French were still resisting. The grenadiers fought valiantly to their front and flank but the enemy sensed victory and were widening their rupture as the rest of the brigade slipped across the French perimeter to join in what had become the main attack. Falling back to the lower edge of town with what troops he could gather up, Teste desperately sought to break the momentum of the Prussian attack and retain his foothold over the Dyle.

*   *   *

"Dismount!"

Count Exelmans, commander of the II Reserve Cavalry Corps, was another man with a reputation to rebuild. Negligent two days before, he had done very little on the eighteenth to aid the cause and now felt like everything was passing him by, including glory and promotion. A man who was reckless to a fault at times, he had received definite orders from Grouchy to lead the transfer of the weight of the attack to Limale and he lost no time in pushing his dragoons at top speed down the road ahead of the marching infantry of Vandamme's corps.

The commander of the II Reserve Cavalry Corps was a veteran soldier but certainly not the best man to have in an independent situation. His overbearing nature and lack of sound command experience at high levels of responsibility could not be readily overcome. At times he failed to use his horsemen like a good leader should, two excellent examples being the disaster at the Katzbach in 1813 and, more recently, the lack of aggressiveness versus Blucher's retreating columns on the seventeenth. His two most obvious traits, bravery and loyalty, reminded some of the Republican armies of the Revolution: one cannot replace training with ardor. Nevertheless, Exelmans found himself commanding a sizeable cavalry corps under a noted cavalry commander and, for the first time and probably because he had firm, simple orders, he acted with alacrity and ferocity.

The lead dragoon regiment of the corps, the 5th, reported that the enemy was in the midst of launching an attack and, to their later dismay, needed infantry reinforcements. Exelmans seized upon this last line of the dispatch to do what he could to "save the day" for Teste and thereby win some glory for himself. Ordering his lead brigade to dismount and join the fight against the Prussians, he figured he couldn't help but look good in the Emperor's eyes.

The dragoons received the order with considerable disgust and the colonel of the 5th, Canevas Saint Amand, found that his men, as they had done over many years, had "lost" their bayonets at some point and so would have to go into battle with only their muskets. Yelling at them that they would have to pay for new ones, he detailed one lucky squadron to round up the horses and get them out of harm's way; a wounded man might survive but a strong mount was simply too valuable to waste. That done, he drew his sword and one pistol and led his regiment, elite company at the fore, towards the fighting.

Teste had expected reinforcements but his surprise was great when the troops that arrived were brass helmeted dragoons fighting on foot. Shaking his head in disbelief, he judged that one foot soldier was as good as the next and he threw them into the firing line to counter a threatened Prussian attack along the river. The other regiment, the 13th, he kept as his reserve with him to be sent in as actions dictated. At the moment, the front had stabilized with the Prussians occupying a good two thirds of the town and a lively firefight erupting over the rest. Several times the enemy had made a great push to sweep them out but every time he had been able to hold just long enough to break their momentum and then recover much of what had been lost. His men were fighting brilliantly but the close action was also using them up. The commander of the 2nd Brigade of his division, Baron Penne, had been killed and the veteran 75th Ligne, his primary defensive unit, had been badly hurt as well. The dragoons, even if they were bayonetless, were a most welcome addition and they shored up his battered defenses enough to allow a counterattack to surround the exhausted Prussians and chase them away once more.

To the north, General Thielemann was anxiously watching the attack from his telescope and he could see that the formations had stalled and pointless brawling continued in the town itself. What should have been so easy would now get even more difficult as the rest of the French arrived from the northeast to reinforce the defenders of the town. Unless they took the town in the next few minutes, he feared that his gamble would not pay off.

*   *   *

Kampfen and Stulpnagel's men were worn out. Fighting in the town had proved decidedly dangerous especially when they were not able to expel the French from it during the first couple charges. They were still getting fired upon from some strong points in their rear and this caused a great deal of anxiety amongst even the experienced men as the French line seemed to strengthen itself to their front. For the men in the streets, the volume of fire from the enemy had grown over the past fifteen minutes and their movements had resumed in the deadly dance of the counterattack. For many veterans, the fierce fighting in the town was like nothing they had ever experienced and it only made them ever more conscious of the fact that they were taking very heavy casualties in the process. Every colonel except the two commanders had at least been wounded while many other leaders were either hiding in houses or dead on the field. The Prussian attack was in poor shape and in danger of falling apart.

The pendulum of battle was quickly swinging back towards the French army. Vandamme's III Corps troops came up twenty minutes behind the dragoons and immediately began make their presence felt along the line. Teste, still commanding despite a recent head grazing by a bullet, ordered them to his right flank where a renewed Prussian effort needed to be thrown back from the riverbank. By placing these men along the water, Teste was also planning for a possible counterstroke at some point if enough fresh troops arrived to allow him to do it. Attacking from every side, he could surround the Prussians and break up their force before they could react and thereby rout the whole attack.

Thielemann saw the danger a little after Teste thought of it and was convinced that the battle had been lost; the French would not be pushed from Limale now. Drawing up yet another defensive scheme, the commander of the Prussian III Corps reluctantly sent out his aides to deliver a message to stop the attack and pull back from the town. The latter, having purchased much of the locale with their lives, was understandably reluctant to leave when victory seemed in their grasp but their officers, especially Colonels Stulpnagel and Kampfen, knew that the French were building up their strength and that a counterattack was inevitable. The longer that the Prussians held on, the longer they courted disaster.

As more and more of Vandamme's men arrived, the firing subsided between the houses of the town of Limale and at first the besieged French refused to believe that the enemy had fallen back but a quick reconnaissance proved them wrong and they cheered their victory. Teste, however, though he was relieved at the sight of the withdrawing columns, could only clasp his fists tightly and give his saddle a soft pounding; the enemy had gotten wind of their reinforcements and had beaten a hasty retreat. The long sought for counterattack would now not go in. He did have a consolation, however: Limale, all pock marked and partly on fire, was his.

*　　*　　*

While the fighting raged anew at Limale, the engagement in the Bois de Paris was getting quite critical for the French as the attack by Bulow was reaching its climax. Every position in the shade of the trees was under heavy assault by the Prussians and, with little support and even less depth, Lobau feared that his men were going to collapse under the pressure of the enemy numbers;

if it was not for the forest itself he knew he would have been thrown back much earlier.

Lobau did not know it yet but the support of the entire Army of the North was on its way. Long columns of infantry, cavalry and artillery crowded the main thoroughfares as they had done since the early hours of the morning and already the first units had arrived on the Ohain battlefield to bring indirect support to Lobau and his men in the forest. Durutte's and Marcognet's divisions were marching north of the forest to take up their positions and a large number of French horse guns had taken their place in the clearing on Lobau's left to duel with the Prussians and keep them honest in the time before the main French army arrived. The whole mass of French troops was marching to the sound of the guns.

The unlimbering horse batteries from the cavalry units arrived one after the other and wheeled into place which in some cases was in very close proximity to the other companies. Dust, grass and shouts of command all mingled together as the troopers dismounted and raced to get their six pounders into place to fire which, under the circumstances, was not easy. The lay of the land at the spot where the battery was being thrown together was uneven and far from ideal but orders were orders and Napoleon was not to be denied the formidable battery he wanted placed here. Looking to the east, the sweaty gun captains saw far more favorable smooth terrain and kept the image in the back of their heads; the Emperor would surely see to it when he arrived.

Napoleon was indeed on his way to the field. Galloping past the marching troops, he knew he was tardy in reconnoitering his future field of battle and he lost no time in seeing all that he could in the time that he had to do so. Furious fighting could be heard by the rumble of muskets in the forest and several aides riding from Lobau's headquarters confirmed that the VI Corps commander was under heavy pressure. Napoleon took in the repeated reports with calm understanding nods which puzzled the excited aides as he seemed to fail to imply the urgency that they felt was clearly needed. They were deceived. The Emperor had already seen to the strengthening of Lobau's force and two units, one very familiar and the other not, were designated to join his "Lion" in the forest and bring relief to the troops fighting in it. General Morand, a fresh bandage covering a wound he received in the arm during the last fighting at Plancenoit, was back in the saddle and leading his veteran Old Guard troops to rejoin their fighting brethren of the VI Corps in the forest. The other support for Lobau was the reorganized infantry division of General Donzelot from the I Corps who was designated to relieve the center of Lobau's line in the forest. Donzelot, a general who had only recently returned to the continent after conducting an impregnable defense of the island of Corfu, was only now getting back into the swing of things and his performance at Mont St. Jean had been uninspired at best. Reflective and worried, he hoped that he could somehow alter the course of events as they were now unfolding in the campaign and at least regain the former luster his name, he felt, had lost. Little did he know how he was going to reverse those very fortunes within the next hour.

The Emperor conducted his reconnaissance of the coming battlefield after visiting personally with Lobau at the edge of the Bois de Paris. The latter reported the Prussians in a quiet lull but he fully expected the attack to recommence soon. Napoleon agreed. More enemy troops were seen massing behind the Prussian battery and it was apparent that another corps would soon be joining the fray. Napoleon reiterated his plan to help his solid VI Corps commander and actually pointed out the marching troops that were coming to join him. This evidence gave Lobau heart as he knew that the Emperor had not forgotten his men in the rush to get the Army of the North to the front. Leaving Lobau, Napoleon rode north along the edge of the forest to observe the buildup of the enemy regiments and then was met by officers reporting their scouting along the Smohain brook and the Bois de Ohain. From this information, a picture of the Prussian position that morning began to emerge. Blucher had taken up a position similar to that occupied at Ligny but with different advantages and disadvantages. The infantry brigades were deployed in the forest between the two brooks and then angled off to the northeast following the track of the Smohain to the town of Ohain itself which had already been prepared for defense. The Bois de Paris was an excellent source of cover for his men but by the same token it was a bottleneck for any potential attack as Bulow was experiencing at the moment. The twin brooks along the Prussian lines limited options of the French in the attack but also constricted the Prussian army into a funnel if they were attacking and left them vulnerable to someone closing in behind them should they have to retreat. What was more, like the position at Ligny three days before, the Prussian deployment left them ripe for artillery crossfire and the Emperor, always a gunner at heart, was very willing to grant their wish; it was amazing to think how often the same mistakes could be repeated. But, as he figured at Ligny, Blucher was too full of fight to let an opportunity like the one he thought he had in front of him slip by. The old man had learned nothing of the art of war. How many times had the French armies moved quicker than the Prussians to snatch the advantage from him? Stopping his horse with an abrupt tug of the reins, he stared into the forming dark ranks in the distance. Now more than ever, it was time to teach old Blucher one last good lesson.

The actual Prussian position changed Napoleon's plans in only the slightest way; one change, like the artillerists expected, was moving the grand battery slightly ahead and into better terrain. As the Emperor returned from his own scouting, he focused on three objectives that would crush Blucher if they could coordinate the attacks with any degree of diligence. Reille would be given Ohain as his target to prevent a Prussian retreat to the north. Gerard was already marching towards Chapelle St. Lambert, well in the Prussian rear, and was confident to reach there before the Prussian could even disengage. Finally, in the center, Napoleon planned to seize hold of Blucher's main army corps and, like a hammer, shatter them against the might of either Reille or Gerard depending on which way they fled. As at Bautzen, Napoleon planned a battle of annihilation and this time he felt confident there would be no one to ruin his plans.

Back at the Mont St. Jean battlefield, the French Service de

Sante, along with some gracious help from captured English and Dutch surgeons, was tending to the untold numbers of wounded men that now occupied every building that possessed a roof in the area. Amongst these hurt men was Marshal Ney and now, as ever, the sound of the guns in the distance beckoned him to get up and join the fight. Staggering to his feet, he made one wobbly step towards the door of the makeshift infirmary before he was accosted by the ever watchful and never resting Baron Larrey who, unbeknownst to Ney, was under orders to not let the marshal go anywhere until the fighting was over. Growling something almost inaudibly, Larrey directed Ney back to the floor to rest and bade him rest.

"It is only a rearguard," he said comfortingly though he knew full well that he was lying. In the next few hours they would once more have their hands full of maimed young men; there would certainly be no sleep for many of them in the days to come.

Ney's eyes opened briefly and focused softly on the surgeon in chief of the army. "Agalae and the boys would like to see me home," he considered before sagging back into a deep and satisfying sleep. The rumble of the guns soon melted into the quiet and sorrowful sounds that drifted through the house.

*   *   *

The Prussian buildup seen by Napoleon was not exactly what he thought it was. Supposed to attack at the same time as Bulow, Zieten had several unexplained delays and did not get his attack off until over one half of an hour later. This might be justified by a lack of confidence in the overall plan or simply by another general enjoying his breakfast but, whatever it was, the Prussian I Corps did not strike against the French in a simultaneous move with the might of Bulow's IV Corps. The half hour delay would make things a good deal different for the opposing forces.

The assembled Prussian batteries of Colonel von Lehmann had been dueling with the French horse batteries for some time as Zieten's infantry massed to the rear of the guns though far enough away so that the rolling cannon balls could not reach them. Behind the guns was the 3rd Brigade of Major General Jagow whose task it was to sweep right around the battery and support Bulow's attack in the woods by drawing off any French reinforcements that were on the march. He was in for more than he had bargained for.

While the thunder of the cannon and the muffled blaze of firing in the forest marked the area as a major battlefield, Jagow's men commenced their advance through the trees and along the upper bank of the Smohain brook. It was a difficult task, as the terrain was steep and sloping, and the advance was tortuously slow for the Prussians who, as any troops would have, lost their formations and became a mob that needed to be realigned as it reached the smoother ground along which the French had placed their guns. The appearance of the Prussian troops, in one of those frequent but lamentable moments in war, caught the French by surprise and two companies of horse artillery suddenly found themselves under fire from enemy infantry. Without stopping to even think about what was happening, they hastily hitched up their pieces up and galloped away. Given where the Prussians had been and the fact that they had to pause to dress ranks and the like, it is difficult to imagine how the French could have been so surprised in their position. Perhaps it was that odd French tendency at times to neglect simple scouting but whatever the cause it left a convenient gap on the hill crest that the Prussians were now able to ascend in peace. Thankful for this prize bit of luck, the Prussians were able to enjoy a small but profitable victory and begin to threaten the rest of the battery in earnest.

The departure of the two companies of horse artillery caused quite a stir in the battery and, to Lallemand's horror, firing fell off precipitately. Gunners looked about in confusion as they thought about riding away to safety but the mighty battery's commander was under no such illusion and he took control of the dangerous but recoverable situation.

"Action flank!" he yelled over the noise of battle in such a way that everyone knew where he was and that they had to move instantly. "Hurry!"

A concrete order can be a god send for troops uncertain of

their situation, probably because it takes their mind off the potential disaster and engages it in some other task that carries the more immediate threat of one's own sergeant and superior officers. This was the case here. Once told, the horse artillerymen lost no time in deploying a company of guns to their flank, loading with canister and then letting fly into the approaching Prussian ranks. They moved like clockwork. The moment the gun discharged, the men were right there to grab hold of the wheels and carriage and push it back where it had been before the recoil while another sponged out the smoking barrel of any debris. Right behind him another man had already snatched another round of ammunition reloaded the muzzle of the gun in order for it to be rammed home. The gun captain then directed the aiming of the piece by shifting the trails of the carriage and then the vent hole, covered until now to prevent a premature discharge, was primed to fire again. When all was done, and this did go very quickly for a well trained crew, the men stepped away from the wheels and the piece was fired. In this case, a burst of deadly double canister shredded the Prussian ranks and they fell under the impact to hide below the crest. In the blast, Lieutenant colonel von Seydlitz of Infantry Regiment #7 was gravely injured.

Stymied by the rapid recovery of the guns, Jagow's troops naturally shifted around to the rear of the battery where Major von Hymmen led Infantry Regiment #29 farther west before making his appearance. Still in the valley, his regiment was favorably placed in a fire and sight dead zone so he pushed ahead in columns of attack to take the whole French position in the rear. Enemy voltigeurs, appearing from the west, engaged his jagers in a furious little firefight but his maneuver had placed his men in a very favorable position in which to engage the battery which had just fired a second blinding burst at the 7th. From his horse he could see the gun teams being led away in haste and he immediately ordered his men to shift once more to the east.

"Sir! Behind us!"

Hymmen turned to look west. To his dismay, the voltigeurs that his men had so easily brushed aside without a second thought had been augmented by more enemy troops. Cresting the hill was a long line of French infantry with their drummers beating the famous (and often deadly) pas de charge. Every second counted at this moment and he yelled for his men to stop though they had already commenced their wheel.

"About face!"

The infantry that faced the trapped Prussians was that of General Durutte, one of the great heroes of the previous day. In one of those odd ironies that sometimes happen in war, the leading unit of the French advance was the splendidly clad 29th Ligne, the same formation that had calmly watched the Prussians of Zieten's corps march away from the battle at Mont St. Jean the previous evening. Still largely in their finery, the 29th looked as if it was on the parade ground as it bore down on the hapless Prussians from the hill with leveled bayonets.

Rousselot's men had been the first unit in the long divisional road march column but when word came from his voltigeurs that the enemy had materialized not more than two hundred yards away he rapidly barked orders for his lead battalion to form line and for his trailing one to form a column of divisions and take position on the right of the 1st Battalion. Rousselot's thinking with the threat ahead reflected the mood and urgency of the advance to the front. General Durutte, the divisional commander, had given strict instructions to his brigade commanders that a battle line for the army was to be established first and that enemy troops were to be pushed back and any penetrations sealed off instead of attempting to trap them behind the lines. Given that the French army had no formed reserves in case something went wrong, this was a sound policy and it was what Rousselot would be following in the next few minutes.

"Fire!"

The 1st Battalion of the 29th Ligne had halted forty yards away from the disorganized Prussians and their first volley of the day flashed simultaneously from every musket with hardly a misfire. The thick cloud that formed hid all effects of the shot but Rousselot knew well enough what lay ahead. Signaling his 2nd Battalion, he watched them begin to charge while the 1st Battalion rushed to reload their weapons.

The carnage was extensive though it could have been worse as the heavy packs worn by most of the men, especially those with metal pans and such, protected their backsides and simply if not gracefully knocked them forcibly over onto the ground. The men scrambled to their feet, surprised at being alive but not willing to gamble quite yet on a repeat performance. Hearing the yelling men of the French 2nd Battalion, they stumbled over each other in a mad dash to get clear of the area before all was lost. Shaken to its core, Infantry Regiment #29 collapsed into a host of fugitives and raced back the way they had come which had the unfortunate side effect of stealing away the ardor of the troops behind them; the retreat of the brigade was precipitate. Given more French troops, the disaster could have been far greater but as it was Jagow had to be relieved with the result. Retrieving his men as best he could, he and his officers set about attempting to rally the rest back behind their own lines.

With the retreat of Jagow's brigade back to its start line, the threat exerted by Zieten's I Corps effectively came to an end though no one quite realized yet that the offensive actions of the corps had actually ceased. Durutte's men, hustling to patch the line and solidify it, lost no time in taking the place the Prussians had given up while Marcognet and his men appeared on the road behind them to give substance to the forming French line. Like it or not, the Prussians were slowly losing the initiative to the enemy and would soon be dancing to quite another tune, that is, after one last crisis in the French center.

*   *   *

By half past seven in the morning, the seesaw fighting in the forest was finally beginning to tell on Lobau's men as the greater numbers of Prussians made themselves felt. Jeanin's division in particular found itself under the heaviest pressure probably due to the fact that, unlike Simmer's men, his formation had not had the luxury of routing the first enemy brigade to its front and instead had been fighting a war of attrition with a more numerous and very determined foe. Casualties, though not crippling, were also not the main problem he was facing. Jeanin's primary concern was the lessening of control he exercised over his men while the fighting continued in the trees. Except for two grenadier companies which he held in reserve, Jeanin's forces were spread fairly thin throughout the Bois de Paris as every regiment he had was in the main line. For this reason, he feared that a strong unseen enemy force might yet turn his position and strike his flank before Donzelot's division could arrive to reinforce the line. His fears would soon be realized.

Prussian General Hacke had, like the rest of the attacking brigades, fallen back to regroup and then renew the attack against the French. The Prussians, though strong in numbers, were having trouble actually being able to deploy their forces in the confines of the trees as, like the French, they were having their own command problems. So far, they had managed to dislodge one French unit only to have in the confusion the men begin a firefight with no opponent anywhere to be found. On another occasion, a shaky group of Landwehr had mistakenly fired into the flank of a line regiment which completely ruined the momentum of another attack. Reorganizations after these mishaps cost more time and energy, being something that the fairly rigid Prussian formations were not highly skilled at doing. Nevertheless, after great exertions, the troops were at last back in loose forest formations and ready to resume the assault. This time they had to break through.

General Bulow was growing more and more discouraged as the time ticked away but he was not in a position to withdraw his engaged men as this would admit defeat and the fact that he was wrong at the earlier meeting. French resistance was lively and fierce and the confusion in the ranks was significant, especially after he was forced to deploy his reserve brigade to fend off the attack of Simmer's division on the Prussian left. That the enemy had been repulsed was a favorable omen but rallying Hiller's men would take time and that was something that he did not have very much of. He fully realized that his insistence to attack the enemy had placed the Prussian army in a potentially dangerous situation and that the supposed weakness of the French had been overestimated.

Be this as it may, if a breakthrough could still be forced against Lobau, even the routing of that one enemy corps would put pause to the rest and allow the Prussian army to disengage while the French were busy trying to concentrate with their various pieces across the Belgian countryside; with a three corps army marching together, no separate French force would be able to stand in their way.

The Prussian focus in the attack had thus now changed to reflect the operational reality it now faced. French reinforcements, for much of the morning hidden behind impenetrable light cavalry screens, were streaming in from across the former Mont St. Jean battlefield on their way to join the forces fighting in the forest. Though Blucher might think otherwise, the other senior Prussian commanders were in full accord with the current intentions of Bulow and Gneisenau and they made sure that Zieten's remaining attacks were first delayed and then canceled altogether. A more sober redeployment was now needed to place reserves in potentially advantageous positions that would allow for a staged withdrawal to be made when the time came. There was, however, the problem of Blucher, and Gneisenau knew that it was his duty to give him the "bad" news that the French beast would once more have to be let go. Current reports indicated that enemy troops were trying to build a bridge at Lasne, others were marching for Chapelle St. Lambert, Limale had fallen and, worst of all, Napoleon was quickly concentrating his victorious army against them.

"Sir, we must prepare ourselves for a withdrawal!" Gneisenau argued as the red faced Blucher threw his arms in the air.

The field marshal was in no mood for another retreat. Could this be? Could the hated French be about to slip away again? Slamming his saddle with his right hand, the old soldier could barely contain himself in his anger. Only hours before, his generals had assured him that the French were strung out and ripe for defeat. And now? Where was the great shattering of the enemy line? "We have them!"

Gneisenau knew he had to press the issue for the good of the Prussian army. To march away intact, he was beginning to realize, would deprive Napoleon of the crushing victory he needed in order to march against the Russians and Austrians who were attacking along the French western border. Probably for the first time in the campaign, the allies were finally thinking like true allies and, at least in the slightest sense, were trying to coordinate their overall efforts. What became apparent, as well, was the fact that pursuit of the retreating Prussian army could only be a stunted affair given a significant Austrian incursion into France which he believed had begun already. "Sir, the enemy has gotten in between us and Thielemann at Wavre. We could be surrounded and defeated without ever having fought a real battle! We have no choice."

Blucher finally bowed to his normal temperament and let fly with every off color word in his extensive inventory. This was all too much for him. The pulsating excitement he felt only hours before was quickly being replaced with a bitter dose of disappointment. Finally, his head sagged as he began to accept what his faithful chief of staff had told him. "But what about Bulow's men? Suppose they crush the enemy in the forest?"

Gneisenau knew he had won. "All the better sir. They dare not pursue us then and we can disengage without their interference." Deciding to throw in another item to entice his chief, he added, "The French are scattered across the countryside in at least three separate groups. There is always the possibility that we might be able to catch one of them on the march. Sir, we will yet march in Paris."

"All right, prepare to pull us back," the commander said quietly, his sadness bordering on the profound. "We almost had them, Gneisenau, we almost had them."

As the senior officers discussed the new plan of action, the fighting in the forest had at last taken a turn for the better for the Prussian army. Hacke's brigade, pressing hard against the division of Jeanin, had found what it had been looking for all day and it hastened to exploit the opportunity. The discovery was largely an accident, the result of a marching error by a Landwehr regiment, but the announcement was one that brought excitement to the staff of the brigade and promised the greatest of rewards. They had found the end of the French line in the forest. This might not seem to have been the hardest of discoveries to make but in the trees, against a clever foe who had positioned himself obliquely in the forest, the news was just what they had been waiting for. Twice already they had thought they had discovered this most vulnerable of positions only to find their own flanks shot up and charged by bayonet toting French infantry. This time, however, was a little different. The Landwehr had become disoriented and marched in a northerly direction before they turned west to strike the French line. The aide sent to retrieve them, realizing that the sound of battle was far behind the regiment, was intrigued and he ordered a small group to go with him and locate the nearest enemy unit. He and the scouts, crawling on their hands and knees, had then seen the rear of a French line company crouching amidst the undergrowth and looking only to their front. Sneaking away the way they had come in, the aide raced back to Hacke's headquarters and proudly saluted before volunteering to lead the way for the single line regiment of the brigade to strike the enemy flank while the rest of the brigade, two Landwehr regiments, assaulted the front of the French line. If they could achieve surprise, they could roll up the whole enemy position. If nothing else, they could open the way for the reserves to exploit the breach and crush the enemy corps.

The fusilier battalion of the brigade, belonging to Infantry Regiment #10, was ready for this change in fortune and they crunched along silently at the head of the regiment as the aide, Major von Messchaert, led them to where the Landwehr regiment, now recalled, had gone in its earlier false trail. Given the newly trampled undergrowth, the path was relatively easy to follow and the major, feeling like the Persian wing commander at Thermopylae in 480 B.C. as they flanked the Greeks in the pass, knew that the move, as yet undiscovered, was going to work. Quietly, the group slipped sideways and around the French.

Surprise for the Prussians would not be total but the result would be all they had hoped for. Jeanin, fearing for his flank, had finally gotten to the point where he felt it necessary to send out a pair of aides to check out this vulnerable sector even though there had not been any reports of enemy activity where it should not have been. Running through the trees, the pair of lieutenants reported out of breath to Colonel Roussel and together they relayed the divisional commander's wishes for the reconnaissance. Assigning the two officers a handful of voltigeurs from the regiment, he sent them on their way to find whatever he figured Jeanin expected them to find. At this point, Colonel Roussel was probably a bit overconfident as his men had already tumbled back two enemy attacks and were ready to strike again should they approach and challenge them. The aides, noticing the nonchalant mood of the colonel, reflected his attitude somewhat and the parties they took with them moved slowly and haphazardly through the trees. It would not take much effort to wreck a good idea already gone bad. The Prussian jagers leading the advance spotted the noisy French reconnaissance and laid an ambush for them that when sprung, gobbled up the whole of the first group. Despite the quiet success, Major Messchaert knew that he couldn't conceal so many men for very long so he ordered a step up in the advance that threw the loose Prussian line into chaos but also made them look like a much greater force.

Colonel Roussel was busy walking his lines when he spotted two of his voltigeurs running for their lives from his deep flank and virtually in his rear. Despite his earlier bravado, Colonel Roussel was in fact a good officer whose worst habit was that he believed his men invincible whenever he was present, a common enough trait in the French army. Roussel, however, also knew how to command his regiment. Instantly ordering up his reserves, one company of veteran grenadiers, he told them to take up a position on his flank. It was a moment too late. From out of the brush and tree trunks along their flank, the men of the Prussian fusilier battalion came running out, bayonets lowered and all howling at the top of their voices. The French center companies, manning the bushes facing east, turned to fire on these men and hold them up but as they redeployed to the flank, they were struck by the charging Neumark Landwehr troops to their front. This double strike was too much for the 10th Ligne and the various companies began to disintegrate into fleeing mobs that Colonel Roussel had a hard time in rallying until even he was carried away with them. Only the French grenadier companies managed to hold up the attacking enemy for a time but they, too, were forced back under the heavy pressure of the assault. Colonel Roussel, finding himself deep in the rear of Jeanin's division, had the dubious and bitter honor of being able to report directly to his divisional commander whom he found after he and his men had ceased running.

The damage to the French line had been complete. Looking for an opening, the Prussians had broken a hole clean through it and Hacke lost no time in securing his position. Stopping his jubilant troops was a difficult task, especially for the Landwehr, as they had gotten themselves scattered all over the forest and were, in turn, ripe for a counterstroke. None came. Not believing his good luck but being a good enough commander to not let an opportunity like this pass, he dashed off an aide to request reinforcements to make the breach a permanent one in the French line. That done, he threw out his jagers to the front and his own flank and proceeded to march due west. At first, the men were slow in their movements, probably because of the earlier French ambuscades, but as they continued and found nothing to impede them, the speed of the advance picked up. Through this new and not previously encountered section of the forest, the men felt their confidence on the rise. They had achieved a remarkable result and it would only take another solid push to win the battle. Hacke, too, felt good and he waited for the magical words he had wanted to hear all morning. They were soon in coming. Jagers at last came running back announcing that they had spotted daylight; they had found the edge of the forest and only the plains leading to Plancenoit were now visible. The lead regiment, the 10th, requested orders.

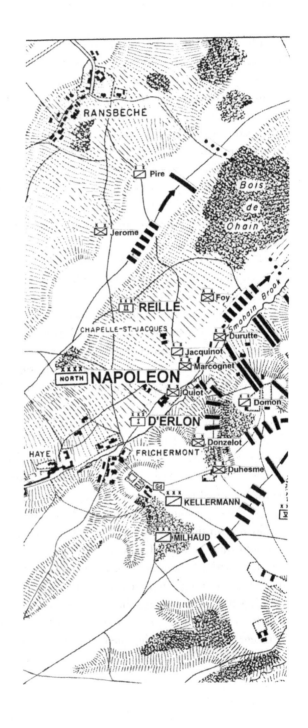

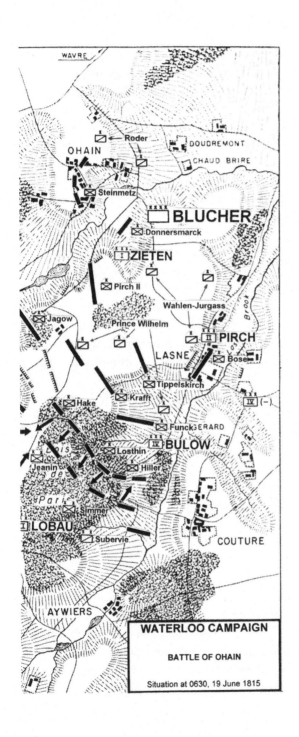

WAVRE

Roder

OHAIN

DOUDREMONT

CHAUD BRIRE

Steinmetz

BLUCHER

Donnersmarck

ZIETEN

Pirch II

Wahlen-Jurgass

Jagow

Prince Wilhelm

PIRCH

LASNE

Bose

Tippelskirch

Hake

Krafft

IV (-)

Funck GERARD

BULOW

Losthin

Hiller

Bois

Jeanin

de

Park

Simmer

LOBAU

Subervie

COUTURE

AYWIERS

WATERLOO CAMPAIGN

BATTLE OF OHAIN

Situation at 0630, 19 June 1815

Hacke's brigade had now swept completely into the rear of the French position and found itself both behind Jeanin's men in the forest and the French gun line which had by this time advanced to better firing fields. French infantry of Marcognet's division could be seen coming up behind the guns and deploying in a large fold in the ground but to their own front there were few visible troops except a cavalry unit screening well to the rear. Hacke himself now came up to the edge of the trees and he, too, enjoyed the view but with an added edge of anxiety in his head. His aide, sent to request reinforcements, had not returned as yet and he openly wondered why that was. He did know that Bulow had been forced to commit the reserve brigade of the corps but Pirch's men were idle at the moment and they certainly could be used to exploit the gap and crush the French. Just as he was about to send off another aide to find out what was going on, the first aide came back to him and faced his commander with a sad countenance. Ashen faced, he explained to his general what had happened and Hacke could only shake his head in disgust: the general commanding the nearest formed but immobile brigade, Major General Krafft, unable to locate Pirch who was at Lasne, had declared that he had no orders and could not move to support the attack no matter what. Bulow, the only other man who could have taken matters in his own hands, was lost to sight several hundred yards away rallying Hiller's broken troops and therefore could offer no help. As a result, the idle brigades of the II Corps stayed where they were and Hacke was left to his own devices. Staring out across the plains, he could only wonder what to do next.

*   *   *

But where were the Prussian commander in chief and his chief of staff? Prussian attention at that moment had been temporarily shifted to another front. At Lasne, French guns had opened fire on the Prussian positions across the river and engineers had splashed into the water to see about fixing the broken bridge with wood stripped from the buildings nearby. Thoroughly frightened by this,

Pirch had halted the movements of his brigades which caused Blucher and Gneisenau to query what was going on at the town. Once more, corps batteries from the II Corps rumbled back towards the high ground and the infantry prepared to fight back against the attacking French.

Gerard's men were putting on a spectacular performance which meant that they were in fact risking their lives down by the bridge. French guns, loaded as quickly as possible and with no regard for real aiming, thundered across the water giving an impression that there in fact were far more French guns than anyone had counted before. Engineers raced to the water's edge and hid behind the pillars of the collapsed structure hauling long planks and boxes of tools. On the slope behind the site, a regiment of French infantry stood apparently waiting for order to advance. For the untrained eye, the ruse appeared quite real and given the obstructed terrain of the area and the constant artillery fire, even the uniformed Prussian engineers had trouble figuring what exactly was happening. Pirch asked for permission to send some battalions down to meet the enemy on the sloped banks but Gneisenau, a careful and cautious commander, smelled a rat and told him to stand where he was for a while and instead to deploy just a few jagers to snipe at the French engineers.

"Let me know the instant they finish the bridge," Blucher's chief of staff said, "but not a moment before!"

Down by the bridge itself, the acting was probably even harder than the real thing. The men, as always feeling harassed by the engineer officers, darted about with their planks under the constant fire from the cannon lining the far shore. Shells exploding in the water around them raised fountains of spray high in the air while the occasional accurate solid shot sent lethal fragments of stone and wood in all directions. Already several men had been wounded, none too seriously though, and the rest, including the same officers, were getting weary of the game they were playing. Nevertheless, they had to keep it up for a little while longer.

Meanwhile, Prussian artillery officers, watching through their telescopes from the north bank, were sensing that something was wrong as well. Puzzled as the enemy engineers removed boards only to place them down again, in the same spot, a few moments later, they did not quite realize yet what was happening.

"What are they doing?" said Lieutenant von Rosenberg, the adjutant to the Prussian army's chief of artillery.

"They are being very careful to match the boards," declared one captain know-it-all to the men around him. "It is very important that the planks be fit with one another to give the bridge great strength and flexibility. All good bridges are built thus."

"Yes, sir," replied a sergeant gunner next to him.

The other officers stared at the captain quizzically, none knowing whether to believe him or not. A lieutenant turned to the gunner standing next to him, shook his head, and said, under his breath, "He is an idiot. They are not doing anything."

"Yes, sir," replied the sergeant.

*   *   *

"Sir! The Prussians are in the woods! The enemy has broken through!"

The situation of the French battle line was in a bad way. Still under heavy pressure in the center and the south, they had settled their northern position with authority only to have the Prussians break through the center of the line and reach the edge of the Bois de Paris. The appearance of these enemy troops in the midst of the French line did not go unnoticed for very long even though only the jagers of the brigade had moved out of the confines of the trees. General Lallemand, the battery commander who had already had part of his command ride off in haste when the Prussians of Jagow's brigade had attacked, saw his right flank train troops begin to run around with puffs of musket smoke originating from the forest. Guessing what had happened, he did not lose his head and his actions began a series of movements that would show why the French army probably had the best command system in the world at the time.

Lallemand's first thought was to move the grand battery away from the danger zone and pull it back to safety. This option was not as detrimental at the moment to the French effort as it might sound. Since a constant flow of heavier cannon were arriving to take the places of the horse artillery companies, the fire from the battery had been diminished in the turnaround and the temporary stoppage probably wouldn't have hurt anything. However, it would be a retreat in the face of the enemy which could very well be misconstrued by both armies. Napoleon, a man who knew a great deal about the minds of men, would no doubt veto the whole idea as unnecessary and potentially dangerous. Deciding against the withdrawal, he instead ordered a just arrived twelve pounder company, ironically Lobau's own, to deploy onto the flank of the gun line to hold the enemy in check. That done, he dashed off an aide to locate the next infantry division coming up the road, Donzelot's, and hurry them along to patch the line. That same aide, along with another dispatched a few minutes later, was also told to report both to I Corps commander Count d'Erlon and the Emperor Napoleon as well.

Hacke's men still were at the edge of the woods. Jagers, deployed to the front and flank, fanned out across the open ground to take the train troops and artillerists under fire while the bulk of the infantry caught a breather and waited crouched in the forest. It was a trying moment for all concerned. The commander of the brigade knew that the French would be preparing for a counterattack like they always did and the longer they waited to attack the poorer their chance of overall success. Hacke knew what he could do. He could wheel his line to the left and march through the forest to face the flank of Jeanin's division who no doubt was ready to receive his attack in the trees and slow him down yet again. This option was a good one but only if they could quickly deal with the French and so far that morning nothing with them had gone quickly at all. Hacke feared getting bogged down in the attack through the trees as he still entertained hopes of leading the breakthrough onto the plains. Dispatching Messchaert again, he told him to hunt down General Bulow wherever he was and tell him what was going on with as much urgency as he could muster.

"Sir!" a somberly clad artillery aide de camp declared as he approached General Donzelot. "Capitaine Lucas reporting!"

Donzelot, casually eating some cashew nuts in his hand, was not surprised to see yet another aide come riding up to the division of the I Corps. One had arrived early in the day to get them all up, another had appeared with orders to move them more quickly and this one he felt must be arriving with a change of position order. In a way, he was right. Donzelot had been ordered to back up the VI Corps in the Bois de Paris and this assignment, to be a simple reserve, certainly wasn't anything that was terribly pressing and his troops, he knew, were highly disappointed at the moment not to be able to get at the Prussians.

The general returned the salute after wiping his hands of the nut shells. "What is it, capitaine?"

"Sir, General Lallemand reports that Prussian troops have broken through the center of the VI Corps and are threatening the great battery," the aide said as he stood in his stirrups and pointed to the east. "He requests you move your infantry to block the enemy advance and restore our position."

Donzelot's eyes widened when he heard the news. Never in his wildest dreams would he have thought that his wish for a second chance would come true but clearly this was such a moment, a moment not to be missed again! No time was to be wasted now! Without waiting for d'Erlon or even the Emperor to confirm the request with a written order, he turned to his chief of staff, Adjutant-commandant Devienne, and clenched his fist in triumph.

"The division will deploy for battle immediately!" he cried out, probably too loud but the feeling in his chest was one that he was loath to give up so soon.

The 2nd Infantry Division of I Corps was ordered to deploy its leading brigade into a column of divisions and to advance right to the spot where the Prussians were stated to be in the shortest possible time. However, remembering his duty, Donzelot did not forget to send aides to his commander and his Emperor to inform them of what he was taking upon himself to do.

The men of the 13th Legere, the leading regiment of the 1st

Brigade and the capturers of La Haye Sainte on the previous day, were puzzled as to why their drummers were suddenly beating a formation call but their sergeants were under no illusions and were all over them to get into position. What had once been a relatively calm march column suddenly coalesced into a real fighting unit. But where was the enemy? 1st Brigade commander, General Schmitz, rode hard over to the very head of his column and turned his glass on the forest. If the Prussians were in the woods, why were they not moving out to attack the French troops? What was going on?

"Quick step! Move!"

The drummers set the pace and the light infantry surged ahead. Perhaps they were going to have some action that day after all. The ground reverberated with the beating of so many shoes along the road. However, so many men in so small a space meant a big dust cloud and the trailing battalions of the division all cursed and moaned at the dry dirt flying through the air. Marching never really was pleasant, except maybe in springtime France and Germany, and now, in the humid heat of a Belgian summer, it was downright uncomfortable. The sergeants, as usual, somehow managed to ignore such conditions and were right there encouraging their soldiers to keep moving and to stay in ranks. Somebody knew something, they concluded, but what it was they had no clue and apparently no one wished to tell them either.

*   *   *

General Bulow had at last managed to round up all the men of the broken brigade of General Hiller and get them back into a semblance of fighting order. Joined by Blucher, who had just returned from Lasne, together they rallied the battered unit so that the commander of the IV Corps once more felt confident that he had a reserve. But for what would he use it? Not one attack had managed to crush the French and his troops were tired from the extreme effort that many of the units had made. Indeed, Simmer's counterattack had shaken his corps to the heart and had upset the whole time table of the offensive (or so he had decided to claim in case of a failure). Riding back to the center of the line at the head of Hiller's brigade, he was deeply concerned for both the army and his own position. Every moment the enemy grew stronger and reinforcements would most likely be funneled into his attack zone thus making any breakthrough an unlikely proposition. The situation was not good.

In the midst of all his gloom, Major Messchaert arrived with the news from General Hacke announcing the much hoped for breakthrough in the French center. "Sir, my general requests reinforcements!"

Bulow's mind raced. They had done it! "The reserve brigade of General Hiller shall back up the attack of your brigade. He may rely on their arrival within the hour!"

Messchaert saluted and raced back to relay the message to Hacke whose only contribution to the battle at the moment was sniping at the French artillerists who had a nasty habit of responding with canister rounds into the trees.

"Within the hour?!" Hacke yelled. "That II Corps brigade is waiting just a couple of hundred yards behind us! An hour will be too late!"

Hacke fumed for a few minutes more before he finally came to a decision as to what to do. They had to try. Ordering his fusilier battalion to deploy on his right flank in semi formed order, he instructed them to engage the French artillerists and keep them from bringing effective fire on the rest of the brigade. His jagers he sent out ahead of the main body while with the rest he began to form a line of battle, hoping against hope that the support of the reserve brigade would be a quicker proposition than Bulow had led him to believe. The troops, confident and determined, marched sharply out of the forest and into the open fields where all could see the leading regiment of Donzelot's division. Clearly, thought Hacke, it was to be a race.

"Form up! Hurry!" the officers yelled as Hacke imparted the urgency he felt for their situation. If opportunity was there, it would not wait for long.

In reality, because of the lack of timely support given to Hacke, the race was essentially over with. Masses of French troops were now converging on the spot to seal the penetration and restore the battle line. Napoleon himself had personally redeployed both horse artillery companies and Domon's light cavalry division to the area and, in addition to Donzelot's men, the Old Guard battalions were on the way from Plancenoit. Like courtiers attracted to a beautiful lady, the Army of the North was off to help its own.

The Prussians, after redressing their loose forest ranks into solid columns, marched out of the cover of the trees and into the plains beyond. The spearhead, Infantry Regiment #10, was supported by only four Landwehr battalions as both flanks had been reinforced to prevent the French from injuring the attacking force. From the trees, Colonel Roussel had cursed his men back into the fight and the ashamed soldiers were now probing the enemy for weaknesses while to the north the gunners of the great battery were still managing to take destructive shots at the attackers despite the heavy fusillade coming from the enemy troops engaging them.

Like a small leak in a great dam, Hacke's attack with only six battalions seeped out onto the plain and stretched out westward. Just their appearance caused Marcognet to angle his flank regiment, several artillery companies to gallop away and one less than careful aide to be shot from his saddle when he thought he was approaching French troops. Despite these small successes, the attack was only a shadow of what it could have been and even Hacke was forced to admit that unless help arrived quickly, his great achievement would be wasted. He could see French infantry, having responded extremely quickly, closing the range, artillery batteries forming up and light cavalry regiments circling behind the guns ready to charge home over any weakness. He marveled at the speed and accuracy of their convergence; surely no army ever moved with such finesse. Holding out until the latest possible moment, he finally deployed Infantry Regiment #10 into line to cover the spear point of the attack but he knew in doing so that he had given up any chance to completely rupture the French front. He would have to fight from there and more than likely without support.

Donzelot's 1st Brigade fanned out slightly to the right while the 2nd took up position behind it in support. The Young Guard, committed by Lobau after he had assessed the situation, moved up along the French right and joined in the assault. All now could see the enemy as he debouched from the woods and it was obvious that he was defending his gains rather than expanding the hole. The colonels wondered if their commander knew this.

He did. General Donzelot, carefully guiding the attack from between the deployed first and second brigades, was on the lookout for any as yet unseen enemy formations but there were none. This was difficult to believe especially since the force ahead of him he estimated to be no more than 3,000 men drawn up in battle formation. Surely reinforcements were on the way, he thought, and thus he came to the conclusion that the enemy must be attacked without losing another minute. Dashing off aides to contact Generals Domon and Duhesme and explain to them what he wished to accomplish, he awaited the first shots of the day's battle for his division.

The 13th Legere, slightly ahead of the other regiment in its brigade, shook out its company of voltigeurs who quickly overwhelmed the enemy jagers with their fire and drove them back on the main body of Prussian troops. From forty yards away, the kneeling and prone light infantry shot the enemy battalions apart but the rest, braving the accurate fire, stood stoically in ranks ready to fire on the approaching French columns.

The light infantry regiment came to a sudden and rapid halt. Orders flew across the drums for the regiment to deploy its three battalions into line. Smoothly executed with the occasional French flair for flamboyance, the 13th Legere ended its short pause and began to come forward again, every musket at the ready but not a shot allowed to be fired. Colonel Gougeon, the commander of this fine unit, emulated Imperial Guard General Dorsenne with his denial of personal danger by riding between the lines to check the dressing of his ranks and actually stopping on the way to tell a soldier to close the flash pan on his musket. Occasional shots came flying their way but the Prussian jagers had been effectively suppressed by the voltigeurs and the issue would now be resolved by the formed bodies of infantry.

The Prussians fired first. Not wishing to have more of his men killed without returning the fire, Colonel von Lettow ordered a volley to be fired at the French who were at about one hundred yards away. Instantly, the line was enveloped in a cloud of thick white smoke.

After that volley, this day became known as the "day of the shakos" in the regimental annals of the 13th Legere. The Prussians, rattled by the sniping voltigeurs and nervous from the numbers of French troops converging on them, had mostly fired high, that is, just a bit high. Taking into account the natural tendency of the musket ball trajectory to sag in flight, the little projectiles had sunk just enough to strike their targets all in their headgear causing severed plumes and punctured shakos to go flying in the air but leaving the light infantrymen startled yet very much alive. Colonel Gougeon, now to the flank of his regiment and pretty much out of harm's way, had his horse hit in the head and killed instantly throwing the surprised officer to the ground. Standing up again no worse for the wear and shaking his head, he took a cool moment to wipe down his tailored uniform of dirt and, only when he was satisfied with the job, then did he draw his sword and motion for another horse.

The 13th, their headgear all over the ground and having taken surprisingly few casualties, continued marching past the ruptured shakos and closed the range while Colonel Gougeon remounted another horse and hastened to rejoin his men. At fifty yards, while the Prussians madly attempted to reload their weapons, the regiment came to a halt.

"Ready!"

Two Prussian musket balls whizzed by followed by an agonized cry.

A split second in the battle became a strange pause that many soldiers remembered years later almost as if time had stopped for men to reflect on what they were doing that day. In a microcosm, the struggle for French sovereignty along the borders of the entire nation was being decided by just these two regiments. That thought was enough to motivate the men in the rank and file to take a little extra special aim this time around . . . .

"Fire!"

Like a blinding flash of lightning, the thin line of French light infantry chasseurs and carabiniers all but vanished in their own smoke while the Prussian front line was swept by the leaden bullets and crumbled to the ground. Colonel Lettow, too, had his horse shot down but was unfortunate enough to have it partly land on his own body necessitating several aides de camp to dismount and pull him free.

Colonel Gougeon, mounted on a singularly unruly horse, struggled with the mount while watching the combat. Proud of his men, he could not help but yell, "That's the way! At them with the bayonet!"

The light troops of the 13th Legere raised a cheer and, moving to the beat of the pas de charge, they ran ahead to engage the wavering Prussian troops. The threat was enough. Infantry Regiment #10, minus its fusilier battalion, took one look at the charging French and came apart at the seams. The 2nd Battalion, the unit which took the bulk of the damage from the terrific volley, lost all formation and stampeded for the rear while the 1st grudgingly fell back around its colors. More French troops began to fire on them and menacing artillery shots sliced through the ranks.

By now, the Prussian Landwehr and regular units, forcibly thrown together by the assault from multiple angles, were getting very intermixed, something that detracted from the overall efficiency of the brigade. Unfortunately, there was little that could be done with the enemy so close and all Hacke could hope for was that the globular mass of troops he had would deter the combined arms enemy from pushing the affair until he was safely back in the cover of the woods.

It was the end of Hacke's bid for a decisive breakthrough in the French center. Brilliantly begun, the operation had quickly lost steam due to a lack of substantial reserves and the very speedy response to the crisis by the French high command. Though his men would hold together in the retreat to the forest and their former start line they would also lose one thousand men as prisoners to the French. The brigade was finished as an offensive tool. Ironically, as a worn and battered Hacke arrived with his men back into the thick of the trees with the French of Donzelot's division somewhere behind them, Hiller's rallied brigade at last arrived to reinforce them. Marching slowly through the trees, it was only able to simply fill the hole in the Prussian line and hold the advancing French. Once again, Bulow was without a reserve.

*   *   *

The defeat of the Prussian breakthrough in the early morning hours of the battle of Ohain had as much to do with the lack of reinforcements as to the rapid response to the emergency by the French commanders on the spot and goes far to show why the French army of the period was so formidable. French officers, allowed to mature in a system that rewarded both skill and bravery, were consistently able to get their men to attack with great élan, rally quicker and react faster to battlefield situations without the heavy burden of rigid structure under which officers of other nations worked. This flexibility made the most of bad situations and one finds that while sometimes they were beaten in battle, French armies were rarely routed off the field. This singular tenacity would pay off handsomely at Ohain.

Bulow's final repulse in the Bois de Paris marked the end of all Prussian offensive activity during the battle of Ohain and it left Blucher's army in a most precarious position. Having made a bid for glory and failed, the Prussians were faced with forcing a withdrawal in the face of an enemy who was bent on their utter destruction. It was a poor situation that even an efficient army would have been hard pressed to get out of and the Prussians, though fierce and determined, were far from that.

Count Gneisenau, informed of the arrival of still more French reinforcements, stared at his maps looking for something that had eluded him all day; the Prussian chief of staff was trying to find a way out of the predicament for his troops. Caught in similar situations during the 1814 campaign in France, the Prussian army had always managed to slip away due to the relative lack of horseflesh that his enemy suffered from. Such was not the case now. Though his army's horse outnumbered those of the French, the latter's regiments were both better trained and, as he had already seen, expertly led. If the Prussian retreat degenerated into a rout, there might be another Jena debacle on their hands and no one wanted that. Soldiers during retreats lost heart quickly and, if even just a little pushed, they would fall apart all the quicker. The Prussian army, having fought just one pitched battle during the campaign and having missed one other major one was preparing to slip away again, surely the sign of an inferior army and a fact that would erode the morale of the rank and file. Another way would have to be found and, indeed, found quickly.

*　　*　　*

Around this time, that is just after eight in the morning, one last detail of the battle of Mont St. Jean still needed to be cleaned up: Hougoumont. After night had fallen over the battlefield, the shooting around the smoldering chateau had subsided and then stopped altogether as the men of both sides sought to get some sleep after all of their exertions during the day. Around five in the morning, Jerome's and Foy's troops had marched away leaving Bachelu's men in possession of the "siege lines" around the chateau. The French 5th Infantry Division, battered from two solid actions against the Anglo-Dutch, was probably the most disorganized and shot up unit in the Army of the North and consequently Napoleon, as he had done with Girard's men after Ligny, ordered them to form the final reserve for the attacking army should they need it. Therefore, by default, it would be Bachelu who received the honor about to be bestowed.

The ranking British officer in the cut off chateau was Colonel Hepburn and upon him would rest the fate of the garrison of the stronghold. Having held the position throughout the battle, he was understandably proud of his men and found it difficult entertaining the thought of a surrender to the victorious French who had swept the rest of his army off the field the day before. While he thought about what to do, a French parley approached the shattered walls under a flag of truce and asked to meet with the commander of the garrison. Hepburn, tired and slightly wounded by a shell fragment that had slashed both his uniform and his shoulder, mounted the wall rampart and told the French to stop where they were.

"What do you want?" he asked in near perfect French though he knew all too well what they wanted.

A French captain walked forward three steps and saluted. "I am Capitaine Morin of the staff of General Baron Reille of the armies of France. My commander asks for your honorable surrender. You are surrounded and your own army is running for the channel. What say you?"

Hepburn looked at the ground, not even noticing the grime all over his formerly white pants or the smelly breeze that carried the scent of the burned out chateau. "We can hold this place indefinitely."

The captain nodded, his flag momentarily blowing across his face. "That may be, sir," he said, pushing it away, "but with your army completely destroyed what is the point of further bloodshed?"

Hepburn felt the weight of all of those watching eyes on him. They might not realize what he was saying but he figured that they knew what the French wanted them to do. Question was, should they do it? Was there any need for his men to hold out? Would not continued fighting just kill off the rest of them? From the lack of firing and the lax attitude of the surrounding French troops it was obvious that Lord Wellington's army was very much gone and the attention of the enemy was entirely focused against Blucher's men near Ohain which basically left them all alone and without support in the chateau. Could he hope that the Prussians, so recently driven away by the French, be able to defeat the mighty Napoleon and then release his own? Somehow, that seemed too much to ask for. Agonizing over the decision, he pointed at the parley flag and asked, "What are your terms?"

Captain Morin, younger brother of Colonel Morin of the 55th Ligne, grasped at what he considered progress. "My Emperor acknowledges your noble defense of the chateau and has graciously stated that five of your officers and fifty of your men may march away unhindered with the full honors of war! The only provision of this offer that he makes is that for the period of one month they may not engage in any military activities of any sort. The rest of your garrison will become our prisoners and any wounded you have will be tended by our doctors. Are these terms acceptable?"

"Bloody hell," said one Lieutenant Pearson who stood a couple of steps back from Hepburn.

The colonel stared at his officer. "Does that mean you want to stay or go, Pearson?"

Hepburn shook his head and turned back to the waiting French captain. "And what will happen if we do not accept your terms?"

Morin frowned. "That would be a most unwise choice, colonel, for this corps of infantry around me will be forced to reopen the fight without quarter. The only certainty would be your own destruction and that would be a great pity for it would be without purpose."

"I need one hour to deliberate amongst my officers," Hepburn said at length. "These things cannot be decided quickly."

"I agree, sir," Morin replied, knowing that his opposite number was playing for time. He held out his watch. "For that reason, I give you thirty minutes to make your decision."

Hepburn wanted to say or do something but knew that he could not; the French, it was clear, held all the cards. Walking off the crumbled rampart, he was immediately surrounded by an anxious group of officers and stared upon by the rest of the garrison. Was there any point to holding out longer? Would not the French guns kill still more of his men, the same men who had held out so brilliantly the day before? There seemed little point to risking their lives, especially in light of the fact that their own army had run away without them. Listening to all the rest of his compatriots, he found that they, too, had seen enough fighting and almost none of them had any faith in the power of the Prussians to decisively defeat the French on their own. It really was over.

"Maybe we should cut our way out, sir," suggested Captain Keane, one of the more aggressive officers. "We might be able to reach the forest before they can react."

Hepburn disagreed. Hitching his thumb backwards over his shoulder, he said, "Those French lancers out there are just waiting for us to do that. We'd never make it."

The group fell silent as most everyone realized that the colonel, though he sounded a bit pessimistic, was unfortunately correct. Unless they wanted to stay for yet another day of bombardment and assault, they had no real choice.

"Well then," the colonel said quietly as he popped open his watch to check the time.

After one last act of defiance, Hepburn slowly appeared along the rampart still holding his watch. Exactly thirty two minutes had passed. Either the Frenchman had really not wanted to start the fighting again or else he simply had a slow watch. "Capitaine!"

"Yes, sir," Morin said raising his arm. "I am here!"

Hepburn, choked with unwanted emotion and frustration, had trouble starting his planned speech and simply threw out, "We accept your terms for an armistice."

Morin looked a bit confused but was smart enough to bow and make a signal to his men not to open fire. "You made a good choice, sir, I did not relish the chance to die without purpose today."

Hepburn pointed towards the sound of gunfire to the east. He couldn't help but throw in one last comment. "You may yet, capitaine."

Bachelu received the news of the surrender with satisfaction but there was a certain sadness in his heart as well. The enemy defenders had fought magnificently only to face defeat even though is was not brought on by their own actions. 'Well,' he decided in his mind at length, 'someone has to win.'

The French general drew up his men at attention along the

road to the main gate of Hougoumont and it was here that the British and allied defenders marched out to lay down their arms and surrender. Not uttering a sound, the French troops stood carefully in place as they watched in fascination as the Guards came out in single file and stacked their arms neatly along the ground. As Colonel Hepburn strode forward with his battered but proud fifty man detachment, his head was bowed and his countenance sad. General Bachelu, recognizing the sight and wishing to do something to redress the moment, barked an order to his men and saluted with his sword. The line troops of the division instantly came to attention and the eagle bearer dipped his staff in recognition. Hepburn, surprised at this gesture but as always wonderfully cool, raised his head and drew his sword as well in salute. Honor to honor, the two great adversaries were now in full accord with one another.

CHAPTER 13

NAPOLEON TAKES CONTROL

GENERAL de Brigade Count de la Bedoyere, Imperial Aide de Camp to the Emperor Napoleon, describes the actions and orders that came from Imperial headquarters during the early hours of the battle of Ohain.

As an aide de camp for the Emperor at the battle of Ohain, I had a better view of the unfolding action than many other people and, of all the engagements I had the honor to serve Napoleon in, it was probably the battle that I worked the hardest. From the early hours of the struggle, during the Prussian attack in the woods, all of the aides of the Emperor including myself were riding clear across the coming battlefield with explicit instructions to get the men moving and to keep them moving in the half light of the morning. My primary instruction from the Emperor was to personally reconnoiter the area north of the Smohain brook and report my findings to General Reille whose corps would occupy the spot prior to the attack on the town of Ohain. I thought this to be an easy task at the time and lost not a moment in examining the area with my own aides, talking to our own cavalry scouts and then heading off to find General Reille and help him in his approach march. The Prussians had not occupied the Bois de Ohain and I determined to use this forest as a fine cover to the advance of the II Corps before actually attacking the enemy. The Prussians did have some guns lining the south bank of the Smohain and I decided against moving in this area.

The morning air was quite crisp and I remember thinking that the day was not going to be as humid or hot as the one previous. Riding west, I soon came across General Foy's division and found this worthy man, though wounded in the shoulder the day before, leading like he always did. Informing him of my reconnaissance and preferred route of march, he readily agreed with my assessment but warned me that General Reille was having trouble getting the other division of the corps, that of Napoleon's head strong brother Jerome, to move out and join in the maneuver. Confused, I searched for and found General Reille involved in an animated discussion with the Emperor's younger brother. The argument, I soon found out, was over who was going to receive the surrender of the chateau of Hougoumont from the British! Jerome, whose troops had been primarily engaged against the fortress, even though this went against the wishes of the Emperor, wanted the honor of receiving what he thought he alone deserved while Reille, caught between being a superior officer and mindful of Jerome's position, tried to get him to carry out his orders. They paid me no heed as I approached and, as I knew the Emperor's desire to move quickly, I deliberately overstepped my orders and addressed Reille in the Emperor's name. I told him that I was there to oversee the movement of the two divisions into action and that the Emperor was anxious for his brother to continue his fine performance of the previous day. Jerome was instantly silent as was Reille and I marveled at the change in climate my few words had managed. This was the last I heard about it from them. Indeed, later that night the Emperor, who never seemed to miss anything, abruptly stopped a meeting and told me I should do well to meet with the great actor Talma and discuss my own "fine performance!"

The concentration of the French army was well under way by the time that Bulow's last attack into the woods had been repulsed. Durutte, Marcognet and Donzelot's divisions of the I Corps were all in line with Quiot's division acting as a small reserve while Jeanin and Simmer of the VI Corps managed to now deepen their defensive positions and for once enjoy a little security in their part of the line. The slowest of the corps to get into action was Reille's

II Corps as Jerome, the master of insubordination, had obstinately tried to disobey orders and remain behind to collect the surrender of the chateau instead of the battered division of Bachelu which Napoleon had wished to leave as a final reserve unit. Finally moving out after a de la Bedoyere stratagem, the II Corps was well strung out and would not enter the battle until later in the morning.

Napoleon could be well satisfied with the way his army had performed over the last day and a half and it was clear to him that the whole unformed mass was actually settling down into a solidly defined whole. Victory at Mont St. Jean had been the ultimate catalyst for the Army of the North and while there remained a few sore spots, like his troublesome brother, for the most part the army was like a ship after its shakedown cruise with all the men and their officers knowing what was expected of them and doing the best job they could. Even Soult was acting more and more like a chief of staff though, Napoleon suspected, this was due more to the scare he had suffered from near defeat than from any love of his fellow officers. Nevertheless, the grand movement of the nineteenth was coming along far smoother than any of the maneuvers previous in the campaign and with greater precision. In part this was due to the Emperor dispatching his own imperial aides de camp to supervise positioning but the fact that the troops even arrived to be positioned meant that his staff was functioning and doing a creditable job. In one rare instance, one aide was reported injured in a riding accident by, and this nearly caused a shock on the part of Napoleon, another aide, carrying the same message, on his way back from the destination they had been both directed to! After the Vandamme incident at the beginning of the campaign, the Emperor had every right to feel pleased at how events were now unfolding and how the internal mechanisms of his army were smoothing out. The Grande Armee, it seemed, was on its way back.

Relieved at the succinct accuracy of the orders sent out by Soult, the Emperor reverted to his old self and once more began a tour of the lines with his returning aides de camp as they arrived to report. Stopping near the gun line and Marcognet's division, he raised his glass to search the open plain for masses of Prussian troops. In between drifting clouds of thick smoke rising from both batteries, he caught sight of deployed enemy infantry directly behind the guns and on the rises to the northwest of the position. Satisfied, he ordered still more guns to be ready to deploy in the center while he rode south to check on his "Lion," the Count of Lobau, whose troops had so expertly held the Prussians in the forest. On the way, he met up with d'Erlon and Donzelot and expressed his satisfaction to the latter for his prompt action in dealing with the Prussian breakthrough. Yes, thought the Emperor, things were indeed on the upswing.

The French line was more stable than ever now and Napoleon found the situation in the forest to be as he completely expected given Lobau's performance. Though battered thin by the repeated Prussian attacks, the proud VI Corps and its commander met the Emperor very enthusiastically when the latter arrived to listen to his former imperial aide de camp. The conversation was brief and to the point; Lobau was to fix the Prussians to his front in place while d'Erlon's men broke the center behind the massed guns of the forming grand battery.

"Well done, Mouton," the Emperor could not help saying in light of the splendid fight that the VI Corps had put up. Against heavy odds, the corps had stopped cold the freshest and largest of the enemy forces. "But you are five days too late for the anniversary of the tree fight at Friedland."

Mouton, Count of Lobau, grinned. If anyone ever had doubts about the ability of his men or their commander, that doubt would now be quelled. "My men were hoping to make another date to remember, sire."

Napoleon's face became deadly serious. "Rest assured, my friend. The destruction of Blucher and his Prussians started in these trees."

"These trees have become our home, sire," the general said as he motioned with his dirty hand. "None of Jeanin's men have yet seen the light of day."

Napoleon nodded in appreciation of his brave aide. "Then it

seems that you have a good objective to fight for. Pass the word. The cross to the first man to step out of the forest on the east side!"

Lobau could justifiably be well pleased with himself and his command. Fighting hard in the forest for two hours against a superior foe, he had been able to slow, deflect and eventually repulse the enemy attack while buying time for the rest of his own army to make it up to the front. Napoleon's comment about the battle of Friedland, where Lobau had been badly wounded, referred to the intense fighting in the forest of Sortlack where Lannes' men held off stronger numbers of Russian infantry while the rest of the Grande Armee marched to their succor. If everything went like that day, June 14, 1807, then a great victory indeed was waiting for them at the end of the engagement.

Napoleon completed his tour of the coming battlefield and established his field headquarters on a knoll approximately in the center of the line. Standing by his little command table, he instantly knew that he would be spending very little time at the spot as it afforded a poor view of what was going on though it did provide an area where his staff could work without fear of being struck by errant cannonballs. The field being largely overtaken with the Bois de Paris, Napoleon had no real effective choice as to where to plant himself and so he chose the knoll while explicitly telling Soult to make sure he emphasized that continuous reporting from his subordinates was crucial to the success of the battle. That done, he turned his glass on the battery of guns in the center and the kneeling line of infantry from Marcognet's division. Aside from the divisions of his brother Jerome and Foy of Reille's corps advancing north of the Smohain brook, all the rest of his troops were just about in position for what he hoped would be the last assault of the campaign in Belgium.

The final French dispositions for the battle of Ohain were as follows. At the north end of the line south of the Smohain brook was Durutte's division which Napoleon expected to perform as well as it had the day before against Wellington. Moving farther south, the I Corps divisions of Marcognet and Donzelot manned the center of the field while the divisions of Jeanin and Simmer and Duhesme held the French right. In support of these infantry divisions was Subervie's light cavalry division on the French right and Domon's light cavalry division behind the French center. As Napoleon envisioned the main battle to take place south of the brook, both French heavy cavalry corps, those of Milhaud and Kellermann, stood in reserve near Domon's chasseurs. The heavy cavalry was much depleted since the day before but enough rallied survivors and gritty veterans had formed up again to make the force one to reckon with especially since the ground here was much firmer now after a day of dry weather. The army reserve was formed up of the Old Guard infantry and cavalry in the center, the detached Old Guard infantry behind the Bois de Paris and, though he planned to use it support the main attack, Quiot's battered infantry division on the French left. Completing the dispositions of the Army of the North was the forming grand battery in the center which Napoleon intended to reinforce significantly before sending in his main assault on the Prussian position.

One interesting aside was a comment heard by an aide as Napoleon met with Baron Radet, the commander of the army's gendarmes. The Emperor, watching small blocks of men, some wounded and some not, marching to rejoin their regiments, had said to Radet that often the quickest reinforcements for an army came after a victory as the lightly wounded, the frightened and the marauders made it back to the field to find their comrades in the ranks. No such thing happened after a defeat.

While Napoleon waited for his troops to finish their final deployment, he went over in his mind the battle plan that he had formulated. Lobau would begin the battle by fixing Bulow in the Bois de Paris. The attack, intended only to hold the Prussians and perhaps draw in some of their reserves, was more diversionary than anything else. The main assault, aimed at the center of Blucher's line, would be begun by a rapid strengthening of the main French gun line followed by the assembly of another battery on the opposite of the brook to bring the Prussian apex under a crossfire. Once done, both groups of guns would begin a heavy bombardment of the deployed enemy guns and infantry. In addition, Durutte's division, operating along the south bank of the Smohain would attack to menace the Prussian guns and draw more troops into the cauldron. Once he felt that enough damage had been done, this preparation would be stopped and the weight of the two heavy cavalry corps under Milhaud and Kellermann would be thrust into the heart of the Prussian position to rupture it while the infantry divisions of Marcognet and Quiot followed up the attack and completed the breaking of Blucher's line. With French infantry behind the Bois de Paris, Bulow's men in the forest would be cut off and ripe for encirclement thus completing the first phase of the grand design. By this time, Reille's corps would have been attacking Ohain and Gerard's troops would be in or nearing Chapelle St. Lambert where the rest of the trap would be finally and totally sprung. As can be seen, the French Emperor was nothing less than totally serious about this battle as he knew in his heart that victory here would mean a possible end to the war as a whole.

But how was Napoleon on this the nineteenth of June, 1815? Probably more than anything else, the Emperor felt emotionally relieved and his personal staff noted that his mood seemed almost jovial; the Emperor in this state, a bit nervous, always checking everything twice and brimming with grim confidence was certainly the Napoleon of old. The Emperor had once said that he was as worrisome as a pregnant woman before he went into battle and this description, though curious, was something that his generals would have agreed on. De la Bedoyere, the officer so caught up in the tension of the moment the day before, commented to another aide, Flahaut de la Billardie, that Napoleon was very much like his old self again. Flahaut, a fervent believer in the Emperor, replied to the effect that he wondered how long he could keep it up given his observations of his commander during the campaign. But de la Bedoyere was more right than he or Flahaut knew. The great campaign had begun under a cloud of impending defeat but, despite all manner of problems, victory as decisive as Austerlitz was within the grasp of the French army. Their great nemesis, the British under Wellington, had been utterly crushed and ruined as a fighting force. Now, with almost all of his army ready to begin the attack, Napoleon was in a position to deal the final blow that he hoped would spell the end of this latest coalition. With Britain and Prussia eliminated from the enemy resource pool, Austria and Russia were relatively minor nuisances given their dependence on English gold and, in the case of Austria, their natural caution. A great victory, a swift march and the Emperor was sure he could scare Schwarzenberg back across the frontier if he had crossed it.

Despite Flahaut's somewhat gloomy forecast, Napoleon actually appears to have been more or less his own self again as now there was no question as to who was going to command the infantry corps, throw in the heavy cavalry or launch the guard should it be needed. He was everywhere and saw everything much like the man at Austerlitz some ten years before. Perhaps he was riding on adrenaline, we'll never know, but his performance on the nineteenth would be amongst his greatest feats. A plan never lasts beyond the first shot and always relies on the commander's ability to adjust himself to the situation as presented to him. Not since the smaller actions in 1814 would the coming battle be so well guided by a hand that was as steady and decisive as Napoleon's though it is all the more fitting given the brilliant strategic plan the French had hatched at the beginning of the campaign. After all the trials and tribulations, it would be a supreme triumph of arms that would produce repercussions throughout Europe. All he had to do now was actually to win the battle!

A rider from Reille arrived to inform them that the two marching divisions were nearing the current French line but on the other side of the brook and would soon be arriving at Ohain to take it under attack. Pire's active cavalry scouts reported Ohain guarded diligently by Prussian infantry who seemed ready to make a stand.

Napoleon nodded in quiet satisfaction after telling the aide to have Reille's men march faster while Soult noted the arrival of the aide and handed him a receipt. As the chief of staff was beginning to realize, their was more to this staff job than he had ever figured and, he thought secretly, the sooner he was away from it the better!

*   *   *

Field Marshal Blucher sat atop his charger without saying a word as his chief of staff Count Gneisenau sent out new orders detailing the withdrawal of the army from the Ohain position towards Chapelle St. Lambert. After the failed attacks in the morning, it was clear to the count that falling back had to be done immediately or there would be no chance at all to do it. Gneisenau was certainly no fool. One of the best ways to keep an enemy off balance was to strike him after a failed attack and he was convinced that Napoleon would attempt just that trick in order to pin them in place for a decisive battle with the rest of his army. The French had proven a stubborn nut to crack and more than a few good men and officers were dead or were prisoners now because of their fierce resistance. He had to admire that quality, silently of course, as even he had thought the attack was a good idea of Bulow's when the latter had suggested it in the conference. But then such was war; things rarely turned out exactly as one had planned them.

Gneisenau, because of the proximity of the enemy, was forced to begin the retreat with Pirch's II Corps around Lasne to clear Chapelle St. Lambert and hold it. This corps would be followed by most of Zieten's men except those holding Ohain itself as these last would be needed to hold the French north of the Smohain in check while the rest of the army fell back. Bulow would have the tricky part in that his men would have to conduct a fighting retreat with a vengeful enemy loose behind them. As he wrote the order, he wondered if they would be able to carry it out at all that day. The morning was still young, visibility was getting better and the French army was getting stronger and stronger by the moment. Reports from scouts noted the approach of all arms towards the center of their line, through the clearing area north of the Bois de Paris, and it pointed to major trouble brewing at that spot. If the French broke through there, Bulow's men would have a terrible time getting out of the trap. Penning a last few words, Gneisenau could only hope that, for whatever reason, the French would hold off on their attack and miss the opportunity presented. He did note one bright spot, however, in all of the gloom. The Prussians had been able to withdraw successfully away from the French after the battle of Ligny when all seemed lost. Here, the situation was much the same. But, as he paused in his thoughts with his pen in his hand, would the enemy allow them the luxury a second time?

More couriers arrived. French troops were seen marching north of the Smohain in large numbers and were closing in on the town of Ohain. Zieten requested reinforcements from the idle II Corps but the latter's commander was loath to lose them for fear that Gerard's men would come storming across the brook. Personally, the Prussian chief of staff thought this very unlikely. Therefore, Gneisenau eventually denied the request when he balanced the pros and cons in his head and realized that spreading the brigades out across the battlefield would be just throwing away his solid reserve. Besides, if Gerard marched instead on Chapelle St. Lambert (as the chief of staff thought the French might be doing), then he would need the striking power of several brigades to push him back and get the enemy away from their lines of communication. Pirch, therefore, would form the central reserve force of the army to be committed only when the troops were most needed and, hopefully, not before.

News of the impending withdrawal spread quickly throughout the army and did nothing good for the morale of the Prussian force. To the soldiers who had fought at Ligny, Plancenoit and Lasne during the campaign, the idea of a retreat without a proper fight promoted the thought that somehow their leaders thought that they were not good enough anymore to face the French. Sixty thousand men were poised on the field to repulse Napoleon's army but the commanders were running scared, they grumbled, sometimes loudly. Where was Blucher? Surely he would fight, surely he would lead them to victory!

Blucher, so often a man of colorful if not polite language, did not have a word to say. Part of his mind told him that they were doing the right thing in abandoning the field to gather strength before facing off against Napoleon again but the soldier in him burned for a chance to strike one more blow, to lead one more charge to glory. Quietly sitting next to the busy Gneisenau, he pondered how to tell his men that they were doing the right thing in retreating. It did not seem fair that they had come this far only to run away from the enemy they sought simply because of the French emperor's reputation. What should they fear? Had they not beaten him before? He pounded his saddle in disgust. Sometimes sensible acts drove him crazy.

Pirch received his orders first from Prussian headquarters but only executed them slowly while keeping a wary eye on those workmanlike French engineers whom he was convinced were ready to move a prefabricated bridge into place the moment he turned his back on them. Organizing the rest of his men, he began to move towards his assigned concentration points though not before he fired on the bridgehead one last time with his cannon. One brigade, Bose's, would immediately march on Chapelle St. Lambert to join Borcke's 9th Infantry Brigade of III Corps and secure the line of retreat for the army while the rest formed a relief line for Bulow's men as they fell back from the Bois de Paris. Judging from the amount of artillery fire to the west of Lasne, clearly, he thought, this was not going to be a simple task especially since darkness was still many, many hours away. No, the army would have to fight this day whether they liked it or not.

At Ohain, the Prussians under General Zieten were preparing for the worst. Ordered by their commander to prepare the town for defense, the men were feverishly barricading the streets, setting up riflemen in second floors and allocating scouts to warn them of the impending French attack. Major General Steinmetz, the commander of the defenses at Ohain, had been told plainly by his corps commander, Zieten, that if the town fell before the army had retreated off the field that they were all doomed. Declaring that he would hold the position till the last, Steinmetz was at least gratified to hear that Donnersmarck's 4th Infantry Brigade would also be in the area to lend a hand if the French assault proved too strong for his troops alone; his enthusiasm would have been a good deal less had he known that the 4th Brigade amounted only to a single battalion of less than responsive Westphalian Landwehr.

Steinmetz was an officer who knew what he was doing and he also knew that to be given a do or die mission was never something that gave anyone great confidence, especially when fighting a defensive battle. To avoid any chance of his men losing heart should they suffer a reverse, he instructed his aides not to mention the true nature of the coming fight to the men and instead to act like they all had great confidence in the outcome.

*　　*　　*

General of Division Gerard, commander of the French IV Corps, was already well ahead of the game against the Prussians. Given definite orders by Napoleon to march to and occupy the critical town of Chapelle St. Lambert, he had begun his march just after seven in the morning and, after a frustrating traffic pileup on one local bridge when a caisson tumbled and wedged itself across the entire span, he had brought his command to within view of Chapelle St. Lambert by half past eight in the morning. Here, however, luck played a role in the camp of the Prussians as his leading scouts suddenly reported back that Prussian infantry and cavalry had been spotted ahead; Blucher's army was being reinforced.

The Prussian troops that the IV Corps scouts had seen were the separate attached units from Thielemann's III Corps, some of whom had only recently marched away from that formation to rejoin the main Prussian army at Ohain. Primary amongst these units was Borcke's 9th Infantry Brigade, the lead unit, ironically, of Thielemann's own corps that had marched away, eluded every attempt at recall and by four in the morning of the nineteenth found passing Chapelle St. Lambert where, an hour later, it received new orders from Gneisenau to march back the way it had come and actually occupy the town. Borcke, a conscientious officer and one who appreciated the value of the town, wasted no time whatsoever preparing the place for defense as he set his men to work loop holing and barricading the buildings and streets. Posting jagers well in advance of the main line, he ordered them to retard the French movement as much as possible and he made sure he explicitly told them to actually report what they saw, a common failing in every army; all too often, commanders on the spot would forget this seemingly trivial but actually crucial part of their duty. That done, he watched and waited, not knowing that the day would hold many surprises.

Two more units from the Prussian army were on the march as well. One was Stengel's Infantry Regiment #19, the ousted defenders of Limale, together with a small force of cavalry which had left the outskirts of that town and traveled by a northern route to reach the main army. The other unit on the road was the 10th Hussar Regiment under Lieutenant colonel von Ledebur who was taking a different, more southerly route accompanied by a pair of guns. These troops, having left Thielemann's force at around six in the morning, were all nearing the town though Ledebur's men had detoured for a moment to collect some much needed forage for their horses. This delay, coupled with the routine problems encountered on any march, slowed their approach enough so that another unit, Pajol's two regiment "corps," would sight them near St. Robert and immediately give chase.

Pajol's cavalry squadrons, all jaunty hussars from the 1st and 4th Regiments, reported movement ahead of them around seven in the morning and their commander ordered them to investigate to see if the force was a friend or foe. Pajol, his men traveling in between the armies, was convinced that if there was a force up ahead it would be an enemy one as he considered it unlikely that Gerard would be anywhere near Chapelle St. Lambert this early in the day. He was so sure that he was right that he decided to push ahead with all dispatch (though the earlier stigma of having gone the wrong way in pursuit of the Prussians probably also still bit him). Sure enough, his scouts reported Prussian cavalry in regimental strength accompanied by two guns which, at the time of the sighting, were being unlimbered around the crossroads near St. Robert. The cannon complicated matters somewhat but he did have six guns of his own to match them with and he was certain that his two hussar regiments could overrun any number of the unwieldy Prussian horsemen so he ordered his tiny "corps" to prepare for battle against the enemy horse.

The retreat of several horsemen in the distance disturbed Ledebur enough to recall his remaining foragers and place his two cannon on the only available rise near the intersection of the roads at St. Robert. If the horsemen were French, which seemed likely, he would hold them here so that they could not approach Chapelle St. Lambert which he knew now to be garrisoned by Borcke's infantry. Then and there, he resolved to ask for reinforcements should the French be more than just cavalry.

The horsemen of Pajol trotted along the dirt road towards Chapelle St. Lambert making good time and eager to renew the struggle with their Prussian opposite numbers. The hussars, fearless daredevils all, kept a keen lookout across the ground until they were graced with the sight that they had been waiting for: Prussian horse. General Soult, younger brother of Napoleon's chief of staff, was an officer of limited confidence who had been uplifted by the great success at Limale the day before. Buoyed with new found pride, the general decided, against the wishes of Pajol, to lift a regiment of his hussars at the enemy and dash them before they had a chance to form up. Taking Clary's 1st Hussars with him, he led them forward as the 4th Hussars, the trailing unit, watched them go straight into action. Pajol, having been with the commander of the 4th and his staff, could only stare dumbfounded for a moment before hastily ordering his remaining regiment, save one squadron, to deploy for action. If Soult had made an error, it would take the 4th Hussars to get him out of it.

The two Prussian guns puffed to life against the advancing wave of cavalry but Ledebur felt that the French had already found him out somehow and realized how small his force really was. Still, feeling that it was his part to try and hold the enemy horse away from the battle, he resolved to meet it in classic style and attempt to roll it up. Not knowing really what to expect of his men, he ordered his own hussars to fall back in a planned feigned retreat in the center while the flank squadrons fell in on the enemy and threw him into disorder. A retreat with these horsemen was likely to produce an unexpected result and he could only hope that their discipline would hold out long enough for him to defeat the attack.

Soult's charging hussars felt that they had suddenly inherited Marshal Ney and certainly not Marshal Soult. Forgetting everything and everyone, General Soult played the role of a regimental colonel, a post he had certainly loved, and led the charge with sword outright. It was a magnificent if foolhardy demonstration; the Prussian guns nearly ended his career as a bouncing cannon ball visibly swept by missing him but catching the horse of some poor fool behind him. Undeterred, Soult neared the guns just before they could fire again and succeeded in wounding at least one man before sweeping by. Up ahead, he could see the Prussians falling back in confusion just like on the eighteenth and he spurred all the harder to catch them and complete the rout of the enemy; that something might be wrong probably never occurred to him until the horse he was chasing turned around to face him. Frantically glancing all around him, Soult could see his glory slipping away.

Catching everyone by surprise, including Ledebur himself, the Prussian horse actually managed to complete the maneuver more or less successfully. As if on call, the flanking squadrons hit the charging French while the two middle ones reformed and moved to reengage in the battle. Soon enough, confusion reigned in the French horse as the exclusively hussar cavalry fight turned against them and their casualties mounted. In the swirling engagement, the fiery French hussars managed to hold their own for a while but the good tactics of the Prussians disordered their formations and scattered the rest into small pockets. Everywhere, the soldiers of the 1st struggled to avoid the local superiority of the enemy and they would have been utterly routed if it had not been for the 4th Hussars, led by Pajol himself, which came to the rescue and once more turned the tables of the combat. Thundering past the silent guns (and chasing away the gunners who dared to try and get their pieces away), the commander of the I Cavalry Corps guided his few horsemen in workmanlike fashion to roll up the previously victorious Prussians and escort them off the crossroads. However,

Pajol held his men to the battlefield and allowed the enemy to retire unmolested down the road again. For his trouble, Pajol had captured two guns but had suffered far too many casualties while gaining an unwanted respect for his Prussian opponent. To Pajol's chagrin, and as could be expected by any real cynic, an embarrassed Soult and his horse emerged completely intact from the fight.

Ledebur's men fell back quickly on Chapelle St. Lambert where they met up with Borcke's infantry and reported their action. Needless to say, Pajol's cavalry was neatly inflated to become several regiments with god only knew what else coming up behind him. Borcke was now faced with the possibility of being smashed by two converging enemy forces as his own scouts had reported that French infantry was approaching from the south together with yet more cavalry. Where were all these troops coming from? Could Grouchy be marching to rejoin the main army? Not being able to answer these questions, Borcke nevertheless sent an aide to tell Gneisenau what was going on and then sat back again in his loop holed town to await the onslaught. Ordered to hold the town, hold the town he would.

By now, Gerard's men were in visual sight of their objective and it was Vichery's troops who knew they would have the honor of starting the battle. Coming under long range sniper fire from the Prussian jagers, this divisional officer requested orders from his chief as he deployed his brigades for action in a series of columns supported by foot artillery. The commander of the IV Corps, hoping that some sort of race might yet be won against the Prussians, told them to advance immediately on the town and, if possible, to take it. Vichery complied readily and quickly sent forward his men with the hope that they might be lucky and catch the enemy off guard; unfortunately for the French, there would be none of that sort of surprise here today. Supported briefly by artillery, Vichery's division assaulted the town and was thrown back after a savage little house to house fight against the Prussian infantry holding the position. Given the élan of the attacking force, Vichery could only think, correctly, that the enemy held Chapelle St. Lambert in fairly good strength and would not be dislodged so easily or quickly. Recalling his men, Gerard knew he would have to settle for a set piece attack and so he prepared to launch a two division assault with one, Pecheux's, in reserve to prevent any nasty surprises.

Shifting his weight on the less than comfortable saddle, Gerard pointed at the church spire of the town. "I want our flag flying from right there."

Loriere nodded. "I suppose it all depends on the strength of the Prussians. They are ready to fight, we just saw that."

Gerard shook his head. "That was a scramble, nothing more. If their commander had more men, he would deploy them and their artillery around the town as well but I have not seen any and our scouts have not either. That's all they have and I'll prove it, too."

The plan devised by Gerard envisioned Vichery's men assaulting the front or southern end of the town while Hulot's infantry, supported by Vallin's cavalry and the bulk of the corps artillery, struck rapidly along the left flank of the town in order to stretch the defenders, potentially cut them off from the rest of the army and then strike them at their weakest link with a quick massing of guns at the vulnerable spot. Unlike many of the Prussian attacks the day before, Gerard was planning from the beginning to coordinate all his arms into one finely tuned assault that at the very least would sever this force from the rest and still place his corps along the retreat route of the main army. At the same time, informed of the Prussian withdrawal from Lasne (the bombarding guns had at last rode away), he ordered all of his men there, the 96th Ligne, most of his engineers and Pecheux's divisional guns, to rejoin the main force though he knew they would not be available for the impending attack.

While the French IV Corps was gearing up for their attack, Ledebur had met with Borcke who had instructed him to post the 10th Hussars along the Prussian right in order to secure communication with the main army. By nine, the first French attack had been driven off successfully though Borcke knew better than to think that his enemy was anywhere near finished fighting for the day. The Prussian 9th Infantry Brigade was a strong unit of around six thousand men and this gave Borcke some flexibility in using it for the defense of Chapelle St. Lambert. The brigade, composed of three regiments, was the best one in Thielemann's III Corps and the quality of its infantry showed. Amongst the units was Infantry Regiment #30 which was probably better known as the former 1st Regiment of the Russo-German legion that had fought during the 1813-14 campaign. Dressed in Russian green tunics, this regiment separated itself both visually and in talent and they would give a good account of themselves during the battle.

The town of Chapelle St. Lambert itself, a narrow north to south type community following the main roads, was a difficult one to hide many men in so Borcke deployed one regiment tightly in the town behind loop holed walls, shifted a second to cover his right and the bridges over the Lasne, and held the third in reserve behind the front or rather to the north. Lacking anything more than eight guns, he could only hope that his request to Gneisenau should be granted and the additional guns delivered before the French attack; given his odd situation, he really had no chance to get any guns from Thielemann! Borcke's only real concern was for the link between himself and the main army and it was exactly there, especially at the Lasne brook crossings, that the French were going to strike.

The French failure in the first attack on the town was pretty much as Gerard described it to Loriere; simply put, it was a hasty throw-together affair that carried a small punch. The fact that it was repulsed was no surprise and casualties were not very heavy because relatively few troops had been engaged. This next attack would be in earnest. Unfortunately, forming up for set piece attacks takes some time and it was only at ten in the morning, when the Emperor's attack had already begun, that he was actually able to begin his own version of the grand assault. Strangely enough, the necessary delay would make the attack nicely coincide with the swell of guns to the west and thus accentuate the urgency felt by both the attackers and defenders.

*   *   *

Napoleon was at last satisfied with the deployments of his army. Aside from the cannon of both parties firing upon one another, the dull rumble of infantry combat had fallen off and all was relatively quiet. Looking about from the Bois de Paris to the Smohain brook, the Emperor made a last quick survey of the ground to see if he had overlooked any crucial detail in his dispositions. Alone in his thoughts, he let a slight breeze refresh his overburdened mind and he removed his hat to pass a hand through his thinning hair. His brain, overworked and under a terrible strain of responsibility, ached badly and he pressed his left hand to his temple while closing his eyes. He exhaled completely, for a bare moment divorcing himself from this field. The bliss vanished immediately. Aware that more than a few eyes were on him, he sharply replaced his bicorne and suddenly swung over to face Soult. His worn eyes stared at his chief of staff. "Start the attack."

Marshal Soult, sitting at the little battle table, nodded respectfully and motioned to a series of aides he had waiting behind him just for that purpose. Handing them the orders for d'Erlon and Lobau, he sent off the first group at a gallop, waited a few more minutes and then ordered the repeat couriers to go. This bookkeeping job, he thought ruefully, never did appeal to him. "And the guns, sire?"

Napoleon watched the progress of the aides as they rode hard across the fields with his telescope. Once the fighting started, he knew that his Prussian opponent, surely the most implacable and probably unbalanced foe he had ever faced, would respond with great vigor and play into his hands. The old field marshal might be predictable in his actions but even the Emperor was forced to extend his respect to the man as he was like a bulldog that never lets go of his prey; this man would never give up. "We'll wait until our friend Blucher makes his reaction. Durutte, I have no doubt, will force him to do that."

The chief of staff remained silent but was in total agreement. Durutte, one of the best divisional commanders in the army, was just the type to seize the initiative on his flank and, by advancing aggressively, draw in the Prussian reserves. When enough of them were exposed, the French guns would quickly deploy and open a withering fire on the masses in preparation for the grand cavalry assault later in the day. Oddly, Soult, unlike the day before, felt reasonably sure that events were actually moving in the way the Emperor desired and he attributed this to the fact that Marshal Ney, his erstwhile rival, lay with the wounded back at the Mont St. Jean battlefield and thus was not around to throw the grand design off its carefully laid track. Still, he above all knew the condition of the Emperor and the great man gave quite a few indications that he was very tired and probably had a formidable headache; another battle like that against Wellington lasting as long as it did would likely ruin both the army and the Emperor. This is not to say that Soult was not confident that Napoleon knew what he was doing. On the contrary, the marshal had been able to witness what he considered the finest plan the Emperor had ever conceived and brought to execution. The only problem was that the man was clearly exhausted from his great exertions, something Soult realized he had not helped in much, and he wondered whether or not Napoleon would be able to finish the battle on his horse or, as he had heard about at Borodino in 1812, simply slumping in his chair while the battle went on seemingly without him. There and then, Soult determined to do what he could to make sure that not only were all the orders presented correctly and on time but that there would be no French need for a repetition of assaults against the enemy. The battle of Mont St. Jean should have been ended far sooner than it had been and he accepted his responsibility (though he would never admit that to anyone). This time had to be different.

*   *   *

Count Lobau, ensconced with his VI Corps in the forest, received his orders from the first courier and immediately sent out instructions to prepare to take the offensive against the enemy. Having been subjected all day to relentless but unsuccessful Prussian attacks, his men were ready to take the fight to their enemy and see how he liked it for once. Napoleon's former aide was under no illusions, however. Just as the might of the Prussian IV Corps had barely crawled through the trees, he could not expect his men to do much better except for the fact that they were more flexible fighting in the trees and might be quicker to exploit any Prussian mistakes. After he sent out his orders, he wrote a short note to Donzelot warning him that the offensive was about to begin and for him to be ready to advance should d'Erlon neglect to release him to move; Lobau had heard about d'Erlon's less than perfect experience the day before and he was adamant not to join that exclusive club.

The fighting in the trees had died down to a mere cracking of muskets between pickets and the feeling in the ranks was that the enemy was going to withdraw. What a shame that would be if the enemy was let to slink off without a proper reception! Such was their enthusiasm that when the order to begin the attack came, more than a few officers raced over to make sure it was indeed what they had been waiting for. Jeanin and Simmer, the divisional commanders, were understanding but cautious although their troops, on the other hand, were ecstatic. This gratified Lobau as his poor men were worn out from all the fighting and still able to cheer for one more assault. Perhaps that's all it would take.

Lobau, standing with the wounded General Morand of the Old Guard, told him, "Mark my words, the Imperial Guard will not have a role to play today."

"You are an expert, Mouton?" replied Morand with false surprise.

"No, just a positive thinker," said the irrepressible Lobau. "Today will see a great triumph, I feel it."

Morand, an old and trusted veteran, raised a hand to the bandage on his head. Confidence in one's self and one's troops could do wonders during a battle. "The only thing I feel is this gash in my skull, but I will take your word for it."

A courier dashed up and saluted. "Sir! General Donzelot is ready to advance with our men. He will move when we do."

Lobau pulled out his watch and clicked open the lid. Quickly calculating, he snapped it shut while the aide removed his. "Tell him we move at forty minutes past the hour. It is half past now."

The aide confirmed the time (actually making a mental adjustment for the minute he was different) and then put spur to horse and galloped away to make his report to Donzelot. Whatever might be said about the success or failure of the attack later, it was going to be started on time.

Lobau, having spent more than enough time in the casualty strewn forest, had a plan for the attack in the trees he hoped would work. The Prussians, he noted, had been fairly good singers but far too obvious, for the most part, in their attacks as their aggressive speed seemed to be lacking. The one attack that had succeeded for a moment, Hacke's, had been a well planned surprise against his flank by troops that had time to use some stealth. Mixing the two ideas in his mind, he came up with his plan for the assault. First, there could be no flank attacks since the Prussian still outnumbered him and finding an open flank would probably be impossible; this left a straight approach. Next, the initial shock would be delivered in such a way that the enemy would be caught off balance thus giving his men the advantage of good momentum. Lobau did not count on a breakthrough; but if he could draw in Prussian reserves like Napoleon wanted him to, then he would be contributing greatly to the cause. Deciding on his tactics, he had sent his commanders their orders. Instructing his men not to use their drums or horns at the outset, the corps would be led by the Jeanin's division in the center. Within this corps was the 5th Legere and these men would crawl along the ground, without their shakos, until they reached a point very near the Prussian line. Once there, they would spring up, give the signal to the troops behind with their horns (or if they did not have them any more, their drums) and fire a volley into the hopefully surprised enemy. Followed up quickly with the massed columns of the rest of the division, Lobau planned to disrupt and even rupture the enemy line.

In the 5th Legere, there was a good deal of mumbling by the men when they learned that they would have to take off their ornate shakos in order to carry out their mission. Many genuinely thought that the enemy could not possibly see them in the growth, plume or no plume. Lobau, however, was even more adamant than they were and in the end, despite the protests, the shakos were placed in the rear to be collected later. Given the delicate nature of this assignment, Lobau mingled briefly with his men as they formed up giving words of encouragement and in general getting a feel for the condition of his men. He was not to be disappointed. Despite the constant fighting both the day before and this morning, the troops, probably because of their success, were ready to take the fight to the Prussians instead of the other way around. Offensives are often very good for morale, provided they work.

Unlike the grand scale attacks during the battle of Mont St. Jean, the start of Napoleon's offensive at the battle of Ohain could only barely be discerned. A few troop movements could be seen, certainly nothing out of the ordinary, but for the most part the occasional thunder of cannon and musket rang out as it had before. Smoke drifted lazily through the morning air, hanging like it always did in the canopy of the forest, and the attention of the Prussians was more or less riveted on Reille's corps which was making a show of their march to Ohain. This march, of course, was partly deceptive. In the undergrowth of the Bois de Paris, where the offensive was due to begin, the most stealthy voltigeurs of the 5th Legere (and usually the smallest of these feisty men) were working their way towards the Prussian sentry line armed with all manner of non firing weapons that could be used to kill or incapacitate the enemy scout line before the main body, formed up in loose battalion columns behind them, made their charge. It was a tense time for these men as no one really knew where the Prussian pickets were and, if they simply ran into one another, the surprise would be total for both parties.

The French light troops advanced with their lead voltigeurs about twenty yards away from the trailing skirmish line with sergeants and junior officers watching intently for the agreed upon hand signals to be given by the crawling raiders. Hanging smoke and the general foliage of the forest cut down visibility considerably which both aided and hurt the attacking force as it kept them under cover but also made communication difficult. A grunt was heard ahead. The skirmishers all cringed in the undergrowth. Everyone waited but nothing happened. The line slowly struggled forward a number of steps, the eyes and ears of the officers wide open and listening for any signal. Captain Aubry was the first to see a signal, actually a knocked cold Prussian sentry, and he was quick to realize that the scouts were all out of visual range. Motioning with his left hand for the line to advance, the group rose slightly and skipped forward a few more steps before he again stopped them and waved them to the ground. Voices could be heard. A shot rang out. The all dark blue clad light infantry flattened themselves on the ground and hugged the dirt. Had they been discovered? Aubry, sprawled like a lizard on the dark earth, held his breath. Only with difficulty did he swing his head around to look ahead, the whole time fighting the natural human tendency to bury his skull below ground to hide. Not making a sound except for his own tortuous exhales, he felt the sweat running in rivers down his face. More voices, speaking German. The moan of a wounded man who seemed to be either badly hurt or violently vomiting. Aubry smiled momentarily; only a Frenchman could be such a bad actor. They were close, very close.

Aubry slowly rose from the ground, once more using his hand to guide the men around him to do the same. All at once, he saw a mustached face, perhaps no more than five yards away, staring at him with more men standing behind him. Their surprise was as mutual as it was shocking and, despite the fact that both men were armed, time stood still for a fraction of a second and neither man moved a muscle.

"Achtung!" the Prussian finally managed, raising his musket to fire. Faces of comrades around him looked very startled.

"Battalion! Fire!" he yelled, in an instant making a split decision to not waste time signaling and instead use the surprise he had gained.

The mass of light infantry rose up in a ragged line and let fly with a volley that woke everybody up for miles around. Bayonets fixed, the men cheered as the regimental eagle was pushed forward by their porte-aigle at the astonished Prussians who fell back in a precipitate rush for the rear; apparently the 5th Legere had ignored the Imperial decree to leave their eagles back home in their regimental depot!

Behind the 5th Legere, another captain had a decision to make. Captain Rutkowski of the 11th Ligne, formed in columns to give sledgehammer support to the lights, was in command of the regiment after his own colonel had fallen the day before. Having had his personal doubts about the chances for the initial assault, he felt that the 5th Legere, their brigaded sister regiment, would need all the help it could get. Consequently, his new found command was in close support of the light troops and ready to move on the given signal. Rutkowski, hearing the volley, considered that signal enough.

"Forward!"

Drums began to beat along the whole front of the 11th Ligne as the battalion musicians made up for lost air time and played with a hearty gusto. The "pas de charge" rolled like a menacingly war cry through the trees, the lack of visibility magnifying the sound and making it seem all the greater. The battalion columns pressed forward with their voltigeurs racing ahead to find the 5th Legere; it would be a relatively long run as the Prussians had taken off with the light infantry in hot pursuit.

The men of Jeanin's division had collided with and routed the 4th Silesian Landwehr Infantry Regiment under Lieutenant colonel von Massow of Losthin's 15th Infantry Brigade. The sudden hole in the Prussian line did not go unnoticed however and the French penetration came under fire from both flanks and ahead as the Prussians rallied and began to counterattack. The deep advance of the 5th Legere came to a grinding halt and, because of the nature of the position they now occupied, they involuntarily formed a rectangle that was manned on three sides as they were now fighting in every direction except to their rear. Soldiers from the Prussian Infantry Regiment #18 began advancing on their left while the 3rd Silesian Landwehr Regiment, recently rejoined by their previously captured colonel, moved in from the right. The French soldiers, minus their distinctive headgear, fought hard to hold open the hole in the Prussian line. Prussian jagers began working around to the rear of the French, threatening the regiment with encirclement. Casualties mounted and all movement stopped on the part of the light troops. Protecting the breach, here they would stand or die.

The 5th Legere was a two battalion regiment of around 900 men which had fought hard now in two separate actions and was becoming quite depleted. Colonel Rousille, the regimental commander, had been wounded the day before but nevertheless stood in the middle of what had now become a square in the midst of the trees. Like his men, Rousille was hatless but unlike them he was also partially unarmed as his wound had been in his right arm and he had never felt very comfortable with his sword in his left hand. As a result, he held a pistol in that hand and gave his orders by waving it in one direction or the other. His men were kneeling in the undergrowth and keeping up a heavy fire that deterred the Prussians from closing but he knew that as their muskets began fouling, the protective wall of flame would grow weaker and leave the two battalions in grave danger.

Rousille called over an aide and together they knelt close to one another only a few yards behind the firing line. "Go to Capitaine Aubry and tell him to start falling back, we can't hold this any longer! When he goes, we will. I don't want any separation!"

"Sir, look! We are surrounded!" the lieutenant yelled as a chasseur to their left fell over with a musket ball in his shoulder.

Rousille stared in that direction. Sure enough, Prussian troops had worked around their rear and were blocking their escape. Still, he thought as he tried to count the puffs of musket smoke, a silly task he quickly realized, the enemy had to be weakest to the rear as the 11th Ligne would be coming up to their support. Safety was back the way they had come.

"Here they come!" a sergeant with two long service chevrons on his sleeve cried out.

This time Rousille stood and ran over to see what was happening. The 3rd Silesian Landwehr, gathering its courage and losing its wits, was charging across the gap between them and the light infantry with the intention of overrunning their position. French fire erupted anew from the right flank companies, shredding the enemy front ranks but the Prussian regiment, using its greater numbers, kept coming almost up to the musket line itself before their casualties finally broke the unit and forced it to fall back. Wounded enemy soldiers littered the ground in front of the bloodied line of French light infantry.

The moment of the repulse of the 3rd Silesian regiment was also the time that Colonel Rousille was hit, again, this time in the other arm; as he fell, his pistol discharged into the trees above. For a moment, everything was confusion in the center of the square as officers and men closed around their colonel. Unfortunately, that time was when the Prussians, attacking with both the regular infantry and the rallied Landwehr, struck again from the front and left flanks in what probably had been meant as a coordinated three side assault on the square.

The 4th Silesian Landwehr Regiment had been partly rallied and led back into the fray. Arriving next after the 3rd's attack had collapsed, they approached to within about thirty yards and then stopped, preferring to set up a firing line rather than risk the same result the 3rd had suffered. A smarter idea, it was not without its dangers and the overcoat clad militiamen came under well directed fire from Aubry's men who picked the standing targets off from their bushy positions. A breeze had picked up and it carried the smoke of all these muskets north.

The lieutenant sent by the colonel arrived and reported to Captain Aubry. "Sir, Colonel Rousille intends to withdraw back to our lines and wants you to start with your companies so that a gap does not occur between our battalions!"

Aubry understood completely and began to set the orders in progress. Falling back after a last volley in all directions, the muskets of the first battalion went silent as the men began to stand in order to withdraw.

"Fire!"

"The enemy!"

Cries of various types were heard in the air as the surprised light infantry were attacked by the last Prussian regiment in the area, #18. These men, benefiting from the battering of the Landwehr and the prevailing wind, had been able to close more or less unseen until their officers could wait no longer and threw them in at the 5th Legere. Covering the distance rapidly, the front ranks got very close before they were mostly cut down by the French but enough closed to disrupt the line and allow the succeeding ranks to come to grips with their enemy. Bayonet to bayonet, the loose French square was pierced in two places by the Prussian regulars who made a beeline right to the eagle standard of the regiment below which Colonel Rousille lay. The porte-aigle, a veteran but illiterate sergeant with four loaded pistols stuffed amongst his person (he had taken two from another sergeant), fired in rapid succession at the enemy soldiers but the four balls, though they found their marks, were not enough in the wave of infantry that collapsed the left flank of the square. A Prussian lieutenant, knocking the French sergeant in the head with the butt of his unloaded pistol, seized the eagle but was immediately shot by a large French carabinier who tried to rescue it in turn. It was not to be. Pierced by a bayonet in the thigh, the man recoiled as the fallen eagle, face down at the foot of a tree, was picked up by the victorious Prussians who formed a group around it and retreated the way they had come. Crying out in frustration, the wounded carabinier shook his fist at the enemy but could do no more as the mass of feet around him passed over and by him.

The piercing of the square by the Prussians caused the French formation to begin to fall apart. Clumps of men, working their way around the trees, fell back to their own lines firing as they went but though many escaped, the rest of the regiment seemed trapped for good. However, that was not to be. The 11th Ligne, its columns having finally negotiated the rough terrain, at last arrived to give succor to the light infantry only to find a confused brawl going on in which the 3rd battalion of the regiment found itself on the Prussian flank which it drove in mercilessly only to be engaged by the Prussian reserve and stopped it its tracks. A firefight developed as the French here began to deploy. The 1st and 2nd battalions had more success as the Landwehr regiments, shaken and mauled, gave way before them. Occupying the position that the 5th Legere had lost, the soldiers of the 11th carefully passed over the sprawled wounded on the ground and Captain Rutkowski noted with satisfaction a chasseur lieutenant caring for the wounded colonel who, though lying in the thick of the area where the eagle had been, was not touched further during the whole fight.

The sounds of heavy fighting rumbled across the shot up forest. The French attack, joined all along the whole line by the full might of the VI Corps and Donzelot's division of I Corps, was being resisted fiercely by the more numerous Prussians. However, along Jeanin's front, the 5th Legere's fight had strained Losthin's brigade so close to its breaking point that this general had asked Bulow for reinforcements to hold the line against the determined French assault. The 11th Ligne, biting deep into the Prussian position, had engaged the remnants of the two Landwehr regiments with heavy fire and made the panicked Prussian commanders believe that, if sufficiently reinforced, the French might force a breakthrough in the line. This reaction, the transfer of available reinforcements away from the selected point of the true attack, was what Napoleon had wanted in the first place even though he had no idea tactically what might be going on amidst the trees. As far as he was concerned, the deep rumble of battle meant simply that Lobau was doing his job.

*   *   *

While Lobau's troops started the fighting again on the French right flank, it was another division, away on the current French left, that would enjoy the greatest attention from the Prussians and cause them to commit more than one brigade to hold it even though they outnumbered it a times by a great margin. This division belonged to General Durutte, the very man who had specialized in turning Wellington's left so recently at Mont St. Jean.

Napoleon realized that in order to offset the numerical superiority of his enemy he would have to draw off the Prussian reserves by diversionary attacks and allow his cannon to blast them whenever they had the chance before actually launching his final offensive. The battlefield of Ohain, wooded and rough as it was, did allow him to employ fewer troops to face off against the enemy, like Lobau's men in the Bois de Paris, but it also had few good zones of fire for his beloved guns. The best zone, directly in the middle of both of their positions, was where he was planning to mass his cannon into a great battery to aid in the forthcoming cavalry strike by the heavy horse. His dilemma was when to play his hand and show the great gun line to the enemy. This is where Durutte came in. The Emperor, on his last ride over the field of battle before the opening of his own attack, had paused to speak with Durutte and emphasize to him the importance of this man's task. Just like the day before, the Count was ready to do his utmost to produce the required result. Napoleon's confidence was not to be mislaid.

The terrain over which the division would attack was a slope leading up to the Prussian position from the Smohain brook which effectively divided the battlefield into two separate arenas. The slope, not as drastic as that around Lasne, was still uneven and would be hard going for the formations having to traverse it. The path along this area did, however, offer some distinct advantages, some of which Durutte learned from the Prussians he captured in the counterattack earlier that day. First, the route was ideal for protection against artillery fire as what artillerists cannot see they generally will not fire at; the French gun line prevented the Prussian batteries from commanding this approach path. Secondly, the small forest directly west of their position would, if captured, provide an ideal place to strike out against the enemy and engage him behind his own guns besides being the best shelter in the area. As Durutte stared at the place through his telescope, he noted how ideal a place it could be, especially for drawing off the Prussian reserves. What better way was there than to really scare him by showing up behind his lines?! Yes, that forest was the key.

Durutte organized his small division with his usual meticulous care. To his regret, he had no indigenous light infantry like most other divisions but happily the regiments he did have were all excellent troops, especially after the great victory the day before. The men were riding high on a wave of invincibility and if he could just harness the energy they were displaying there was a good chance his mission would be a success. Riding his lines to check on morale, he found it very high with the 29th Ligne still shining like a new coin in the midst of ordinary pocket change. Reflecting for a moment on his troops, Durutte realized that he had never been more proud of them and this revelation gave him great confidence and intense motivation. Surely these regiments would add the battle of Ohain to their other victorious battle honors and secure for France the success she so desperately needed.

The 4th Infantry Division prepared for battle. Because the division did not have any light infantry regiments, Durutte ordered the 85th Ligne to fan out in a heavy skirmish cloud not only to cover the advance but also to try and secure a footing in the trees at the top of the slope. Leading with his more intact 2nd Brigade, he planned to attack along a narrow frontage using the woods to cover his initial moves and confuse the enemy as to whether he was attacking in earnest or not. If the Prussians could be led to believe that he was only bothering them rather than trying to crush them, his men could close with them before they realized their mistake and figured out what was going on. A few critical minutes might prove all the difference for his first strike.

The French artillery companies to the right of Durutte were dueling successfully with the greater number of Prussian guns and ravaging parts of Jagow's brigade which was unlucky enough to be in the line of fire. Under Napoleon's strict orders, Lallemand had been plainly instructed that the enemy columns would be his primary target no matter how many guns the Prussians might bring up against him so Jagow's men, being the only target worth firing at aside from the cannon, was swept ruthlessly by the forty two gun battery. This battery, made up of mainly the guns of the VI Corps which were worthless to them in the trees and a few from the I Corps, was soon to be supplemented by the remaining guns of the I Corps which had been ordered across the Smohain brook and into the wake of the French infantry marching to Ohain. Taking the road to that town, the guns would unlimber on the high ground to begin a crossfire against the tip of the Prussian position much like they had at Ligny. This new battery of nearly fifty guns, commanded by the talented Imperial aide de camp Lebrun, the Duke of Plaisance, was not yet ready to fire when Durutte began his attack but the fire from these cannon would soon add their weight to the French assault.

The 85th Ligne's two battalions broke formation and, by company, spread out across the slope to begin their quick advance. Behind them, the next regiment in line, Colonel Garnier's 95th Ligne, was kneeling along the slope waiting for the signal to follow along with their battalion columns. Thinning out across the rough fields leading to the brook, the 85th Ligne didn't look like a very great force and to the Prussian defenders of the woods (where they had hidden from the artillery fire) it appeared that this was simply a skirmish line coming to harass them because the guns could no longer reach them. They would have thought different if they had heard Lallemand giving the order to have his company commanders switch their fire to new targets and let Jagow's brigade alone. The voltigeurs, always the fastest, ran up to nearly thirty yards of the trees before dropping down and letting fly from a prone position. The Prussians, irritated but not really concerned, returned the fire with their own jagers but refrained from leaving the safety of the trees and dealing a hard blow to the French. Things changed slowly but surely. More and more infantry began to appear around the western edge of the woods all firing at the trees until a rather substantial force of men was formed, or rather unformed, in front of them. The firing was creating quite a racket but none of the officers thought to do anything about it. Casualties amongst the troops in the wood were light but steadily mounting.

The Prussians hiding from the gunfire were from Infantry Regiment #7, the same unit that had unsuccessfully tried to engage the French guns before being blown off the ridge by the accuracy of their enemy's fire. Since then, they had retreated back to their start line and the wounded Colonel Seydlitz had been carried off to be tended to in the rear. Sullen and leaderless, the men now fell under the command of the feared but respected Major von Werner whose reputation for discipline was well known. This officer, sensing the low confidence of his men, energetically tried to instill some spirit amongst the troops whose morale had sunk after the wounding and he went so far as to near the firing line at the edge of the woods to encourage his men to fight harder and hold the position. This act of bravado was just the right thing for the moment and the men began to respond with more and more of them joining the jagers in the latter's firefight with the French. However, no more than a minute had passed when that almost inevitable shot rang out over all the others. Hit in the right thigh by a decorated French center company man who was too tall to be a voltigeur and too small to be a grenadier but nevertheless an excellent shot, Werner went down against a tree and was caught there by a jager corporal. As several men pulled him back through the woods, the 7th found themselves without a leader for the second time in the battle.

"Charge!" an order rang out from Colonel Masson, ironically right after the downing of the Prussian officer.

Almost as if out of nowhere, the entire body of the 85th Ligne raised up from the ground and hurtled themselves at the Prussian troops guarding the edge of the forest. With bayonets fixed and the men howling at the top of their lungs, the infantry used every last ounce of adrenaline to push up the slope and engage the enemy hand to hand or scare him off. The Prussians were surprised but ready. Despite their officer troubles, the 7th was a good unit and they met the French with a heavy fire which, in places, stopped the charge cold. Only on the Prussian right did any troops give way but for the most part they held firm and refused to give an inch. With few places to go, many of the French troops hit the ground again, feeling that the earth was a safer haven than being in the thick of the enemy fire. Some, however, reached the edge of the woods. Yet again, a bayonet fight occurred, a rare event on the modern battlefield but almost common between such equally determined foes. The French attacked savagely but the enemy would not have anything to do with it and began to use their greater numbers and tenacity to turn back the attackers and halt the attack. Some Prussians began firing into the flank of the attack while a few junior officers managed to put together small company size counterattacks. However, no call for help was given by the Prussians as most of the senior officers were either disabled or actively defending the line. The French, surprised and disorganized, began to feel the pressure and give way.

Suddenly the tables were turned. Pounding up behind the heavy skirmish line was the 95th Ligne and they produced a profound shock on the enemy as the French actually gained a numerical superiority and held momentum on their side. The battalion columns, arranged one behind the other, slammed into the woods line with the grace of a wheelbarrow and in a stroke ruptured the front line of the 7th. The jagers turned and ran while the rest of the luckless regiment lost heart and also fell back before the onslaught. Breaking formation, the 7th crumbled and bolted for the safety of its mother brigade. Following up the attack, Durutte's men spread out in the trees and winkled the Prussians away from every hiding place before expelling them completely from the woods and the hamlet of Genleau which they took as the enemy retreated in confusion.

Durutte was there when the capture occurred and he could not believe his success. Instinctively, he whirled through a rapid consolidation of the position just in case the Prussians returned. The disorganized troops were in need of orders and no one was to leave the shelter of the trees unless Durutte himself authorized the action. The last thing he needed was some idiot to blunder out of the cover and trigger a serious offensive action before he was ready to defend in place. However, Durutte's concept of defense was not always what others might think it to be. This commander, riding on a wave of aggressive brilliance, was out to do his job as best that he could.

The French commander wasted no time in reorganizing his men. In the attack his overall casualties were fairly light, probably due to the speed of the attack, but any sense of formation had been lost by the 85th which Colonel Masson hurried himself into rallying. Durutte certainly expected a counterstroke by the Prussians and in this vein he deployed his 2nd Brigade in the woods and held the weaker 1st in reserve along the reverse slope of the position. If the Prussians succeeded in flinging his men out of the forest then the 1st Brigade would be well placed to launch a counterattack and catch the enemy off balance. At Genleau, Durutte massed several grenadier companies along with their accompanying sappers in the buildings to act as a breakwater while the rest of his men lined up along the edge of the woods.

General Jagow was stunned at the speed of the French attack which had struck as if out of thin air. He really should have been used to it, though, as the French had always attacked in that manner whenever they had met. To his credit, the Prussian general was not slow in ordering a counterattack against the forest which was in full accord with the defense of the position occupied by the Army of the Lower Rhine. The capture of the forest site and the hamlet had seriously compromised the Prussian gun line which was now coming under fire from French voltigeurs; to be fair, the Prussians did to the French what the latter had done to them and turned a battery on them to keep away the skirmishers. Shattered branches and leaves fell on the cowering heads of the French soldiers though the determined Durutte ordered his men to sidestep to the right and engage the guns anyway.

The Prussian infantry, perhaps sensing the urgency of the situation, reformed in good time and stood ready to attack the earth hugging French. However, the cannon presented a problem as Jagow couldn't strike until the guns stopped firing for fear of losing men to their own artillery fire. To this end, he sent a mounted aide with a request for the cannon to cease firing so that the brigade could expel the French and restore the situation. Galloping off, the aide had to ride in front of the new French position and from there, about half way across, his horse was struck and killed, the ensuing crash spilling the rider onto the ground completely unconscious. Not having watched the aide while the troops were finished forming up and dressing their ranks, neither Jagow nor his staff could tell what had happened and they waited while the guns continued to rip into the trees. Finally, after another fifteen minutes had passed, Jagow sent off another aide and watched him go as far as he could. This one made it. The cannon, under increasing fire from the slope, were swung around to fire canister at the pesky sharpshooters.

The delay in the Prussian attack helped the French secure a little assistance in their defense of the woods. Rolling into position along the slope on the opposite side of the brook was the first company of French artillery of General Lebrun's new battery and the Imperial aide de camp, spying the target presented by the forming Prussians, ordered his men to hurry and take the enemy under fire. General of Brigade Desales, the I Corps chief of artillery, quickly estimated the range, which was about 300 toises or six hundred yards, and the gunners went about their business as real professionals, loosing their first shot within minutes.

"Over and left!" yelled Captain Bourgeois, commander of the 9th Company of the 6th Foot Artillery Regiment, strangely enough Durutte's own divisional guns.

The artillerists, recovering their cannon, wheeled them back into place and sighted them once more. The process, very much a team affair, was executed smoothly and with admirable precision. "Ready!"

"Fire!"

Most of Durutte's men were still face down in the dirt when one of the officers at last realized that the Prussians had stopped their cannon from firing at them. "They're getting ready to attack! On your feet!"

Cautiously at first, the men rose up to a crouched stance and found that the officer had been right; the guns were now blasting the light troops along the slope. Hustled forward across the broken pieces of the trees around them to face the stiffly visible Prussians, they rapidly gathered together to give the enemy a hot reception. One or two muskets fired but the majority obeyed their orders to hold until the order was given; breaking the Prussian attack was imperative if the advance was to continue.

General Durutte noted with satisfaction the first puffs of white smoke from the guns across the brook from him and, riding safely along the reverse slope of the ridge, he waited for the first sign of the pending Prussian attack. Already he was prepared to resume the advance and he needed to block the Prussians in such a way that they would ask for reinforcements to dry up their available reserves. This is not to say that General Durutte was in any way suicidal; experience had told him that if he harried the Prussians as long as he could, the momentum would give him an advantage against an enemy that was constantly off balance. Besides, he had already seen part of the Guard's artillery forming up to join in the duel of cannon on the ridge.

At last they were ready. Jagow, irritated by the delay but knowing what must be done, had finally sent an aide to tell General Zieten what was happening along his part of the front before he rectified it himself. His plan, intended to utilize his superior numbers of men, envisioned an advance to the woods and along the slope to the brook so that the French could be neatly trapped between his infantry and the shattering fire from the guns on the other side. His regiments, battered but good troops, were prepared for a stiff fight.

Supported briefly by a Prussian I Corps battery that lobbed a few rounds at the woods and the buildings, the 3rd Infantry Brigade, reformed and ready, began to advance along with the general himself who rode behind the last column. As the regiments forged ahead, cannon shot from across the brook began to come down on them, the ricochet effect slicing through the ranks killing everything in its path. Screams rose from the men hit but the others simply closed ranks, iced their hearts and kept moving, even if that meant pushing aside their wounded comrades and stepping over their agonized bodies. Drums beat the step and the jagers, overworked and definitely underpaid, took up their traditional forward posts though more than a few had simply vanished from the ranks.

"Forward!"

More cannon shots came raining down, these now hitting the

flanking battalions who were even closer to the French. The 7th came up to Genleau and split up to try and seize it and the woods.

"Fire!"

The French infantry line at the edge of the woods erupted in flame and smoke. The front rank of the fusilier battalion of the 7th, the best of that regiment, crumbled to the ground and immediately fell into complete disorder. Fire seemed to be coming from every angle as mounted officers found themselves shot at from tree tops, the bushes, nearby buildings and even the ground itself. The few jagers hid wherever they could. This part of the attack collapsed before it had a chance to achieve anything. The 3rd Westphalian Landwehr Regiment, the unit next to them, observed what happened and suddenly seemed reluctant to engage. Instead, they formed a line and volleyed at the French from afar.

It was Infantry Regiment #29, the same unit that had almost broken the French gun line before being struck in the rear some hours earlier, that was to prove to be not only a fine regiment but also the most dangerous in this particular attack. Advancing in spite of the cannon balls raining down on them, Major Hymmen pushed his men hard to confuse the range of the enemy guns and close the distance with the open flank of the French position. Moving quickly, they swept passed their crumbling sister regiments and made a controlled dash across the slope.

The Prussian maneuver was not lost on the French and Durutte spotted the Prussian deployment early enough to do something about it. Taking stock of his reserves, he ordered the 8th Ligne from his 1st Brigade into line to defend this critical junction. It was probably Durutte's poorest decision of the entire campaign. The 8th, victim of the great British cavalry strike at Mont St. Jean, had been much reduced in strength and really only presented the culmination of a single battalion of men and that not even at full establishment. Nevertheless, as ordered, the 8th formed up and marched off followed, at a safe distance, by the 29th Ligne which was in better shape but wanted by Durutte as his divisional reserve. Rousellot, the commander of the regiment, fumed in his impatience; if the 8th was hit hard, they might not be able to hold a strong enemy attack.

As the Prussian advance against the woods shifted into a stalemate rather than an assault, the 29th reached the flank of the French position and came across the small French unit ordered to defend it. Hymmen, in command of perhaps 1400 troops, was facing a little over 400 Frenchmen defending in place. He could see no others in the vicinity.

The French, in line and not moving, leveled their muskets on command and aimed at the advancing enemy. The line flashed and the Prussians cringed but surprisingly few of them fell. The enemy had fired high! Raising a cheer, they pressed forward with renewed ardor, their dark uniforms forming an evil spectacle. The French, worn out and distraught, gave ground, firing as they went. Hymmen stopped the regiment to deploy into line leaving one battalion in reserve behind the lines to support the attack or, if things went poorly, help them retreat. That accomplished, the whole unit began to move ahead again but immediately came under a heavy fire from the massing French guns on the ridge across the Smohain brook. Three balls performed a brutal cross section through the 1st Battalion killing its captain instantly and knocking over the national flag. The battalion, shaken by the sudden loss, began to lose cohesion as some men stopped while others continued on. Sergeants yelled over the din of musket fire for the men to close ranks.

The potential crisis on the French right was taken very seriously by General Durutte and he rode personally over to the area to bring forward the 29th Ligne and rally the jumbled pieces of the 8th as they attempted to form up again.

Beseeching the troops as he reached Rousellot's men, Durutte cried out, "Who will be the first to take the eagle standard?"

Several "we will" calls came from the ranks and the 29th marched again to the attack against its counterpart which, once more, was in difficulties. Rousellot called to his men. "Forward 29th! The day is ours!"

Rousellot could probably be forgiven his preemptive cry but

his men understood the urgency of the situation as they had seen the 8th fall back in disorder and knew there were no more troops to back them up. Therefore, while Durutte turned to getting the 8th back in order, the 29th grimly advanced on the attacking Prussians.

The attackers were in some confusion themselves. The fusilier battalion had passed the 1st Battalion by some thirty paces when it stopped, waiting for the other to catch up. To their credit, the men of the 1st Battalion kept to their ranks and stayed calm under the increasing fire from the French guns. Dressing their battered ranks, they attempted to join in the assault again only to find that the French in the woods had shifted positions and were peppering them from the flank now. Stopping to engage, the regiment ground to a halt in three distinct pieces. Judging from the advance of the 29th Ligne, which could clearly be seen now, they were faced with a foe who was doing his best to stop them and, if given the chance, to crush them from the front and flank. Cursing over the lack of ardor from the other regiments, Hymmen reluctantly ordered his men to fall back, an act that he had simply not been ready to do just a few minutes before. However, the cannonballs from across the brook were raining down with some regularity and it was either now or never to escape from the trap.

The Prussians fell back in excellent order thanks to the diligent service of the regiment's second battalion which held the French at bay and allowed the unit to retreat out of harm's way. Hymmen was not happy as he saw that the other two regiments had already abandoned the assault and would have left him in the lurch should he have needed their support. More than once today, a lack of overall coordination on the Prussian side would rob them of tactical success although at least part of the credit for the repulse must go to the rapid response by the French higher commanders who reacted with decisive moves and remained prepared for any eventuality.

As Jagow's men retreated for the second time, Durutte reorganized his veteran division. He had successfully rallied the 8th Ligne and, for safety, had switched the role of reserve to them instead of the far better motivated 29th Ligne. In the woods, the 2nd Brigade still hid but now came under heavier artillery fire from the bent Prussian gun line as the latter became more fearful of the potential damage that this upstart French division could cause. Genleau had barely been touched thus far. Convinced that the bombardment was a softening up exercise, Durutte began to feel there was not a moment more to lose and that, if he did not attack, the Prussians would take the initiative and try to expel him from the woods again. As can be seen, Durutte, the consistent professional, was taking his role very seriously even if his was not the main focus of the overall French battle plan.

Another man had been watching the progress of the attack and he was one who could influence the progress of the 4th Division. Corps commander d'Erlon, a far more alert and diligent general the day after Mont St. Jean, was carefully monitoring the advance of his subordinate and was quick to spot the Prussians wheeling their guns out of line to take the 4th Division under fire while they still could. Knowing that the Emperor was counting on his corps to draw in more enemy troops under the arc of fire of the guns, he realized that Durutte had to be left to do his job without direct interference, but if there was anything he could do to help his subordinate, then he had better do it. Directly, he was under orders to keep his main strike force out of harm's way and ready for the grand attack later in the day. Indirectly, he had a free hand. If he could get the Prussians to switch their fire away from Durutte then the latter could renew his advance and draw in the Prussian reserves. To this end, he ordered Jacquinot, who up until now had done very little except sit in reserve well behind the gun line, to move in support of Durutte along the slope and threaten the guns with his light cavalry troopers. To be quite honest, the slope was no place for a cavalry charge to begin since it would make any charge very slow going. However, like many things in Napoleonic warfare, appearance did not necessarily translate into reality. Like Durutte and Lobau's attacks on the flanks, the move by the cavalry was designed to threaten a charge but not actually make one. If the Prussians believed their guns were in danger they would have to wheel them back to face whatever force was about to attack them which in turn would leave Durutte to his own devices. For once, d'Erlon got exactly what he intended.

Jacquinot, his men fresh from the victory on the previous day, was up to this assignment and did not waste any time in moving his division to where Durutte had begun his advance. He could see plainly through his telescope the powder blue gun carriages of the enemy facing in two directions and while he wasn't exactly thrilled with the prospect of having those same muzzles face his troopers, he was ready to do his duty. Excellent officer that he was, he already had a plan. For greatest effect, Jacquinot led with his second brigade because it included two regiments of light horse lancers, the 3rd and 4th. Advancing in a skirmish line with their lances in the air, his intention was to make the Prussians react and then get his men out of harm's way before the gunners had a chance to fire. If the Prussians turned back, he would repeat the process thereby leaving them in confusion as to what he was going to do. If they ignored him, a limited charge might do wonders for everyone concerned.

The French light horse rode off just as the guns of the Imperial Guard were accumulating en masse ready to concentrate in the center of the line. Heavy twelve pounders pulled by laboring six horse teams were pounding their way ahead and the sheer quantity of cannon made the chasseur and lancer troopers feel both proud and glad that the Prussians would be on the receiving end of that brutal salute. It seemed that even the lowliest private could feel the battle ripening.

Napoleon, sitting in his field chair at the headquarters table behind the lines, listened to the thunder of the guns with his eyes closed and his hands clasping the front quarters of his head. His strong headache, a throbbing pain in his temples and a drastic dizzying feeling that left him wobbly on his feet, had been with him since the early morning and it was robbing him of what he needed most in battle: personal sight. The pain having escalated from the time he had woken up, he now had to pay the price and he sat almost dejected in his command chair, his ears almost but not quite oblivious to the sounds of battle in the air.

A current reconnaissance was needed but the energy from his body was lacking as it fought the ache in his brain. Still, he had to do something. The day before at Mont St. Jean, his inattention had left parts of the army leaderless at times and had cost him dearly when events had taken off on their own and sabotaged his plans. Not having completely shaken the exhaustion (he really hadn't done anything to shake it anyway), the ache had returned almost as if it wanted to force him to rest. Silent and unmoving, he was watched by his officers but they saw no good reason to rouse him if the battle seemed to be progressing in the right direction. The Prussians had been heavily engaged on the right and preliminary reports from d'Erlon suggested that Durutte was trying to win the battle by himself which meant that the enemy would have to react soon or pull back their guns to a safer haven. Soult, always the pessimist when it came to everyone except for himself, felt that Durutte had bitten off more than he could chew and fully expected him to be driven back though when a report came in stating that they had captured the woods and thrown back an enemy brigade, he was forced to reevaluate.

A rider galloped up to the small mound upon which was the French headquarters. The officer, a man dressed in a dark green and white laced chasseur elite company outfit, brought his hand up under his busby and saluted. Reaching into his sabretache, he produced a message from General Lebrun whose artillery had finished deploying on the ridge across the brook.

Soult received the message quietly, one eye on the paper and the other on the Emperor who still did not stir from his head down position. Lebrun stated that his guns were in place as ordered and that Prussians troops were massing against Durutte's men in the forest. Pondering for a moment, the French chief of staff knew that the time for the massing of the guns was certainly near.

"What does it say?" Napoleon said suddenly though his head remained motionless.

Startled, Soult stuttered for a moment before explaining what was written on the dispatch. "Allowing for the time this took to reach us, the enemy is more than likely well advanced. Durutte will be heavily outnumbered," he added.

The Emperor raised his head, his forehead visibly strained and his eyes closed. Forcing the pain away for a moment, he took a deep breath and squinted in the sunshine at Soult. "Durutte can take care of himself. Tell Drouot to take his guns to the center and prepare to begin the bombardment."

"Sire, should we not wait for confirmation . . . ."

Audible hooves to his left made Soult stop his speech and roll his sarcastic eyes as another dispatch rider arrived from d'Erlon with, as he knew it already, the same news. The enemy had reacted to Durutte's attack just as the Emperor had known he would. Perhaps this was why he was the greatest soldier in Europe. "Yes, sire," he ended quickly.

Napoleon reached for his famous unadorned bicorne hat and placed it on his sweaty head. Somehow, he had to force himself to take control of the battle, if only for a few more hours. Standing abruptly and knocking over his chair, his legs felt wobbly and the dizziness struck him but he steadied himself on a nearby chasseur and collected his strength. "Gourgaud, bring my horse."

Soult stood as well, though he was careful not to topple his chair. "Are you all right sire? Should I call the doctor?"

The Emperor, partly sagging and his grip on the chasseur strong, smiled sarcastically as he almost managed some of his usual humor associated with the medical profession. "So that he can kill me?" he said loudly before adding, in an undertone, "Larrey has enough patients without me. I need to see for myself what is happening before something goes wrong."

As the Emperor mounted the horse with the help of Colonel Gourgaud, Imperial aide de camp Flahaut turned a mischievous eye to la Bedoyere. "He thinks that Maréchal Ney is still about."

*   *   *

As the French I and VI Corps were becoming heavily engaged with the Prussians, Reille's marching II Corps was finally nearing its destination: the town of Ohain. With Pire's men riding ahead to prevent any unexpected surprises, the II Corps had split into two halves that now traveled on opposite side of the Bois de Ohain. While this maneuver might seem dangerous, especially if the Prussians could manage a sudden attack, there was one surprise that the French had received that allowed them to split the two divisions. Aside from a few annoying jagers, the forest they were passing had no troops in it at all; with the fight in the Bois de Paris still raging, any forest position would have seemed to be a good one for delaying an enemy but the French were never one to argue with Fortune, all the more so when she had favored them on this day. Nevertheless, the march to Ohain was not all so easy. While Jerome marched to the north accompanied by one light cavalry brigade from Pire, Foy's men marched to the south escorted by the other of Pire's brigades. Moving up the road to Ohain in skirmish order, the latter came under heavy fire from the Prussian batteries lining the banks of the brook. Moving fast, they crossed this dangerous zone only to find themselves shot at again by another battery which had neatly picked up where the other had just left off. Reille, marching with Foy as he wanted no more of Jerome, took the opportunity to count the enemy batteries and report his findings to the Emperor. It appeared that whatever Prussian corps was occupying the ridge had its artillery attached at the brigade level as no more than ten or twelve guns lined the intervals between the infantry blocks across the brook. The French infantry, apprehensive and with a twitch in their necks that made them keep looking over their shoulders to the right, became a perfect target for cavalry had there been any as they swarmed ahead in a formation that lost cohesion with every step they took. The Prussian gun batteries, without a real target thus far in the day, took the opportunity presented and bombarded the jostling ranks of French infantry as the latter moved almost at a run to clear the fire zone and escape. French artillery, guns of the II Corps destined for the attack on Ohain, wheeled into place at intervals to return the fire and distract the enemy but the Prussian fire was well directed by Colonel von Rohl who was in charge of these guns of the Prussian I Corps. Reille, seeing the trouble his division had gotten into, ordered the men to make for the Bois de Ohain where they could reorganize and reform in relative peace. However, an order made and an order received are often two different things and, until everything was straightened out, the French would suffer under the fire of these Prussian guns.

The bombardment was a difficult and confusing time for the French and it opened up the possibility of a counterattack by the Prussians. However, the same bane the French had endured for some days now, the wetness of the ground from the heavy rains, now actually helped their cause. The Ohain brook, not normally a great problem for troops to cross, was swollen like the Lasne though its banks were not as high. Additionally, the ground was soft and marshy along the course of the waterway which further discouraged anyone from moving from one side to the other. In a sense, this suited both sides as the French were not inclined to attack there and the Prussians could sit back and shoot at them without fear of any retaliation. About the only activity from Blucher's army was from a small group of jagers that tried to get closer to the French but ended up being stuck in the disagreeable mud. The riflemen, disgusted and dirty, fired off a few shots before heading back to their parent units.

When Foy's division at last reached the safety of the woods, his men were scattered all over and even with his most energetic exertions he doubted that he could reform them in less than an hour. Reille, cursing his bad luck, rode through the forest to catch up to Jerome and order him not to attack until Foy could get his men into proper formations again. One might question why Reille did not just send his aide to the Emperor's brother and leave it at that. With a commander as knuckle headed as Jerome, however, the personal touch was often the only way to get one's desired response. As he picked his way through the trees with his staff, Reille couldn't help but think that the nineteenth was starting out just like the day before.

Back on the southern ridge, Zieten was watching the marching French with growing concern as they made their way to attack Ohain. However, when his artillery scattered the French unit in front of it and chased it into the trees he was able to give a grand sigh of relief and relax for a moment. Perhaps things were working out after all. Steinmetz, his troops calmly waiting for the oncoming enemy at Ohain, had been worried about a heavy attack in his direction especially when he found out that Donnersmarck's "brigade" amounted to only a single battalion! His request for reinforcements, however, had met a polite refusal from the corps commander as the threat had been thrown into disorder. Zieten, free to concentrate against his primary enemy, would be able to press the attack against Durutte's men to his front and patch up the battle line. To this end, he had asked for, and received, permission to move Krafft's brigade of the II Corps, currently deployed in the Prussian center behind the gun line, into an assault against Durutte to be supported by the battered Jagow; the latter's troops, beaten and thrown about, were becoming something less than effective by now.

Jacquinot's lancer regiments, the 3rd and 4th, riding to the front with their whipping red and white pennons in the air, provided an attractive spectacle of quite deadly troops. Attractive uniforms with their brass crested helmets and their respective pink and crimson facings, they echoed of the knight of the middle ages in his armor and colorful tunic. Trotting into position along the slope that Durutte had used to begin his attack, the light cavalrymen had been ordered to threaten the enemy guns with their presence and cause these batteries to defend themselves instead of firing on Durutte's men who were trying to form up again to attack out of the woods. Jacquinot, a light cavalry expert if there ever was one, knew how to play this game as he had learned the hard way at Neumarkt some years before. Collecting his regimental commanders for a short talk, he told them what he expected and exactly how they might achieve their aim before letting them loose; the coming action would at times require more finesse than martial prowess and Jacquinot was certain that unless he ordered it some of his less clever commanders might get a little over zealous.

The chasseurs and hussars of Jacquinot's 1st Brigade were initially dismayed at the plan thrown together by their commander, especially Colonel Marbot of the 7th Hussars, but were quickly won over when their role, in a possible later phase, was revealed to them. As it was, the lancers trotted off to begin their harassment in long skirmish lines while the mass of the 1st Brigade moved to their left to watch and wait.

The Prussian reaction to the French cavalry advance was immediate. The gun captains spotted the lancers riding towards them and did not lose a moment in informing Major von Bardeleben, the commander of the IV Corps artillery in the absence of Major General von Braun, of what they had seen. The young major, not at all pleased at this turn of events, rode over to his gun line and looked for himself. Sure enough, a mass of lancers was clearly advancing on his position and he hastened to halt the firing on the woods in favor of the defense of the grand battery. Just as he had made that order, a French ball shattered a gun carriage near him and a piece of it neatly sliced open his cheek from his mouth to just below his eye. Bleeding profusely from the long cut, he placed his handkerchief over the wound and courageously held his position while his gunners manhandled their powder blue pieces into line against the cavalry. A backbreaking task, the artillerists obviously felt the urgency of the moment and gave their all to wheel the cannon back into the firing line.

"Ready!" yelled a nearby lieutenant.

A distance away, another voice was raised in command. "Fall back!"

The French lancers, nearing the guns at a trot, suddenly stopped and wheeled their mounts around, effectively breaking off their maneuver and high tailing it in a great cloud of dust for their start line. A crash announced a retort from Bardeleben's guns but the salvo proved to be a hasty and ineffectual blast and which caused few if any casualties. The Prussian major, elated at having scared off the French horse complimented his men and then, after a minute pause to watch the French, ordered the same guns to be moved to fire at the French infantry in the woods. For their part, the gunners, when they could see through the smoke, raised their fists to the retreating French horse and taunted them from the ridge. Bardeleben, at last satisfied with the repulse, tugged at the reins of his horse and walked it back to the spot where he had been watching the firing against Durutte. The gunners, meanwhile, tired but now at least a little pleased, began the laborious task of moving their heavy equipment again.

Colonel Martigue, commander of the 3rd Legere Lanciers Regiment, ordered the reform and the trumpet blast sounded for his men to rally their squadrons and get organized again. Waiting for about seven minutes, he gave another prearranged signal and his veteran troopers swung around to face the ridge and then dressed their loose line. Taking his position in the lead, he raised his sword and pointed it at the vulnerable guns again so that the harassment could continue. The troopers, intrigued and spirited, did as they were ordered and in an automatic motion they began to coax their mounts up the slope again just like they had before.

"They are coming back, sir!" said a surprised Lieutenant Pfeiffer as he directed his chief back to the west. "Look, sir!"

The major uncomfortably rode over to his spot occupied only minutes before and with a painful groan he cursed his luck. His battery, dueling on and off with the French guns for many an hour now, was tired and battered. Positioned to cover the gap in the army center, just like the French, his targets had been few and far between except for Durutte's division which had unfairly hidden amongst the trees and then thrown out snipers to shoot at his artillerists. This annoyance was compounded by the growing number of cannon balls falling around his guns and teams. The firing from the large French battery was both heavy and accurate especially as the horse batteries he saw in the morning were replaced with heavier cannon from the line. He had lost eleven guns to outright hits while more than a dozen had taken visible damage to their carriages and, more importantly, their crews. Infantry volunteers from the brigades had been called to be ready to join the gun crews although as yet everything was more or less under control; hitting a cannon was not an easy thing for an enemy gun but the French, to their credit, had proved that it indeed could be done.

"Move the guns back!" he ordered.

The artillerists again responded with energy but less enthusiasm as they mightily pulled their pieces out of line and wheeled them back over to fire at the lancers. This time, however, the gunners timing was better or the French worse as a the volley from the guns actually emptied a few saddles which broke up the retreat of the horse and caused them to scatter in small groups across the slope. Bardeleben felt better about that defensive fire as the French cavalry troopers seemed to have been convincingly thrown back. Now, with the cavalry out of the picture, at last they might have some peace if not quiet to destroy the hiding French infantry in the woods.

It was not to be. The gunners had managed to lob one round each at the woods when yet another cry went up that the French were advancing. This time, Colonel Bro of the 4th Legere Lanciers Regiment, acted the familiar role of decoy and he approached the ridge doing the same thing that the 3rd had done some fifteen minutes before. This time the game, however, was more in earnest as the men passed their dead comrades who had not escaped the fire from the enemy guns. Collectively, they gave a shout as they neared the enemy artillery position and for all the world looked like they really were going to charge.

"Hurry!" Bardeleben yelled at his men as the latter shook their heads and grumbled something inaudible. It was clear the French were playing with them. "They'll just ride away again!"

Bro watched carefully the cannon being slowly pushed back and he noted the loss of speed in their movements. When at last they sighted their pieces and seemed ready to aim the guns, he raised his sword and ordered the trumpet sounded to mark the withdrawal. The line of pennons slowed and stopped until it recoiled as before back to the start line without the Prussians even being able to fire.

"What are they doing?" yelled one man in the battery.

"They are afraid of us!" another declared.

"Shut up and move the guns!" yelled a veteran sergeant who did his best to keep focused on their primary task at hand.

Bardeleben was just as irritated with the French horse as his gunners were and he intended to do something about it. Sending a rider to General Bulow, he asked for cavalry support to dissuade the French from trying their little antics again. Motioning to an aide, he pointed at the cavalry in the distance. "If they come again, move one gun and only one gun. Do you understand?"

As expected, the lancers returned to the game again though this time, after an interval of some twelve minutes they were a bit more massed than they had been. No one really noticed either that the French guns were concentrating on the Prussian left instead of the whole position. Durutte's men, taking advantage of the breaks in the fire, deployed more skirmishers and began to really hurt the two Prussian batteries aimed against their position. Lying prone in the grass, they had become experts at suddenly rising, firing their muskets and flattening themselves on the dirt again while the Prussians retaliated with balls against the trees. In turn, Bardeleben ordered canister rounds fired next to help clear the skirmishers in front of the guns and allow the battery to engage the trees unmolested.

The French cavalry approached in exactly the same fashion as it had before. Lances upright, mounts barely trotting, it appeared to be a remake of every other phony charge they had tried time and time again; the troopers even raised a great shout to announce their presence. Bro, watching and waiting, saw one gun turned on them but without any of the crew actually loading the piece while the rest blasted another salvo at Durutte in the woods. This was what Jacquinot had been waiting for and would demonstrate the great utility of light cavalry; the chasseurs and lancers might not win great battles but they would always play their important role. Bro looked quickly down both sides of his advancing line. Now was the time.

Across the area a new sound was heard that brought chills to the Prussians. The sudden lurch of two hundred and fifty horses shook the ground and the trumpet blast announcing a charge echoed like a death knell. The troopers of the 4th Lanciers bellowed another call and lowered their long lances in anticipation of the assault. Pennons whipped in the air and horses pounded the ground beneath their feet. Despite the slope, the squadrons gathered speed probably due more to the spirit of the men rather than the tired condition of their mounts. The dark green line of cavalry charging in desperate fury was as impressive as it was menacing.

Lieutenant Pfeiffer, watching the cavalry with his face aghast, shook himself from the trance he was in and slapped the back of a gunner sergeant. Pushing the man towards the one gun they had brought up, he yelled, "Load the gun. Canister! Hurry!"

It was in vain. Several gunners ran off in a panic while more just stood there waiting for an order to do something yet powerless to do anything at all. Hearing everything but not listening, they dove underneath their carriages to hide forgetting the fact that they were facing veteran lancers who knew how to deal with artillerists. In seconds, the cavalry was upon them piercing everything in their path and scattering the crews of the guns. Bardeleben, faced with the disintegration of two of his batteries, rode off to a safer haven while the Prussian horse of Prince Wilhelm of Prussia, the commander of the IV Corps Cavalry, heard the call and rapidly approached from the east.

The French used their cherished opportunity to the utmost, pushing their mounts to catch as many of the enemy they could. No place was secure from their depredations as they rode between the silent guns and stuck the unfortunates in the back who had thought that the gun carriages were proof against the deadly lances. Some gunners just cringed on the ground, holding their hands over the ears as the thunder of the cavalry rushed by while others fought back with ramrods and even the occasional wooden bucket. It was not nearly enough. Piercing and hacking anyone in their path, the quickly disorganized lancers succeeded in upsetting the entire Prussian gun line as train troops attempted to escape and all fire quickly ceased.

"Get the train!" yelled an officer of the lancers as the limbers and caissons for the guns began to retire behind a pair of reserve batteries which were beginning to deploy in the rear of the line.

The lancers chased down the supporting vehicles shooting drivers and horses with their pistols or slicing the traces with their sabers as they swept on past. Several limbers, deprived of a lead horse at a critical moment, careened over spilling their contents all over the field. One crashed quite spectacularly with men flying, horses flailing and one lancer clearing the wreck by jumping clean over it. Everywhere, Bro's men were split up and hunting at will while the colonel himself, watching from a standing horse in the midst of the abandoned Prussians guns, at last ordered the recall.

Cheers could be heard from the woods as French infantry, invigorated and reformed, began to debouch from the trees in attack formations. With the removal of the guns, Durutte's men were set to begin their advance once again though by now Jagow's brigade was in better shape than before. Still, the general needed to force the issue and an attack deep in the heart of the Prussian position was just the thing to get a reaction.

As the French lancers returned from their wild chases, they came under fire from the deployed reserve batteries of the IV Corps and took their most significant casualties of the day. Voltigeurs, surrounding the flank of the guns on the ridge, used their bayonets to loosen the earth at their feet and then, carrying it to the abandoned guns, pushed it deep into the touch holes of the pieces so that they could at least delay the enemy when they were forced to abandon them back. No one was under any illusion for that particular event. A large mass of enemy cavalry was moving to engage the lancers and so they hurried as best they could to sabotage the cannon in some way before running hard to rejoin their battalions that had by now fully extended from the forest.

Durutte, watching the clearing of the hill from the relative safety of the trees, had rode ahead to see what was going on with the deployment of his troops when he spotted the mass of Prussian horse approaching the apparently hapless lancers. Thinking that a good demonstration was worth a thousand unexplained words, he formed his right hand regiment, the 95th Ligne, into a series of three squares instead of withdrawing them to the protection of the trees. Hoping the Prussians would pause to think for a moment instead of charging home on the lancers, Durutte wanted to return the favor from Jacquinot in the best and fastest way possible.

"Form square!"

Prince Wilhelm of Prussia, the commander of the IV Corps Cavalry Reserve, had his regiments formed up by brigade in the order of their experience. In the lead, therefore, was the 1st Brigade of Colonel von Eicke, a brigade of regulars, and bringing up the rear was the 3rd Brigade made up of five regiments of less than proficient Landwehr which the Prince wanted kept as far as possible away from the coming fight. Some of these latter units weren't so bad but a couple had no experience whatsoever and would prove to be quite unpredictable. One, Major von Kameke's 2nd Pommeranian, would go down in history.

As the Prussian horse neared the battery, the French lancers were at last reforming into something resembling a line. Scattered after chasing gunners, limbers and, in one case, a mounted officer, the lancer horses were blown and in need of a good rest but would soon be in action again. The 3rd Lanciers under Colonel Martigue had reformed solidly and General Gobrecht, the 2nd Brigade commander, held them motionless as the enemy closed with the 4th. Cavalry actions are often matters of timing and finesse and this one was going to be no different. Rather than striking an enemy all at once, good commanders kept a reserve to influence the tide of battle for their side and roll up the enemy line. It was not unheard of for cavalry actions to go back and forth in this manner as each commander threw in one more regiment until the one with the last won the fight. The fight at Villadrigo in 1812 was decided by the last French regiment as it neatly skirted around the flank and collapsed the British line as the latter were out of reserves. Thus, Gobrecht held the 3rd Lanciers tightly under his personal command and waited for the clash to begin.

The 4th Lanciers of Colonel Bro were not as confident as their brigade commander would have wished them to be. Exhausted and momentarily disorganized, their officers were doing everything they could to reform the squadrons into cohesive units before the enemy fell upon them. They nearly had their task completed when the lead brigade of Prussians announced that time had run out.

One regiment each of lancers and hussars broke into a gallop as Colonel Eicke led his men to retake the hill for Prussia. Cresting a very minor rise in the ground, the infantry squares of the 95th Ligne were clearly seen and then and there Eicke wished he could have angled his attack more to the west to clear those bayonet bristling nests of fire but it was too late for that. What was worse, the unit best for dealing with squares was posted on the left of the line instead of the right! Nevertheless, the die was cast. Breaking into a run, the light horse troops crashed over the debris of battle and at the enemy horse and infantry. The squares of the 95th flashed with well aimed fire and cleared the first troopers from the periphery of the position though at least one horse still charged even without its rider. The hussars, angry but impotent, reached hard to strike the kneeling infantry but could not make any impression on the bluecoats within. Swirling around desperately, they looked to find a hole of some sort or an imperfection in the formations but the 95th Ligne left no such opportunities. With their eagle defiantly in the midst of the middle square, they beat off every attempt to shake them and littered the ground with downed enemy horsemen.

Unlike the hussars, the Prussian lancers found their counterparts an easier group to deal with as the latter were blown and many were missing their lances which they had left scattered about the hill, usually in the back of some unfortunate Prussian. However, a nut is still a nut and it took everything Prince Wilhelm's lancers had to finally crack the green coated French and force them off the ridge. The French, despite their condition, had managed to get that last ounce of energy from their horses to make a final charging burst before being ridden over. However, help was on the way. Guided by the expert hand of Jacquinot, the 3rd Lanciers entered the fray catching the Prussians in pretty much the same condition that the latter had caught the 4th. Having swung in from the front and flank of the fight, the more ready 3rd, still with lances and full of spirit, routed the enemy horse after a brief struggle and continued on to relieve the squares from the attempted depredations of the enemy hussars. Quickly enough, there was a large mass of horsemen traveling in every direction such that one couldn't figure who was attacking and who was retreating. The French infantry, used to only seeing Prussians, fired a few times at their own cavalry before understood curses made them realize what they were doing. Musket shots became cheers.

Prince Wilhelm watched the rout of his 1st Brigade calmly knowing full well that the casualties sustained would be relatively light especially when he made his next order to launch his ready reserve regiment of the 3rd Brigade to extricate the others. This regiment, the 1st Neumark Landwehr Cavalry Regiment, was probably the best of his questionable militia horsemen and so Prince Wilhelm was keen to see them in a full fledged charge. General von Sydow, the commander of the 3rd Brigade, begged to be allowed to charge the enemy with the rest of the troops as well but the Prince refused, noting that the remainder of the general's cavalrymen were inexperienced and that he needed a reserve, even if it was a poor one. With that, the 1st Neumark was sent ahead to relieve the 1st Brigade.

Charge and counter charge. The French had played the first hand and the Prussians the second but it was time for the next round. The 1st Neumark, charging past the retreating elements of their sister regiments, approached the French lancers who took one look at them and fell back down the ridge towards their own lines. Thinking that a great rout was ahead, the Prussian horsemen followed in pursuit right past the stationary infantry squares and right into the open sword arms of Jacquinot's 1st Brigade which swept into their flank with two fresh regiments of men. The 1st Neumark was quickly in a bad way. The French 7th Hussars and 3rd Chasseurs, denied for so long, took their opportunity and crashed headlong into the enemy with tremendous force. In short order, the 1st Neumark's commander was killed and their standard taken by the marauding French horsemen. Once again, the Prince was able to see remnants of his horse flying away and General Sydow asked to charge again.

"And lose all these children?" the disgusted Prince replied to the request as he eyeballed the waiting regiments. "Don't worry, their mere presence will help our cause but I dare not use them yet."

The cavalry fight, so long in actually starting, was now over. Jacquinot, having given strict orders to not pursue the enemy, saw his cavalry rally to the sounded recall and fall back down the slope while Durutte's division prepared to advance again with a safe flank. In a sense, both sides had gotten something they needed. The French, having removed the threat of the guns to their flank were able to continue in their diversionary attack while the Prussians, in delaying Durutte, were able to deploy Krafft's men into the gap and prepare to halt Durutte. Napoleon's army came out the better, however, as the Prussians decided to pull back their gun line and the new infantry brigade in the area immediately came under fire from both French batteries on either side of the brook. Additionally, the French Emperor noted that Blucher's center was slowly being denuded of troops as the reserves were deployed to the flanks. Tucking that piece of information away, he waited for more reports.

Prince Wilhelm, gathering in his beaten horse, fell back beyond the forest to rally his men and prepare for the worst later. This time they had faced light horse. What would happen when they met cuirassiers?! With this thought in mind, he sent a messenger to his 2nd Brigade, well to the south behind Losthin's and Funck's infantry brigades, to summon them to the center and, once they had arrived, to replace them with a pair of his Landwehr units from the 3rd Brigade. The 2nd Brigade, if it could be called that, was made up of one regiment, the 8th Hussars, as the companion regiment, one of dragoons, was not with the army. Replacing it with two militia units seemed a fair bargain.

The end of the cavalry action marked the finish of the second phase of the battle where the French completed their deployments and began their pinning attacks in earnest. Blucher's position remained largely the same but it was clear that the French army was outfighting them and forcing the commanders to commit more and more men to hold the line against the aggressive enemy. Troop quality was partly responsible in that the Prussians had strong contingents of Landwehr regiments but what was the more significant item was the quality of overall leadership from the level of the regiment on up. Blucher, a man not unlike the Russian Suvarov, plainly believed in the fighting spirit of his men and their ability to sustain repeated attacks against the enemy. This thought entailed close action against the French where firepower, the strength of the British infantry, would be less important. As we have seen, in built up areas the Prussian infantry performed well but when the situation became more open their efficiency against the more mobile and imaginative French fell off allowing smaller French forces to retain the upper hand even against far larger Prussian formations. This is not to say that the French commanders were all better; the French simply were able to utilize the organization of their army as a single unit and coordinate their arms whereas the Prussians had difficulty doing the same. A good example of this is that the Prussians assigned their major cavalry units at corps level instead of retaining a reserve that could influence the course of battle. As a result, most Prussian horse was scattered across the field supporting the infantry and thus could easily be outnumbered by a concentrated cavalry strike force like that of the French army. At Ohain, given the tight nature of the terrain, this might not prove critical but, like Napoleon's grand cavalry attack at Eylau in 1807, such a force could possibly tip the balance of any battle.

CHAPTER 14

THE TRAP BEGINS TO CLOSE

HAUPTMANN Hirsch, a staff officer to Count Gneisenau, describes the feelings abounding at Blucher's headquarters as the tempo of Napoleon's attacks increased.

What a swing in mood had occurred in the past few hours! In the early morning we were full of confidence as Blucher himself told us that the French would be broken and driven from the field. Even our normally reserved chief of staff, Count Gneisenau, had the same expectations as our great leader. When the French, fighting with admitted skill and extreme determination, foiled our first attacks everything changed and I sensed a feeling that no one seemed to know what to do as success had been absolutely expected, even taken for granted, whereas failure had been completely discounted. For some time we acted as if we were in some other world as we neither attacked again or retreated off the field and the whole while our reserves were being committed one after the other against the growing French army. I know our field marshal did not want to retreat in the face of Napoleon but we just sat like pumpkins in a field! All of the other aides around me did as I did and waited patiently for something to be done.

Feldmarschall Blucher, a normally boisterous and inspiring man, sat on his horse several feet away and, as I watched him, for the first time ever in his service, I actually noticed that he was old. This may seem to be an odd statement for one of but twenty-five years to be saying about a seventy year old man but the fire that had constantly burned so brightly in him appeared to have dimmed all at once and the effect was noticeable. I believe he felt betrayed by God, whom he had damned so often, for this lack of success against the hated Napoleon and was fighting with himself as to what to do. It was Graf Gneisenau who finally convinced him to retreat off the field but by then, especially when Chapelle St. Lambert had fallen, it was getting far too late. A definite nervousness now gripped our little group of aides but Graf Gneisenau's energy revived us as he set himself to the task of getting our army out of this battle as he had done at Ligny two days before. After that moment, there was action without stop for the staff and no more chance to consider our situation.

Napoleon galloped across the field of Ohain followed by his faithful aides and escort of chasseurs to feel for himself the pace and action of the battle thus far. Reports to him indicated that the diversionary attacks were going well and that the Prussian reserves were being drawn into battle. The Emperor, always a realist, took some of these reports with the proverbial grain of salt but when a similar report came from Drouot who was with the grand battery, he knew he had to act quickly. Drouot, called the "Sage of the Grande Armee" for his religious conviction and humble honesty, was a man who could be trusted under any circumstances and Napoleon greatly respected him. Meeting the Emperor behind the gun teams of the Imperial Guard, he saluted perfectly and calmly, if a little awkwardly, gave his personal report.

"Sire, Blucher is committing his reserves against Durutte," he said simply without expanding on the idea but then he probably knew that Napoleon would.

"In what strength?" the Emperor questioned.

"About four to five thousand men."

"You are sure?"

"Yes sire, as if they were my own troops."

"What of the Prussian cavalry?"

"They have fallen back out of range."

"Then Blucher has only his guns and infantry deployed in his center?"

"That is my impression and belief, sire."

"Very well then, Drouot. Deploy the cannon of the Imperial Guard."

Thus the battle of Ohain entered its next phase. As if on cue, the teams of the Imperial Guard artillery, replenished and rested, shook themselves into motion and began to move towards the existing gun line. It was a majestic sight. The teams, all large well fed horses, pulling large wheel limbers and caissons, moved like clock work towards the existing French line to deploy as Drouot had ordered: wheel to wheel. Napoleon's intention for this massing was very simple and straightforward. With so many guns lining the French center, he would be able to literally blow a hole in Blucher's line and then fill it with his own cavalry. Thus engaged, the enemy position could be easily breached by the trailing infantry divisions and victory gained before noon.

As the Emperor rode on, his headache began to fade away. A feeling of strange well being overcame him for a moment and for the first time in the whole campaign he began to think that everything just might go their way yet. Wellington had been routed, Blucher was on the verge of defeat and if those two were finished then the Austrians and the Russians would be comparatively minor nuisances. Catching himself, he quickly realized that he would have to think about the battle at hand rather than a possible battle down the road against other enemies. Too often one might think days ahead only to lose the day at hand. Extending his glass as he came to an abrupt stop, he raised it to spy on the Prussians in between the cannon blasts. Thirty yards away was the 54th Ligne under Colonel Charlet and, for once, all eyes were not focused on the Emperor but on another phenomena, a natural one.

The weather had been an odd mixture of rain and sunshine on the eighteenth which had left its mark on the battlefield of Mont St. Jean. Today, the moisture in the ground had given way to mist and a slightly overcast sky had obscured the sun. As the Emperor sat quietly observing the Prussians, the sun finally crept out from the clouds to engulf the field with its full force, almost as if to lend him a helping hand. This perceived omen was not lost on the soldiers and a man, it could have been any Frenchman, called out from deep within the ranks of the 54th.

"Sire! Look, the sun!"

Startled, the Emperor closed his telescope with a sudden snap and, not finding the face within the staring ranks of the line infantry, turned his attention to the sky. Raising his hand to shelter his sensitive eyes, he took in the brilliant rays. Sure enough, the morning sun had arrived and with a startling beauty even a cynic like himself had to admit. Napoleon couldn't help but grin a little. It did seem like a good omen, much as it had back in 1805.

The soldiers, so often a thinking body onto themselves, began muttering with each other as if trying to find an answer to a puzzling question. What did this mean? Did the sun predict another great victory as it had back in that cold December ten years before? The answer was a resounding "yes" from the ranks (and why not) as they cheered and waved their shakos in the air. The nearby Imperial Guard rankers just shook their heads in regal dignity but more than one felt the same way.

"Austerlitz! Austerlitz!"

Their repeated chants filled the air and even Napoleon had to agree with their sentiment. Turning towards la Bedoyere, he pointed at the smoky center of the Prussian line. "We will break their line there," he said as he waved his arm along the gap north of the Bois de Paris. It was difficult in the light of the soaring enthusiasm right beside them to not posture even just a little bit. "He's gotten himself into the same predicament as at Ligny. This time he won't be so lucky. Let's go back."

*   *   *

"Sir, we must withdraw," pleaded a downhearted Gneisenau as yet more reports came in of the pressure building along every portion of the front line. "Bulow is barely holding, Zieten's men are being savaged by the enemy guns and Ohain is being threatened. Napoleon is preparing for the final blow! Sir, as I respect you I must ask you to allow us to fall back."

"Napoleon! Napoleon!" Blucher yelled. "That is all I hear from you! His army is at the end of its rope and we will beat him! Where are our reserves? Commit them!"

"But if we have to fall back, what will cover our retreat?" the chief of staff said though his voice indicated his heart wasn't in it.

"No more talk of defeat! Here we conquer or die!" finished Blucher after which he walked his horse a few steps forward to create distance between them. They could not fail now, not when victory was within their grasp. All they had to do was hold and the battle would belong to them.

The Prussian position at this moment was shaken but not yet a disaster. Bulow, entangled with Lobau and now d'Erlon in the Bois de Paris, was holding his own and still could count on the morale of most of his men even if they were getting very tired. At the moment, Zieten's men were under the most pressure as Krafft's newly arrived brigade came under heavy fire from the French artillery companies and began to take casualties even before it had made it into actual battle. Pirch's corps, not so much an actual unit now, was being used as the "pick and choose" reserve for the whole army. The situation was not yet hopeless but it was starting to slip out of the grasp of the Prussian command.

A rider from General Zieten came up to the old field marshal and saluted. His news was not good. Krafft's men, deploying into a cauldron, were taking a terrible beating from the French artillery deployed on either side of the brook. Blucher, frustrated at the lack of success so far, cursed the man as a defeatist and turned away in fury. The lieutenant messenger, bewildered and cautious, looked at Count Gneisenau and handed him the written version of the report that he had not been able to finish.

The Prussian chief of staff took the proffered paper reluctantly and began to read the badly penned note. Suddenly, his eyes widened almost as if he had just experienced a revelation. Zieten's artillery commander, Colonel Lehmann, had apparently done a quick survey of the French gun positions and had noted how the cannon on the north bank of the brook were situated in such a way that they would not be able to strike the Prussian line if it was pulled back as the guns would be blocked by the saddle slope of the hills. What was more, pulling back the line might also lessen the blows from the battery directly ahead as well. Knowing the importance of this information, Gneisenau knew he would have to approach the field marshal and impress upon him the need to pull back, even if it was just a small withdrawal.

Walking his horse up slowly, Gneisenau found Blucher contemplative and in a low tone he read the pertinent part of the dispatch from General Zieten. "Sir, we will still be holding the line and saving our men at the same time. If we will not withdraw, at least let us straighten our defensive line to protect the soldiers."

Blucher, his head partly sagged, turned to Gneisenau, his faithful comrade, and nodded in quiet agreement. A million images rumbled through his worn head from the defeat at Ligny to his dismissal by Frederick the Great to the entry into Paris in 1814 to his drunken stupors. What was happening now? Was his army dying?

As the Prussian commander sat in reflective thought, his chief of staff acted on the nod from his general and drafted the necessary orders for Zieten and Pirch to pull their men back to form a new line out of harm's way and for the cavalry of these two corps to start concentrating in the center to cover the withdrawal; he probably would have written even faster had he known how Krafft's men were fairing under the fire from what was now a huge number of enemy guns. Still, the order to fix the line was just the ticket he needed, just the primary concession he wanted, to pull back the Prussian army a little at a time until it could all be brought away.

Despite this clear sign to abandon the battle, Gneisenau should not be viewed as a man who gave up so easily. More to the point was the fact that Blucher's chief of staff was a realist who was only willing to take risks when the chances for success were quite high. This trait he had already demonstrated during the march to Waterloo on the eighteenth along with his deliberate modifications of the orders given by Blucher that day and the next. Given the chance, Blucher would gamble everything away with one throw of the dice no matter what the odds; Gneisenau, it is clear, wanted the best odds and an extra throw or two as well. The Kingdom of Prussia, bankrupt and tired after years of war, was funded by English gold and he knew that a knockout blow delivered here would ruin the work of both he and Scharnhorst and leave his country without support of any kind. France was not the only enemy Prussia had on the continent; both Austria and Russia commanded great quantities of men and both empires were always looking to expand. If this army was lost, what defense would they have then? Would the Tsar decide to partition their country like he had done with Poland? Where would the money come from to create another army?

*   *   *

Along the front, the situation had already become desperate. Colonel Lehmann, watching the French gun line was horrified to see a huge number of uncommitted French cannon all at once joining the other guns and begin to unlimber. It could only be one thing, he surmised; Napoleon was throwing in the fabled Imperial Guard artillery. He had seen them at work before; at Ligny, the French Guard artillery had blown a path through the Prussian center allowing the enemy to break the position and rout his army. Staring at the muzzles in the distance, he was hard pressed to say that they wouldn't do the same again. Yelling orders like a madman, he told his men to open fire on those dangerous enemy guns as fast as they could without regard or pause for accuracy. If the French were allowed to deploy unmolested, Lehmann knew that they would be smothered.

A Prussian twelve pound ball smashed into a caisson wheel just feet away from where General Drouot sat on his horse watching the enemy batteries. His guns, the "beautiful daughters" of the Imperial Guard foot artillery, had been waiting all morning for this event and the men were anxious to at last take an active part in the battle. Given the delay in deploying, the men clearly knew that their commitment was a preparation for a grand assault and their animation reflected this knowledge. Rightly acclaimed as the finest cannoneers in the world, the evolutions they performed were as smooth as if they were on the parade ground. Never mind the occasional soft piece of ground where the rain had not yet evaporated; the strong veterans in their tall bearskins just ignored it and manhandled their pieces to point directly at the Prussian masses to the rear of the enemy guns. Never mind, too, the blaze of fire from these cannon directed at them; nothing could stop this force once it was on the field. Cannon balls screamed at, over and before them while shells sizzled as they landed just waiting to explode. One gunner, unfortunate enough to be near one landing howitzer shell, watched in horror as it bounced against his gun's wooden cartridge box and came to a stop at his feet. Frozen for a brief second, he then bent over and snatched the smoking fuse from the ball. Holding it in his hand, he threw it into a nearby small puddle without a second thought and went about his work. Surely that was a good omen.

The French battery, very much a "grand battery" now after the addition of the Imperial Guard artillery, counted seventy two guns under the command of General Lallemand who was quite pleased to see the might of his very own Guard twelve pounders joining his firing line. Joining Drouot, he pointed at Krafft's unfortunate brigade but the former noted another more interesting phenomena.

"There, at the very end of the Prussian line, where the firing has stopped," said the more senior general.

"What do you see?" questioned Lallemand.

"They are not rolling their guns back in between shots," replied Drouot. "They may be attempting to retreat."

Lallemand raised his glass to observe the enemy only to have the lens blurred by a smattering of blood as an artilleryman beside them took a hit from a ball and was cut in two. Having had one commander killed in the same way, Lallemand suggested to Drouot to check on Lebrun's setup across the brook giving the valid reason that the terrain would check his firing unless he was able to deploy farther east. The Guard commander, not recognizing the reason for Lallemand's concern, agreed and left the other to conduct the firing against Blucher's center. Lallemand breathed easier inside.

The Guard foot artillery's commander now regained his focus. Wiping his lens of the blood, he looked through it again to watch the enemy gunners doing exactly what Drouot said they had been doing. So that was the reason that their fire had been so erratic; the Prussians were indeed pulling back and in a most ingenious fashion at that. Lallemand slowly retracted his glass, a plan formulating in his head.

French orders for the artillery bombardment had frowned on counter battery fire as it was considered wasteful of ammunition but Lallemand, like all gunners very protective of his men and cannons, wanted to knock out those enemy guns or at least cause them to retreat. Coming up with an idea given the compact nature of the ground, he took another approach to fulfill both aims. Instructing his gun captains to ricochet their first shots along the line of the Prussian guns, he intended to bounce the shots from there and onto the infantry beyond. Given the number of shots that would be flying in Blucher's direction, it was quite apparent that the enemy guns, only about seven hundred yards away, were in for the deadliest of times. As the first company of the Guard artillery announced that it was ready, he gave a nod. Seconds later, the throaty twelve pounder roared to life, a cloud of dense smoke declaring to the world that the battle was about to be rejoined. Lallemand checked his watch. It was ten minutes past eleven in the morning.

*   *   *

"General Gneisenau reports heavy French attacks along the battle line. He says that he can only spare a single battery of cannon to help us," read Major Count von Finkenstein, a staff officer of the Prussian III Corps who had become attached to Borcke's brigade. "That's not very much."

Borcke was more positive. "It is eight more guns than I had before, major. We will have to make do with that."

"Seven, sir, the battery lost one cannon already," corrected Finkenstein as Borcke flashed him an annoyed face.

The Prussian officers were glad to have the support of any troops at the moment. The brigade commander, watching the French form up with a sense of impending dread, knew that he was faced with a very difficult assignment. To his front was the corps of General Gerard, clearly an able enemy officer, and to his left were more enemy troops in unknown strength. How many regiments had Ledebur's cavalry reported? Was there infantry and more guns, too? He couldn't answer the questions posed to himself but his duty dictated what he had to do. His orders were to hold the town and the adjacent bridges for as long as possible as the roads that passed through his position were critical for any retreat that might take place. If the French took the bridges, they could descend into the rear of the army and cause all sorts of havoc and that was something that had to be avoided. Borcke, however, was under no illusions. His position was not a strong one and the fact that he had to defend two separate targets made his job that much more difficult. Nevertheless, he calmly deployed his men for battle with the emphasis on his right flank where he posted Infantry Regiment #8 under Major von Zeppelin. The orders for this regiment were simple: hold the bridge approaches. The next in line was Infantry Regiment #30 who occupied the loop holed center of the Prussian formation and defended the town itself. Leaving one squadron across the brook to maintain communications with the main army, he redeployed Ledebur's cavalry to the Prussian left and then posted his sparse number of guns in pairs across the front of the whole line. In reserve were the men of the 1st Kurmarck Landwehr who waited in apprehension over the coming assault.

The French infantry columns approached the start line just before ten in the morning and were greeted with the first shots of the few enemy guns in front of their position. Pausing to dress ranks and throw out skirmishers, the two French divisions waited for the word from their commander to begin the assault. Morale was high amongst the troops and for once the French actually had numerical superiority (though they had no way of knowing that).

Gerard arrived amongst his forward regiments in time to see the voltigeur companies fanning out ahead to take out the enemy jagers and open the way for the attack columns. French artillery struggled into position having found, as Baltus de Poilly wryly put it, every single pothole and mud slide in the area to drive through. Their cannon, deploying one by one, prepared to bombard the Prussian positions along the edge of town near the bridges.

Gerard planned his assault carefully with the thought that a little deception could go a long way. He could tell that the Prussians knew what he was about and understood what it meant if the French seized the bridges. Therefore, he planned to take the bridges in a most direct manner by attacking in true Hannibal form with his center refused and both flanks sweeping ahead. Figuring correctly, he believed that Borcke would post his best troops to secure the crossings as the open ground would be dangerous country to rely on poor quality infantry. To answer this, he planned to send in Berruyer's dragoons to force the enemy into square and then crush them under the weight of Hulot's 14th Infantry Division. On the center and right, Vichery's 13th Infantry Division would be posted, mostly already deployed, and thus appearing to be in greater strength. Vallin's 1st Brigade of cavalry would take up positions on the right flank while Pecheux's men would remain in reserve behind the main lines. Satisfied with his plan, he ordered Loriere and his staff to send out his commands.

Just as Gerard's staff was finishing their work, a rider pulled up to their headquarters and dismounted in some haste. Pausing for a moment to catch his breath, he approached Gerard and saluted while handing him a message.

"Lieutenant Laden reporting from General Pajol's I Corps, sir!" the man declared.

Gerard, fearing that the man was actually from Grouchy, took the paper snappily and unrolled it. Reading the message, he stopped on one word, obviously a name, he could not quite make out. "What is that?"

"Robert, sir," the lieutenant said.

"Robert?" Loriere broke in. "As in St. Robert?"

"Yes sir," the lieutenant replied as he tried to assess why the two generals were so surprised. "It is just down the road."

"We know where it is lieutenant," Loriere said, cutting him off again. "You mean to tell us that General Pajol's corps is practically on our flank?"

They didn't know! Understanding flooded Laden's face. He smiled. "Yes sir! Marshal Grouchy instructed us to come to your aid though I must add that our corps is really only two regiments of horse with a third still with the marshal at Limale."

Gerard nodded. Things seemed to be getting better and better and he did not understand why. Perhaps it was the axiom that lady Fortune follows the bold or maybe it meant nothing at all. Either way, help had arrived to bolster his situation and make him even more confident, justifiably, that his mission would be successful. "True enough," he said as he turned to his chief of staff, "the other division is with the Emperor. Change Vallin's orders and switch his men to the left to support Berruyer. I think that our right is in good shape now."

The sound of heavy gunfire to the west was rising and Gerard guessed that the Emperor was more fully engaging the enemy before committing his hammer blow to finish him off. Along his own front, only the Prussian guns fired as his own were having great trouble getting into position to fire. Only now were the last of his field pieces taking their places opposite the town and bridge areas while the heavy ammunition caissons were having the same difficulties negotiating the mud. Judging from the terrain around Chapelle St. Lambert, the French assault point was in a shallow area that had as yet not drained so the initial move might be a bit slow and unsteady until dry ground was reached. However, the ground was good enough now to attack and that they would do, regardless.

"Give the signal to open fire," Gerard ordered. "I want to get this started."

As the last gun rolled into place, Baltus de Poilly ordered his crews to begin the bombardment. Gerard was waiting for this and, always an impatient man, he paced back and forth on foot as the guns came to life and announced the beginning of the assault on Chapelle St. Lambert.

The Prussian guns fired back gamely with their spaced out cannon but the preponderance of the fire was directed against them by the French. Borcke watched with concern as a solid shot struck one of his few guns, crunched the carriage and then cut down a few artillerists as well. His resources, limited as they were, could not take such losses but there clearly was nothing he could do beyond taking the punishment and hoping his men would be able to hold their ground against the French infantry. It appeared to him that Gerard was going to simply swamp him with numbers as he could see the whole French battle line stretched before him and it did look impressively large with all of its men lined up and ready to march. He had no idea that Gerard would be taking a page out of Hannibal's plan book by refusing his center and crushing the enemy flanks.

After a twenty minute bombardment, General Gerard felt that the enemy had been softened up enough. Concentrating their fire on the Prussian center and right, the French cannon, as always well served, silenced the Prussian guns and battered the exposed infantry battalions. Thankfully, thick hedges in the area helped conceal some of Borcke's men and thus not all the news was bad. Prussian jagers knelt in position along these obstacles ready to take on the expected French voltigeurs.

Hulot's well used 14th Infantry Division was deployed in single company columns and presented an odd spectacle for the watching Prussians as they were more used to the two company French column or the mixed order. Even odder was the fact that no French skirmish troops, practically a Gallic trademark, were out in front of the columns to pepper the formed Prussian units with their fire. Following discreetly behind the leading brigade of infantry were several squadrons of cavalry but beyond that they could not see due to the taller posture of the horsemen. What Prussian guns were left began to fire again.

"Prepare to charge!" ordered General Berruyer from his position in front of the 1st squadron of the 6th Dragoons. The troopers instantly stiffened and their throats dried out.

"Draw swords!"

The flashing of several hundred straight polished dragoon swords played on the sunlight as they were unsheathed in one quick motion; if the Prussians were watching with any care, then they knew what was coming.

"At the trot! March!"

The squadrons of the 6th Dragoons shifted slightly to follow the lead of the first squadron and from their position between the infantry brigades they aligned themselves into the gap between the 9th Legere and the 111th Ligne. All the while the infantry kept marching steadily forward though the pounding of so many hooves so close made more than a few take a tentative look over his shoulder just to reassure themselves that this was indeed part of a greater plan.

Major Zeppelin, commander of the Prussian Infantry Regiment #8, watched nervously as the French formation changed and their intent suddenly became very clear. A trick, it was all a trick!

"Cavalry!" he yelled to his adjutant who froze and said nothing. "Move, damn you! Everybody into square!"

"Forward! Gallop!"

Trumpets sounded along the column of horsemen filling the air with urgency. The dragoons dug their spurs in and their mounts lowered their necks and swept ahead at increasing speed. Small puffs of smoke appeared along the fractional hedge to their left as the jagers targeted them but certainly no skirmisher was going to stop them. As the last squadron of the 16th Dragoons, the second regiment involved, thundered by, the infantry came to a planned halt. Drums, the very voice of the infantry, rapped out another beat and soon the columns were deploying into the more normal column of divisions with two companies forming the head. The formation finished, the drums beat again and the battalions finally threw out their impatient light infantry who suddenly were feeling much more like run of the mill center companies than voltigeurs! Even as they sprinted out ahead, the first man fell, wounded in the thigh by a rifle bullet from the Prussian jagers; his comrades pressed on. The drums began beating the pas de charge.

"Forward!"

"There they go, sir," said Loriere to his chief as Gerard followed the distant movements of his men against the Prussian right. "Shall we commit the 13th?"

"Has Pajol arrived? I don't want them to be unsupported," replied the IV Corps commander. Since the battle of Lasne against the greatly superior enemy forces, Gerard had thought about how his command could have been forced to retreat or even routed had the Prussians been able to coordinate their men during the action. His own handling of his men had been careful and deliberate and now, when he felt he had overall numerical superiority against a part of the enemy army, he fervently believed that he needed to control his men as best he could and not throw away a definite advantage. His plan called for the 2nd Brigade of Vichery's division to advance against the Prussian left to fix his cavalry in place and any infantry posted there as well. However, his flank was in the air and he relied on Pajol's present arrival to fill this void and anchor his infantry line.

Loriere clicked open his watch and did some quick mental juggling. "Given that they were at St. Robert when the aide reported in, they should be very close by now."

Gerard nodded. "Very well then but make sure an aide is there to meet them. God only knows I don't want Pajol running all over the countryside like he did before."

"Yes, sir," his chief of staff replied though he was not even looking at his commander. Handing two previously written letters to nearby aides, he said to one, "Deliver this to General Pajol and make sure he stays on our flank."

Gerard's main attack was on the Prussian right flank but he did not want the enemy to know this for sure so he postured and threatened with the rest of his forces. From scouting reports he knew that the Prussian left was lightly held and against a combined infantry and cavalry assault was sure to be driven back. With any luck, the retrograde movement of the Prussian troops would force the enemy general to peel off forces from his center and right to avoid being encircled and then the bridges and town would fall of their own accord. If done correctly, French losses would potentially be very light.

Pajol's men were in fact very close to the scene of the fighting and his own scouts had reported back to him that French infantry was deployed before Chapelle St. Lambert in line of battle and that the guns were already in action. At this moment in time, General Pajol could not complain about any lack of intelligence at his headquarters. His own scouts had described the situation accurately and only minutes later the aide from General Gerard arrived with his dispatch asking him to place his horsemen along the French right and to join in the battle. Sometimes one could be thankful for not having to make the hard decisions any more. Pajol sent aides to his regiments and to Gerard acknowledging his part in the greater plan; this was no surprise as Pajol was always a team player and it suited his wounded pride to find a battle and stick with it.

As the infantry of Vichery's 2nd Brigade prepared to advance, the first hussars were seen cantering along the road towards their position. Like always, the whole formation ground to a halt as everyone thought they had been flanked by what appeared to be a handful of enemy cavalrymen. Colonel Herve of the 69th Ligne, standing in his stirrups, yelled at his men to rise off their collective butts and get moving again; it was a common thing for infantrymen not to trust their horse bound counter parts. The infantry, sheepish but reassured, responded and continued on.

The Prussian commander, Borcke, viewed all of these movements with concern. Ahead of him was deployed a strong French corps with plenty of guns and horsemen to use to smother his forces in the town. More enemy troops were clearly joining his foe from the forces under Marshal Grouchy to the east and that alone told him that his flank was now in the air. Feeling suddenly undermined by the strength of the enemy, he changed his plan of defense. Dashing out an aide to Ledebur, he instructed him to fall back to a post just to the northeast of the town where Stengel's men were coming from and then he ordered his reserve regiment save a single battalion, all Landwehr troops, to join in holding the town north of Infantry Regiment #30's position. This move was a sensible one as it shortened Borcke's lines though he had to make sure that he was able hold the brook line lest he be surrounded in the town between two French forces. That proposition was immediately put to the test.

Infantry Regiment #8, the unit charged with holding the bridge approaches, was a regular unit and it formed quickly into the squares Zeppelin had ordered just moments before. Their professionalism saved them. The same hedges that hid the infantry from the artillery fire also shielded the men from seeing what they were up against. Moments after they completed dressing their ranks, the sword points of several hundred French dragoons burst onto the scene in a frenzied rush for the infantry. Luckily for the Prussians, the hedges had helped funnel the attack and the French were hard pressed to wheel their mounts before coming at the formed infantry. Nevertheless, the charge was a fearsome one. Erupting with musket fire, the Prussian infantry emptied many saddles and killed a score of horses before the wave of French cavalry vanished from view due to the heavy smoke. Frantically, the foot soldiers began the process of ramming and priming again. Another group loomed out of the haze.

The Prussians had formed into three battalion squares and they met the French dragoons with a heavy and costly fire. Holding firm, the ground around the squares began to fill with dead horses and wounded cavalrymen as the desperate dragoons swirled around the solid formations looking for openings and only finding more musket blasts. Prussian musketry quickly dissolved into a free for all individualistic fire but they remained staunchly where they were without caving into fear. The noisy, brutal ballet around the squares was enough to make any man nauseous and want to flee but these men held their ground like Frederickan infantry of old and refused to be intimidated.

If Borcke had any cavalry to spare, he would have used it to relieve his hard pressed infantry but Ledebur's horsemen were all he had and he needed them to meet Stengel's Infantry Regiment #19 which had been retreating from Limale. From his command site, a simple tree stump that was tall enough to hold one man sufficiently high to view the battle, he watched the swirling cavalry and knew he was powerless to help his men; the squares had to hold firm on their own. French infantry was marching up behind the cavalry, obviously to exploit the confusion and the poor position of his men but so far in the center the enemy had only demonstrated against the town itself without actually launching an assault. Borcke found this curious but he had no way to act on this information for any move from one end could leave another exposed and he was too weak to risk it. As he watched, word came to him from Ledebur that the French had been joined by at least two cavalry regiments with more probably on its way. The odds, it seemed, were mounting rapidly.

Amongst the squares, the fight continued as the dragoons, fierce, angered and frustrated, tried vainly to overrun the firm foot soldiers that stood as immovable as large rocks. Striking from all angles repeatedly, their horses at last became blown and jaded; both rider and beast were exhausted. Regimental integrity, hard to maintain at the best of times, was utterly lost and the squadrons of both regiments were mixed badly with one another. Unexpectedly, they were faced with a single formed Prussian uhlan squadron which charged them with great vigor. Momentarily fractured in confusion, they broke and fled pell-mell back down the paths they had come, an act that would cause a complete upset in the plans of General Gerard.

The squadron of uhlans that Borcke was at last able to deploy onto his right was the group of horse that had been attached to Stengel's infantry as they retreated from Limale. Riding ahead to make contact, they had found the battle in full swing and reported to the brigade commander on their own to take a more active part against the French. Borcke liked such initiative and immediately gave them the duty of ridding the 8th of the tired out French dragoons. What seemed to be a daunting task actually proved quite easy as the enemy was blown and some had already begun to fall back to their own lines. Mostly through a show of force and a brief charge, they relieved the infantry, which cheered them, and then wisely chose not to follow up the attack as yet more enemy cavalry stood ready to join the fray and alert enemy skirmishers shot at them from the hedge row. Chasing the dragoons up to near the broken hedge row, they inflicted few actual casualties but nonetheless managed to cause a stampede. The winded French dragoons, having lost Colonel Mugnier of the 6th, fragmented and raced away at the best speed their tired but desperate mounts could take them.

Hulot's infantry was just nearing the hedge line when the incident occurred that stalled the attack of the IV Corps before the bridges. Not expecting anything out of the ordinary and with the air heavy with smoke, they passed two abandoned guns and prepared to take on the infantry. There was really no way to tell what had happened to the cavalry as they were out of sight and both colonels felt that the former had managed to ride to the bridges or else they would have streamed back in pieces by now. Obviously, neither man realized that the dragoons had met with surprisingly heavy resistance and were determined to break it or be beaten back.

"Attention! Cavalry!" shouted a veteran sergeant of carabiniers.

Caught open mouthed by their own horse, the 2nd Battalion of the 9th Legere was struck by wild horses careening right into their loosened ranks. Front rank soldiers dodged out of the way of the mad beasts and the formation of the battalion quickly came apart and dissolved into a mob. More and more horses, some riderless, followed the route of the others and the 9th Legere found itself completely engulfed by what it thought at first was a hostile cavalry charge. The 1st Battalion, where Colonel Baume was, immediately stopped and formed square while more dragoons swept by as if the devil himself was behind them. The stricken 2nd Battalion was quickly rendered hors de combat and a large gap appeared in the midst of the line of French infantry as that battalion was positioned between the two leading regiments of the division. As a result, the two battalions of the 111th Ligne continued forward only a few more yards before they, too, came to a halt for fear of enemy cavalry following up the rout of the dragoons. French soldiers, both mounted and on foot, were scattered all over the plain.

"Ninth! Form up!" yelled Colonel Baume as he saw the extent of the disaster and forced his horse out into the open. Nearby, a dragoon was shot from his horse and fell to the ground with a wound to his arm. "They're our men!"

"Damn it all!" Gerard was heard to yell as he pounded his fist onto his saddle. Plans really did have a way of unfolding in the face of the enemy. What had happened? "Where is Berruyer? Taking a deep breath, he waved to Loriere. "Have Vallin move up with his men and cover the withdrawal of the first brigade. Rotate them with Toussaint's second brigade and continue the attack."

Loriere knew Gerard was having a difficult time with the ruin of his plan and he had to admire his forced calm in the presence of the premature repulse. Nodding but saying nothing, he sat down to hurriedly write the orders to get the movement in progress.

Veteran regiments often do things on their own that less experienced regiments are not able to do. For one, they have the ability to rally far faster and ready themselves to attack again. Both the 9th Legere and the 111th Ligne were excellent regiments with long service records of battles in which they had fought and from that experience they had produced a hard core of iron willed soldiers that seldom gave up on the field. Colonel Baume was to be gratified by this fact in just a few minutes. Coming across a sergeant with the battalion fanion, he was pleased to see that the darkly clad light infantrymen were already forming around him as they gathered their wits and realized what had happened; no doubt a bit of wounded pride was in the mixture as well. To be routed by one's own cavalry was a bad thing and would make any regiment, even the 9th Legere which had gained glory a day before, the laughing stock of the Army of the North. Colonel Sausset of the 111th met him in between their stalled regiments and asked what he wanted to do. The Prussians, it was clear, were not about to attack them though if they stayed put for long the enemy might yet get the idea. It was either forward as soon as the 2nd Battalion was ready or fall back and hope the enemy did not follow. Baume was loath to stop now as both regiments had shaken out their skirmishers who were now owners of the hedge row and the 9th was rallying very quickly as more and more of the men returned to the ranks. Perhaps the mess wasn't as bad as he had first thought.

"I say we go," Baume declared. "The Prussians would have attacked by now if they could and they have not."

Sausset smiled. "Good, then we move on your signal."

As the colonel of the 111th Ligne rode away, Baume suddenly realized that his counterpart, whether intentionally or not, had placed all the responsibility on his shoulders in case something else went wrong. Wondering if only for a second how that had transpired, he shook his head and turned his attention to the 2nd Battalion as the men raced about like ants in a nest trying to find their proper companies.

"Sir, do we go?" asked a lieutenant of the 2nd Battalion.

Baume locked his jaws to hide any nervousness. "We go!"

The Prussian were elated at their unexpected success and at least one aide pressed Borcke to counterattack the French infantry but Borcke would have none of it and simply ordered his men to resume their former positions. So far he had held the bridges open as ordered and he figured the French were safely out of contention on their right flank for some time. His belief was confirmed by the advance of more French cavalry, a sensible move made to protect the blunted and disorganized infantry spearhead. The repairs being conducted by the French here were the least of his worries now for the enemy had launched another attack, this time on his left with more infantry and cavalry. Changing his perspective with a bias to his left now, he waited for word that Stengel's nearing regiment had arrived to bolster his position.

All was not finished on the right, however. The fire fight continued between the jagers and the voltigeurs as each kept the other busy and the parent formations were able to redeploy in peace. The three Prussian battalions reformed their lines and all seemed normal save the blocked vision due to the loss of the hedgerow to the French. Not being able to see was frustrating for Major Zeppelin and he determined to find out what was happening on the other side. Riding ahead, he found a gap in the hedge where no French soldiers were hiding and he raised his ornate glass, a gift of his father, and watched the enemy reforming with cavalry approaching from the rear. The next moment, he was on the ground with several plumed shakos hanging over him and one musket muzzle pointed at his chest. Nodding dejectedly as he slowly nudged the gun away from his body, he knew he was a prisoner of war.

Colonel Baume's men, spirited and a little ashamed, reformed very quickly and the second battalion, commanded by one Captain Durso, reported itself ready for duty again. The broken off attack would now be able to resume. Giving the order, the 9th Legere rapped out a new beat and, followed by the 111th Ligne, began marching ahead.

General Hulot, the 1st Brigade's actual commander but now responsible for the whole division, sat on his horse between the two brigades, a look of pride on his face. Hit by a bizarre calamity, his men had held together, reassembled and returned to the attack. Commenting with approval to an aide, Hulot was quite pleased.

A courier now rode up to them with Gerard's order from a few minutes before. Hulot read it with alarm and his head suddenly jerked up to watch as his men arrived at the hedge row and began to launch their attack. "It's too late, lieutenant, the first has begun the attack!"

Through the smoke of the nearby guns, another officer watched in amazement at what was happening. "Where are they going?"

Loriere grinned and shook his head. "They are following your orders, sir. That is, your *first* orders!"

Gerard pounded his fist again. What about the next batch of orders? Suppose they followed them now? Shaking his head over his curious luck, he dismounted and walked over to his chief of staff. "The die is cast. Countermand our orders, the latter set. The second brigade will advance to support the first. Vallin's cavalry will join the reserve."

Loriere stared at him. "But sir . . . ."

Gerard shrugged. "We at least must follow through. The enemy is in front of us and that is where we will strike him, now."

While the rest of the 14th Division wallowed in a little

marching and countermarching, the 1st Brigade swarmed around and over the hedge row taking the Prussian fusilier battalion under a heavy and destructive fire. The Prussians, recently reformed in a column, had been deploying into a newly ordered line when the 1st Battalion of the 9th Legere appeared and interrupted the movement with a surprising though ragged volley. Raising a cheer, the French lights pushed forward despite the return fire and the Prussians gave ground rapidly as the disjointed companies attempted to get to safety. To the right of this little fight, a sudden volley brought the French 2nd Battalion to a halt as they ran into the Prussian 1st Battalion deployed into a line and they struggled to extend amidst the carnage of the defeated dragoons whose horses were lying about liberally in the field at their feet. A fire fight ensued between the ready Prussians and the chastised French with neither giving any ground.

The 111th Ligne of Colonel Sausset had a tougher time of it coming through the hedges but, despite the fire from the hidden jagers, they managed to push ahead along the flank of the town, part of which, having been hit by howitzers, was ablaze. With the wind blowing the smoke westward, visibility fell off which did help to conceal them from the attentions of Infantry Regiment #30 in the buildings. Nonetheless, the regiment flushed out the jagers with their own more numerous and experienced voltigeurs and pressed on their heels towards the deployed Prussian 2nd Battalion. This battalion, partly ensconced in a few farm buildings which lacked high walls, was waiting for the French but obviously not prepared for the speed of the 111th's attack. Having dispersed the jagers in short order, the infantry swept right up to the farm area and directly engaged the defending Prussians. What should have been a good blocking position proved anything but and the Prussian battalion was ejected after a short but savage little tussle that left the French spearhead disorganized and the Prussians retreating. Sausset, feeling the need to keep up the momentum of the attack, nevertheless ordered his reformed 1st Battalion into line but left the second in column to flank the enemy position if the opportunity presented itself. That done, the drummers set the pace to move ahead again. Neither French colonel knew it, but both were about to make precisely the same maneuver with the quite different results.

Baume's first battalion, in column, chased after the retreating Prussians who finally cracked and ran off towards the town. This movement left the French with the bridges to the west and the rest of the Prussians to the east; the thick smoke just to their right suggested the presence of another enemy unit probably blocking the 2nd Battalion. Choosing to keep his regiment together, he ordered the battalion to wheel to the right and attack the enemy there. The Prussians were about to be rolled up from both ends.

Borcke was rudely awakened to the heavy fighting on his right flank again and his eyes were able to witness the rout of the Fusilier Battalion of the Infantry Regiment #8. Without any hesitation, he ordered the reserve battalion, the 3rd of the 1st Kurmarck Landwehr, to immediately march to cover his right while he himself rode over to see what was happening first hand. It was not a moment too soon. As the broken pieces of the 8th fell back towards the safety of the town, the sound of musket fire grew. A French unit, no doubt the one that had crushed the fusilier battalion, had flanked the whole line and was closing in the next battalion as it was engaged to its front. The view decided him. Dashing off more orders, the rest of the 1st Kurmarck was withdrawn from the town to shore up the right flank and counterattack the advancing French. Likewise, the single uhlan squadron, recently so decisive, was recalled as well.

Despite their setbacks, the men of Infantry Regiment #8 were good troops and they showed their mettle with their stand against the 9th Legere. Faced with the enemy light regiment on both front and flank, the 1st Battalion of the 8th found itself in an angled deployment as it tried to fight along two sides without exposing itself too much. French voltigeurs circled around the enemy unit to hit it from the rear while the rest of the 9th attempted to close the distance and drive the enemy away. Instead, the battered 1st Battalion formed a square of sorts around its regimental flag and prepared to die in place. Casualties grew and the wounded bodies of the soldiers piled up along the ground just like they had the day before at Mont St. Jean. It was an act of desperation and pure sacrifice. Unable to see a great deal, the able men simply grabbed muskets from dying comrades and discharged them at the French who were very impressed with the heavy fire they continued to receive even if it wasn't very well aimed. The battalion's captain went down and then the standard bearer but the plucky Prussians closed up their ranks, picked up the shot torn banner and defied the French to do it again. The 9th Legere, in almost a reluctant manner, edged closer to the enemy square.

The 111th was also getting nearer to the Prussians they had chased away and a company of horse artillery pushed its way between the regiments almost heedless of the enemy fire. Dashing and grim at the same time, the efficient artillerists did not lose a moment unlimbering their cannon in preparation to add to the Prussian's misery.

"Forward!" yelled Colonel Sausset to his men as they approached the enemy position. Benefiting from the fire of the French foot companies which had been able to take this part of the enemy line under direct bombardment, they found their unlucky previous opponent to their front definitely wavering and Sausset knew cracking morale when he saw it.

"Bayonets!"

Cold steel puts the fear of god into any man. Two solid battalions of elite French line infantry proved unbearable to the 2nd Battalion of the 8th. Involuntarily falling back at first, they back pedaled under the threat of the shimmering triangular blades losing formation as they went. Sausset's men charged after them. To be fair, the 8th's men had very little going for them at the time with French artillery fire raining down on them and a very aggressive and strong enemy not allowing them time to properly reform and rally. Hoping they had broken through, the soldiers of the 111th Ligne cried out the usual victory slogan, "Vive l'Empereur!" and got exactly what had happened so often at Mont St. Jean: a volley and a quick reappraisal of the situation.

The Kurmarck Landwehr 3rd Battalion marching from the

reserve position stopped the immediate French advance as Borcke redirected the unit to where he thought the greatest danger was. The tip of the 111th Ligne, messy and confused from the merry chase with their bayonets, was fired upon by the line of militiamen and they realized that another enemy force was entering the fray. Recoiling just enough to gather up their strength, the 2nd Battalion of the 111th Ligne pressed ahead again and the Landwehr, impressed and caught up in the dark atmosphere of the battle, started to fall back as well. Sausset's first battalion, having taken a few casualties from the flank, paused to strike whoever had shot at them thus adding a third battalion to the attack against the Prussian 8th regiment's only remaining formed unit. The situation was critical.

Borcke needed time and with all of his units on the verge of routing, he had to resort to desperate measures. With the two additional battalions of infantry marching up the road to the right flank, he saw the third battalion in a very real crisis with no other support. As soldiers began to trickle off, he rode out ahead of the battalion, brandished his light sword and yelled, "Where are you going? There is the enemy!"

The effect was what he had hoped for. Despite the hail of lead bullets that passed through the air beside him, the Kurmarck seemed to shudder in place as the men realized that things weren't that bad. Galvanizing themselves and reforming, they paused to load their empty muskets and come to the ready. On Borcke's command, they fired. The forthcoming volley of balls and a few accidental ramrods rippled past some of their running comrades from the 8th and stopped the elongated French battalion. Caught by surprise, the pursuing French fell to the ground wounded or were quick to retire knowing that the game of chase was up for now. Falling back on to its center companies, the 2nd Battalion of the 111th had to stop to reform its ranks before advancing again to complete the rout of the Prussians. In any event, Sausset did not want his regiment to be split up and open to defeat in detail.

As the rest of the Kurmarck approached to rebuild a new Prussian line, the men of Infantry Regiment #8's first battalion were in their death throes. Surrounded by three enemy battalions and now being shot at by a French horse artillery company, the ground around the battalion was so thickly strewn with dead bodies that recent victims simply flopped over on to the gruesome remains of the rest of the unit. Through the smoke and haze, the piles of corpses and badly wounded men looked like able bodied soldiers crouching and the French, caught in a seeming blood frenzy, poured shot after shot and canister round after canister round into the unit before realizing that the Prussians were no longer firing back. Colonel Baume could see through the thinning air what he could not before and a sick feeling crept up his spine as he stared at the shattered and cut up bodies.

"My god," he was heard to mutter before ordering, "Cease fire!"

The racing blood of the French infantry halted after they had seen what had happened. Normally iron stomachs were dismayed at the carnage and it was with relief that they heard the order to advance against the approaching enemy. Taking as wide a berth as they could around the terrible sight, even the most hateful of them could not but admire and pity what these Prussians had tried to do on the field. Regimental records would remember the action of the Prussian square at Chapelle St. Lambert.

The death of the Prussian 1st Battalion was not entirely in vain. Profiting from the delay, Borcke hurried up his two other battalions and covered them with the uhlan squadron which threatened to charge the 9th Legere. Forced to a stop, Baume whistled up the horse gun company which, like the infantry, was only too glad to get away from the handiwork they had performed on the square. A few shots sufficed to convince the small cavalry unit to seek greener pastures and this left the Prussians once again with three battalions facing the advancing French.

The men of Hulot's 1st Brigade were in a confused state and needed to reform before continuing the attack. Under the cover of the horse artillery which pushed itself ahead to bombard the Landwehr, the two regiments stopped to put their ranks back in order and get everybody under control again. Sausset and Baume met again at this point and agreed to approach this new Prussian formation in the more traditional fashion as their momentum had been all turned around by the crushing of Infantry Regiment #8 and the lost time had obviously been put to good use by their opponent. Retrieving all of their men, the two regiments prepared to deploy their voltigeurs but only after they had given the artillerists time to "soften" their targets to be.

In Chapelle St. Lambert, the burning buildings on the southern tip of town had forced the Prussian defenders away though there was no way for the French to take advantage of this as fire is wholly indiscriminate of who it burns. Baltus de Pouilly, Gerard's artillery chief, sent a message to this effect to his commander and suggested splitting off his guns to allow them to continue firing on the enemy. Gerard's answer was to allow two companies to separate from the battery and move to support the respective infantry divisions engaged in the attack. Heavy smoke now made visibility poor on the French left.

The battle had lulled momentarily but the advantage still lay clearly with the French. One Prussian regiment had been routed completely and, given some more time, so would the Landwehr troops in the second line. Major General Borcke knew this as well as Gerard did but he did not give up the idea of defending his position. Having been forced to abandon the southern edge of town, he hit upon the idea of using the troops thus released to counterattack against the French and drive them back while he rallied what could be rallied of #8 and used them to cover the town. In this way he could retake the initiative and force the French to use more time to seize the town and inflict heavy losses on them as well. Meeting Major Ditfurth of Infantry Regiment #30, he told him what he was planning to do and was met with an enthusiastic response. Leaving one battalion to guard the town, the two remaining battalions would join in on the attack and recapture the ground lost before the French right came into play. The 30th, having been shelled during the whole battle was only too ready to actually fight on the field.

Borcke rode his lines prior to the attack to reconnoiter the enemy position and also to stiffen the Kurmarck troops again as the artillery fire was becoming quite galling. From his experienced eye, he could tell that the French were preparing to resume their advance in short order as the pesky voltigeurs began to break formation and head out in pairs across the fields. Returning to the smoking town, he was in time to see the Russian uniforms of the 30th as they emerged from the buildings and formed up along the right flank of the Landwehr. Given the tight nature of the terrain along the banks of the Lasne, the 30th was formed in columns one behind the other ready to take the enemy with the bayonet.

The Prussian preparations to strike back against the French were not lost to the eyes of the IV Corps officers but Gerard was confident that against Hulot's 1st Brigade the enemy attack would be repulsed. The 14th Division was now formed in two lines of infantry represented by the two brigades and then was backed up by Vallin's cavalry. Berruyer's dragoons were only just starting to reform after their disastrous charge. Over on the French right, the attack, delayed by the arrival of Pajol's men and the customary greetings, had developed far more slowly and Gerard was forced to send an aide over to get the attack moving again. He could only guess what they were waiting for though one clear indication that he felt the French left was the critical area is shown that he never left that flank or removed his watchful eye from it to supervise personally on the right. The battle, he knew, would be won by slicing between the Prussian forces and not pushing them together.

An objective observer might have thought that the coming match up on the French right was the clear money winner given the strength of Gerard's men. Once organized and ready (and the infantry at last trusting that the horsemen were also French), the attack swept ahead in a wheeling motion in more or less the traditional style. A single Prussian gun located at the edge of town took the 69th Ligne under fire causing a storm of cannon fire to descend on its position when Baltus de Pouilly spotted the flash from afar. The 69th deployed its voltigeurs and one center company liberally to screen the parent unit but the pause in the advance was an indication of how things were going to progress on the

French right. Slowly and cautiously the division edged ahead causing Gerard to swear more than once and send aides to hurry things up.

The lack of speed in the attack of Vichery's men was a curiosity to the commander and staff of the IV Corps but they might have understood better if they had been there and could witness what was happening. With no enemy troops save a few cavalry to their front visible, the regimental and brigade commanders felt that something was obviously wrong with the situation as they had not been faced with numerical inferiority in battle throughout the entire campaign. It was too easy. The fear that the enemy was going to strike from somewhere else and catch them unawares was very prevalent and any officer who had been at Salamanca in Spain in 1812 knew exactly how uneasy this feeling could be. At that battle, a surprise British counterattack by cavalry charging out of nowhere had reduced Marmont's army to a rabble in short order and had cost them the battle. Still, given the strength of Pajol's cavalry and the obvious heavy fighting along the French left, the division should have had enough confidence to march with a little more alacrity.

The 2nd Brigade of Vichery's division wheeled gracefully with the cavalry posted on its flank and closed on the town itself. A few shots could now be heard as the jagers and voltigeurs exchanged pleasantries though, fortunately, the cannon had been knocked out by accurate fire from the light troops who had made the gun an unhealthy place to be. Like the jaws of a great animal, the IV Corps was ready to trap its prey.

But it would not happen quite yet. The Prussians had not given up and were about to try and turn the tide of the battle. Borcke was gambling on the French not being able to take advantage of the momentary weakness on his left as he launched his own attack along the right; Stengel's marching regiment also played a part in his plan as these men would slip into the vacancy left by the two battalions of the 30th. This connecting event was not wishful thinking on the part of Borcke either as Stengel's men were indeed very close by and preparing to at last rejoin the main army and, conveniently, help in the defense of the town.

Both Baume and Sausset had reformed their lines again after the crushing of the 8th and the ubiquitous voltigeurs had dispersed ahead to renew the action. So far, Hulot's men had succeeded in taking the ultimate objective and now they could concentrate on seizing the immediate one. With the 2nd Brigade appearing behind them, at proper intervals of course, the force was well prepared to finish the job and snap the jaws shut.

The Prussian attack took everyone by surprise. Pouring out of the town in columns of attack while the Landwehr madly raced ahead to strike the front of the French line, Borcke was throwing his best blow at the attacking French force. The voltigeurs came racing back the way they had come sounding the alarm and taking up better hiding places while the rest looked on in astonishment. Having just beaten one enemy regiment, no one had quite expected an enemy counterattack so soon.

Sausset's exposed 2nd Battalion was the first to contact the enemy and they were driven back when they saw the Prussian 30th curling around their flank. One good volley checked the enemy advance for a moment and then they hustled back to reform some yards away thus giving up a good deal of the ground they had just seized. The Kurmarck Landwehr, carried by a tidal wave of emotion after Borcke exhorted them in the name of Blucher, charged the French line with great elan and refused to break after taking a solid volley from their enemies. Seeing that they were in earnest, Hulot's men fell back as well. Only the horse artillery company gave any trouble but when some hidden jagers on their flank started knocking off their horses, the gunners limbered up and rode off to a safer haven leaving the firefight an even one. Borcke's plan appeared to be working.

Baume's 9th Legere fell back quickly before of the weight of the Prussian assault but reformed just as fast when the colonel ordered them to do so. Dressing a neat line, they thundered a volley at the advancing militiamen and halted the wild charge with a crumpling of overcoat clad bodies. Coming to their senses, the Prussians hastily began to deploy into a crude line to return the fire but this was not their strong suit and the 9th rapidly gained the upper hand, their voltigeurs heckling the enemy at every turn. Here at least, the Prussians would be brought up short.

The 111th was in tougher straits. Pinned in front by the attack of the Kurmarck, they watched with a pensive eye the 30th starting to flank them though the latter was hounded by the French artillery which spotted and then let fly against them with every tube. Held for a moment, the 111th gradually pulled back. Sausset rode behind the lines exhorting them and keeping a lookout for any men who were about to take off for the rear. He reached the very right flank of his regiment to see what the enemy was up to when he abruptly received a message that he was in the wrong area. As he observed the enemy, he felt a jager's rifle bullet pass through his left tunic arm without harming him and, more dangerously, a French cannon ball neatly decapitated his horse's head before sailing too close to his own men. Strangely, he was able to simply step off the dead beast before it slowly collapsed and, aside from the blood splattered on his tunic, he was no worse for the wear. Aside from his being alive, the next best thing was the realization that the ball had been an errant one as no more of the projectiles came near his men for the rest of the fight. The 111th now maintained the line that the Prussian 8th had held initially, including the small farm. How quickly battles turn.

The French artillery fire probably saved the 111th Ligne from being flanked and forced back off the field. Spotting the enemy troops deploying away from the town, Baltus de Pouilly directed the fire of every company save one and planted a pair of shots directly in front of the first enemy battalion which sliced right through them in a bloody swath. The Prussian 30th, victims of the barrage, shook out its fusilier battalion into skirmish order and opened an annoying fire on the 111th but in doing so lost some of its initial momentum as the second battalion struggled to get clear of the town. The French voltigeurs returned the fire but really were stretched fairly thin.

Coordination of all arms is what makes a battle winner. The

Prussians, because they lacked any guns and had virtually no cavalry support, were pure infantry and subject to its good and bad points. The French, on the other hand, enjoyed artillery and cavalry superiority and had the know how to use them. Watching the beginning of the Prussian attack, Gerard lost not even one minute in ordering Vallin's cavalry to execute a charge en masse through the intervals in the French line and along its left flank to relieve his men and allow them to fall back to their start lines. Without the support of the 2nd Brigade, this first major assault had failed and not gotten anywhere but perhaps the tables could be turned now. What was more, Gerard was definitely getting a better idea as to the strength of the Prussian force in front of him and it clearly was not numerous. Having just routed one regiment, there could not be many left. As was becoming customary, Gerard fired off another aide to get Vichery to move faster.

The 9th Legere, facing an equal number of enemy battalions, stubbornly refused to budge an inch and inflicted heavy casualties with their fire on the Kurmarck troops. The Prussians, having lost momentum, became disorganized and, their morale sagging, started to give way under the volume of fire they were receiving. Already a line of bodies marked their furthest advance from which they could go no further. In an ironic note, part of Baume's men, the 2nd Battalion again, was forced to defend around the mangled bodies of the Prussian 8th Regiment which did nothing to alleviate their stress; the bodies, however, did act as a form of protective rampart. The Prussian standard bearer was hit and fell but this tempting prize was too far away for the French to do anything about it and the colonel restrained his men from wanting to advance before he had word as to what the 111th had done (at this point, the 2nd Battalion really wanted to be away from their horrid "fort"). For the moment, because of a sudden wall of horse flesh, Baume would not be able to know what had happened.

Vallin's cavalry brigade, unemployed since the day before, was ready and eager to do their best. With the battle unfolding around them, they were anxious to not only play a part but to avenge the rout of Berruyer's dragoons should the Prussian horse decide to make another appearance. Leading with the 6th Hussars, the two regiments advanced in columns, one around the French left and the other through the gap between the two infantry regiments. Vallin's orders had been relatively simple: move through the lines and angle east. The hussars, taking the long way around, had to pick their way through a few hedges before arriving in the open field and thus were not the first into the fight. Instead, and to their chagrin, the 8th Chasseurs, following the now traditional straight up the field approach, burst onto the scene between the fighting foot soldiers, passed all the bodies of horses and men and finally arrived before the 3rd Battalion of the Kurmarck Landwehr. Catching them as they formed square, the cavalry, mistaking them for the 8th's solid squares, really put them to the fury of their swords as they broke the formation apart and cut down anyone within reach. The savagery of this particular small action probably saved some of the Prussians, especially the fusiliers of the 30th who now scrambled to reform. The enraged chasseurs did not let up on the Landwehr and, after running over them with succeeding squadrons, chased them right back towards the town. In a few short moments the battalion was nothing more than running fugitives and they only found salvation when the Prussian uhlan squadron showed up after having arrived from the left flank. Deploying as they approached, the small unit of horsemen spied a torrent approaching them.

The Prussians that survived the wave of cavalry formed their squares properly and, of course, the counterattack came to a swift close. The 30th found the change of formation especially galling as they were pounded by the French guns who had been frustrated when the fusiliers had broken into skirmish groups. Now, with the enemy more solidly formed, they could do their deadly execution. On the French left, the hussars were also making their presence felt as they arrived to put the fright into the remaining two battalions of Landwehr and root them in position. To their credit, the Kurmarck troops remained steady and replied with heavy, if high, fire.

The arrival of the French cavalry on the field signaled the transfer of the initiative to the French again. Trapped in their protective squares, the infantry was vulnerable to every sort of fire and the jagers, many of whom were cut down by the charging horse, had mostly joined the massive formations to avoid being chased down; rifles had no bayonets and were notoriously slow to load, two serious detriments when cavalry was in the area. As it was, the squares were both safety and danger for the troops in them as the French infantry and the single horse artillery company approached to take them under fire. Chapelle St. Lambert was about to fall.

Events now began to unfold at an ever increasing pace. On the French right, the unchecked advance of Vichery's division, even with its lack of speed, was making Borcke's position increasingly untenable. Stengel's infantry did arrive when it was supposed to but could only file into line to slow the French; the regiment, #19, was badly mauled from the fight at Limale and weak in strength. Ledebur's troopers put up a credible defense against the steadily advancing French but could do nothing to stop them. Firing now erupted along the edge of the town and Borcke found his brigade formed into a "V" that was fast becoming an "I". It was almost half past twelve.

Atop his horse, General Borcke was reaching the end of his rope. His attack having failed, he would soon no longer be in a position to dictate his own fate unless he did what he had no orders to do: withdraw. With the thunder of cannon all around him and his troops being savaged by the enemy, he lowered his head onto his chest for a moment before rising stiffly in his saddle. With all eyes on him, he motioned for Major von Muggenthaler.

"Yes sir?" the staff aide asked as he nudged his horse forward a few steps.

"The brigade will prepare to fall back behind the brook to the north," Borcke replied sharply. "Ledebur's men will be the last to cross."

"What about the squares of the Kurmarck? Only a counterattack can possible relieve them," Muggenthaler queried as he looked back over his shoulder in the direction of the fight.

The Prussian commander bit his lip. "They are our rearguard."

Borcke's decision to withdraw from the trap came from necessity as further resistance would only result in his men being pocketed and forced to surrender by the superior French force. Thinking realistically, he had done all he could and his choice would save at least part of the brigade from being taken. Some accused him of cowardice but given the situation he was in, there was no other option available as the Prussian army could neither support him or relieve him later. His decision was the right one even if it was difficult.

The plan drawn up by the Prussian commander was a good one though it did deliberately sacrifice the Kurmarck Landwehr that was surrounded by masses of French cavalry. Forming a battalion sized unit from the parts of the 8th Regiment, he used them as a rallying point for the withdrawing 30th which fell back into the town and pushed north to join up with the 19th which was on the verge of collapse. Fresh blood helped stabilize the line for a moment while a feigned charge by Ledebur's men bought some more time. It was not an entirely clean process but one that demonstrated Borcke's ability to take advantage of Vichery's lethargic troops and the unfortunate sacrifice of the Kurmarck Landwehr. Withdrawing by stages, his troops filed unmolested over two nearby bridges. The last men over were Ledebur's cavalry who did an admirable job as the rearguard and set both bridges on fire as they passed.

Only too late did Gerard see what was happening north of the town but by then there was little to do about it except order his men to occupy the town, secure the bridges and wait for further orders. The two battalions of Kurmarck Landwehr, separated from their parent unit, faced by infantry and cavalry and now staring at gun muzzles from redeployed horse and foot artillery, laid down their arms and surrendered rather than be annihilated like the 8th Regiment. The strange action was over and with it, for the moment, the IV Corps' direct involvement in the battle of Ohain itself.

Gerard was not pleased with the results of the battle as it had cost him far higher casualties than he had cared to take but there was no denying that he had completely achieved his objective and had earned the rest he could enjoy for the next few hours while the battle of Ohain swirled around him. Reporting to Marshal Soult about his seizing Chapelle St. Lambert, Napoleon's chief of staff, in his final staff foul up of the campaign, promptly forgot about him in all of the excitement at Ohain itself and failed to issue new orders for his or Pajol's corps. That it was not such a bad thing to the troops was evident as they were able to relax for the first time while the cavalry scoured the area to find feed for their worn out horses. For Napoleon, the mistake was not such a bad one either as whether Gerard moved or not, the IV Corps was in a position to shut the door on the Prussian line of retreat.

The battle of Chapelle St. Lambert had cost the IV Corps some 900 casualties, mostly in the 1st Brigade of the 14th Division and Berruyer's dragoons; Vichery's men came away quite lightly. They had inflicted almost 1,600 casualties on the Prussians, captured another 1,000 prisoners and seized six serviceable cannon. Though their commander had wished for a good deal more prisoners, he could not complain about the elan and skill they had displayed. Gerard's troops, inspired by their victory the previous day, had fought splendidly even in adversity and had earned their victory against a good opponent. Gerard himself, by not directly assaulting the town and wisely exploiting his superior forces, was able to minimize his risks and those of his men while frustrating an obviously competent commander. Even in these hectic days, Gerard, a veteran of many years, had been able to learn a few things too. On the Prussian side, Borcke, too, could be praised for his handling of the battle. His lack of numbers left him few options but his defense and wise withdrawal saved the rest of his command for Prussia and these men would end up being, except for parts of Thielemann's corps, the most solid part of Blucher's army to return to Germany after the campaign was over.

CHAPTER 15

CLIMAX AT OHAIN

Gᴇ́ɴᴇ́ʀᴀʟ de Division Kellermann, commander of the III Reserve Cavalry Corps, gives his impression of the famous charge of the French cavalry at Ohain. (Note that the narrative fails to mention that General Milhaud's IV Reserve Cavalry Corps charged with him or that there was light cavalry backing them up!)

My corps had been deployed behind the artillery of the Imperial Guard for two hours when an order came from the Emperor to charge the enemy lines. The Emperor, having guessed that the enemy intended to withdraw, had decided to entrust me with breaking their center so that the following infantry of Comte d'Erlon could complete the rupture of their line and crown our efforts with victory. I was at once anxious and proud at the responsibility placed before me as it exhibited the highest trust a commander could have in his subordinate. Determined not to fail that trust, I brought my men forward with alacrity and wasted not a moment like other commanders in our army. This was the moment that the whole army had waited for!

My corps was in high spirits. Though we had suffered somewhat the day before, I was pleased to see so many of my men who had been captured or wounded at Mont St. Jean rejoining the corps for its decisive charge; with such men behind me, I could not fail! I organized my men into three lines, roughly of brigade strength in the first two and a third to follow up the others. We advanced in echelons of squadrons so necessary for mounted attacks with myself posted with the elite carabiniers in the lead of the whole. The artillery fired one last great round before we started and suddenly we were off! Gathering speed, we reached the Prussian gun line before they could inflict much mischief on us and great was my satisfaction when I sabered two gunners, something that should have happened the day before. Once past the captured cannon, I directed my charging horse at the great mass of Prussian cavalry directly ahead but their first line refused to stand and instead made off in great haste. Their second line was not so cowardly but also could not stand against my men and they, too, broke and fled. However, the numbers of the enemy were great and we were soon heavily engaged by them. Heavily outnumbered and our horses blown from the constant action over the past days, we parried all of their grand attacks and held the center of the enemy line until the infantry broke it. I was very proud of my corps that day and we were congratulated by the Emperor himself for having won the battle!

*   *   *

The fall of Chapelle St. Lambert was crucial for both sides. For the Prussians it meant that not only was their main line of retreat cut off but also that if they didn't start moving soon, that force in their rear was going to make any withdrawal later an almost impossible ordeal. Gneisenau, upon hearing the news, was beside himself for letting it happen and he pressed his desire of a retreat on Blucher with very uncharacteristic force. The latter, knowing that all had been lost for the moment, agreed to the retrograde movement reluctantly but even old "Marshal Forward" knew when he had been bested by position. There was little else to do except decide along which route they would go. Steinmetz was holding firm at Ohain itself and therefore this seemed to be the right spot to head for before swinging east for Kleist and the path for home. However, even Steinmetz reported advancing enemy troops and this put a definite electricity into the air for everything to be moved as quickly as possible. Consequently, orders were drawn up in a hurry detailing which units would move when and who would cover the rear of the army as it marched away.

It may seem at first glance that the Prussians had for the most part wasted all the time they should have been using for retreat but the fact of the matter is that it was not entirely their fault. Napoleon's battlefield strategy envisaged escalating attacks along the entire front if possible in order to rivet the enemy's attention and force him to commit his reserves piecemeal into his line. So far, Blucher and Gneisenau had done just that; Pirch's II Corps had been effectively frittered away as reinforcements to both the I and IV Corps and only one brigade, Bose's, remained as the army reserve along with the cavalry brigades. French attacks, by Durutte along the Ohain brook and d'Erlon and Lobau in the Bois de Paris, had pinned those friendly brigades destined to be withdrawn and thus had tied the hands of the Prussian high command. Now, with the momentary lull in operations along the whole line, Gneisenau was actually quick to seize the opportunity to get his army out of what he now recognized to be a growing trap.

The lull in the fighting at Ohain came about through a couple of different circumstances. First, Durutte's fight against Jagow, the Prussian grand battery and the cavalry had ended with the retreat of all of the Prussians concerned and the re-establishment of their line farther to the east, thus giving the French more room to deploy as they fought up the "funnel." Secondly, the forces in the Bois de Paris had settled down to a skirmish affair as both sides were exhausted and in want of organization. For the French, fighting since around six in the morning had taken its toll and even Lobau had a tough time getting his men to continue their attacks. The Prussian line, still numerous if a bit shaken, was not going anywhere, forward or backward, yet.

Back at Blucher's headquarters, his chief of staff was sitting inside a nearby farmhouse with his aides drafting orders to move the army away from the battlefield. Gneisenau's problems were complicated, however, by the position in which the Prussian army found itself near noon of that day. Both bridges across the Lasne had been either lost or destroyed and those at Chapelle St. Lambert were in enemy hands. To launch an attack there with Napoleon poised against their rear was courting disaster and so that option was given up as not being viable. Gneisenau's deliberations eventually left only the route through the hamlets of Chaud Brire and Doudremont, both behind Steinmetz's position at Ohain, as a possibility. This route, directly out of the "funnel" to the north, was relatively free of French troops for the moment and, with Steinmetz holding Ohain supported by Roder's cavalry, promised to be the safest and quickest possibility.

In order to prepare for the withdrawal towards Doudremont, the Prussian chief of staff took stock of what troops he had left to commit and for once was almost pleased at what he discovered. Of Zieten's I Corps, only Jagow's brigade had been in action, though it had taken a beating, and the same was true of Pirch's II Corps as Krafft's was the only brigade that had seen action there. Bulow was fully engaged and was now relying on Tippelskirch's brigade of II Corps for his own reserve. Steinmetz of the I Corps was the unit holding Ohain, backed up by Donnersmarck's questionable Landwehr battalion (the rest of this brigade was with Borcke at Chapelle St. Lambert). Judging which unit would be the best for being the pivot unit against which the rest of the army formed up, he chose Bose's brigade which was the only brigade left in reserve for the whole army. Having merely watched the French and their building exercise at Lasne, they were completely rested and fresh and therefore the best choice for this task. Studying his maps, he realized a lucky stroke had been granted to his army in that the II Corps, despite being dismembered for reinforcements, was essentially the unit holding the Prussian center even with two brigades uncommitted to battle. These two brigades were the key to the retreat since they could hold, along with the cavalry of course, the center and allow the flanks, especially Bulow's left flank corps, to fall back unmolested to the north.

Gneisenau's last problem was what to do about Gerard in

Chapelle St. Lambert. Long suspecting that Borcke would not be able to hold the town against the French, he had written it off as lost. He was, however, determined to hold the French to the brook line and not allow them to take advantage of the captured bridges. The troops of Gerard might have cut off this route of retreat for the army but the damage would be limited to that and no more. Gneisenau's solution to the problem was to take some guns from Pirch, attach some cavalry from Wahlen-Jurgass' cavalry reserve and then position them across the brook so that they could cover the area with their fire and counter any French attempt to cross the river. Even if the French did attack with their corps, it would take some time for them to get a foothold, like at Ligny and Wavre, and by then, he hoped, the army would be in a more favorable situation.

While the Prussians madly planned for their withdrawal from the Ohain battlefield, Napoleon and the Army of the North were not idle. Reports from Lallemand, Durutte and Lebrun all gave indications that the Prussians were going to break off the action and attempt to fall back. Lebrun, an experienced imperial aide de camp, had been watching the movements of the Prussian cavalry and guns across the brook for some time now and had stated that the enemy was slowly moving out of the angle of fire for his cannon. Durutte, positioned in the very front line of the French army, noted that the enemy had ceased his attacks and seemed content to bombard his position in the woods with guns being withdrawn from the battered Prussian grand battery and angled to the right. Lallemand, watching through his glass from the gun line, reported the Prussian center occupied by cavalry without infantry in position. These tidbits of information prodded the recently returned Napoleon to ride his lines again to see for himself what was happening; this was the job of the commander in chief and Napoleon, getting stronger as the day progressed, was going to be there this time to supervise the commitment of the strike force he had assembled. If indeed the Prussians were about to fall back, it was imperative that the heavy cavalry corps be launched immediately into the weakened enemy center to stop the movement and bring about the breaking of the Prussian line.

Napoleon's plan followed the good sense he usually employed in battle. Disliking fancy or overly complicated tactics, probably due to his studying the campaigns of the ancients, he relied on sound basic tactics that would secure his strategic objectives. At Ohain, his pinning attacks and deployment of the guns of the Imperial Guard were all in the truest form of the Emperor and were deliberate stages leading up to the final attack. By extending his bombardment of the Prussian center, he had two objectives in mind. First, his troops, some in battle since the early morning, were tired and in need of food and reorganization. Second, the presence of two large Prussian infantry units, a line of guns and a body of cavalry in the line of fire of his heavy guns was too great a target to let pass easily; Napoleon, a gunner at heart, knew that the fire of his cannon could so seriously weaken the Prussian center that it would make the assault by the two heavy cavalry corps that much easier when the time came. However, if the Prussians pulled back before the cavalry was ready, they might have time to rebuild their gun line, support it with cavalry and then be in a position to negate the advantages gained by Lobau and Durutte.

Napoleon mounted La Desiree, especially brought over to him by the Master of Horse, and rode out to inspect the front. Soult, riding uncomfortably next to him with his pen and notebook, followed with the army of aides and the hustling duty squadron of chasseurs. The Emperor could hear the thunder of the guns at nearby Chapelle St. Lambert and knew that Blucher could hear them too; if the Prussian was smart, and indications varied on this, the capture of the critical town would be a very clear signal that it was high time to escape and leave the field to the French. As he rode, he mentally went over the plans he had already drawn up. Kellermann and Milhaud, commanding the two heavy cavalry corps of the army, were positioned behind the cannon line as they had been for an hour already. Domon's light cavalry division, posted to the right of the guns, had orders to support the charge when it went in as Napoleon knew that the Prussians had considerable numbers of horsemen available to them and that both of his heavy corps were not only worn but depleted as well from the losses they had suffered at Mont St. Jean. Backing up Domon, just in case and completely hidden from Prussian view, was Lefebvre-Desnouettes and the Imperial Guard light cavalry. Stationed well back of these cavalry bodies was the Imperial Guard heavy cavalry which had received orders, strict orders, not to move a muscle unless ordered to by the Emperor himself; no repeat of the day before would occur on this battlefield. The Guard heavy cavalry, always an arm of decision in themselves, were too valuable to lose to a wild charge as they were that last reserve of horsemen that could stem the tide of disaster or tip the scales of victory in their favor. As for infantry, Soult had aides standing by to ride like the devil to every French foot formation on the front line the instant the cavalry strike went in. The orders they carried were simple: attack the enemy to their front and once more pin him in place. Denying the Prussians the luxury of maneuver would leave them helpless in the face of the attack and almost guarantee victory.

Obviously, battles are not won by just great masses of cavalry alone. A proper coordination of all arms was the key to battle, as it always has been, and for this Napoleon had his last force ready, too. The great mass of decision for the French army was the reorganized divisions of Marcognet and Quiot. Standing by to the left rear of the gun line, these troops had been unengaged for the entire battle, had eaten breakfast and were impatiently waiting their turn to enter the contest. Whether because of the victory the previous day or because they sensed the critical nature of the battle today, the divisions were rejoined by a multitude of returned prisoners, wounded men and even the occasional soldier grabbed by the gendarmes. Some of these prisoners, interestingly, had spent most of the evening watching the routed Anglo-Dutch army swarm north; their guards had let them go to join the race for the coast and they figured the safest thing to do was to just wait until morning before enjoying their freedom. In the hustle and bustle of a rout, especially at night, it was too easy to get trampled or even killed for no good reason by either side. Wellington's army had collected some 3500 prisoners during the course of the afternoon and now these men, or at least a good chunk of them, filtered back to their regiments to rejoin the fight. The comradeship of the Grande Armee was standing the Army of the North very well.

The guns bellowed like thunder across the field and the officers of the battery were down to using hand signals to make sure that their meanings were clear to their gunners who proceeded to communicate in the same manner. The area behind this great gun line was strewn with the equipment of the artillery as small arms, ammunition boxes and tools lay scattered almost haphazardly on the ground. Gun teams, large and small, waited patiently as the pieces continued the rolling bombardment of the Prussian position. The companies themselves, positioned virtually wheel to wheel, appeared like a well oiled machine as all the actions of gun and crew alike had become automatic. To their front, several hundred yards away, lay the remnants of the Prussian gun line which had been destroyed one cannon at a time by Lallemand's ricochet fire throughout their position. The volume of fire from the French companies had so completely overwhelmed the enemy that fewer than half of their guns were in any condition to fire and their ammunition caissons and limbers had been repeatedly struck making it difficult for them to effectively get reloads or even to do such a simple thing as move. Despite this problem, the remaining Prussian cannon held on manfully and returned the fire as much as they could. The time was one in the afternoon.

Napoleon rode into the dense cloud of smoke that had drifted in from behind his cannon and, coughing for a moment, burst out the other end of it to clear his view and allow him to judge the condition and intent of the enemy army. General Lallemand met the Emperor and pointed out to him the Prussian line. "You can see where their guns were before."

The Emperor's experienced eye could tell immediately that not only had Lallemand done some counter battery work but also that the enemy had slowly pulled back his line as the wrecks of the carriages and horses showed where he had been. "They are hurt, general, but they are also about to retreat. Soult! Release Milhaud and Kellermann! The infantry will attack all along the line. Reille will attack Ohain. Lallemand, redouble your firing until the cavalry pass you. Give them all the support they need."

The die was cast. As imperial aides galloped in all directions with the orders, Napoleon remained where he was, mounted and with his telescope firmly planted against his eye. For Blucher, he was determined that there would be no escape this time. Indeed, if they could crush the Prussian army and drive it out of Belgium, there was the chance that the war would effectively end in an afternoon and that was certainly a gamble that the Emperor was willing to take. To have an end to the long wars would give him the time he needed to spend on France's affairs and, for once, his own; Napoleon's son, a captive Austrian at the moment, was always on his mind and one of the great personal driving forces behind his campaign.

La Bedoyere stood by the Emperor holding the bridle of his horse. Napoleon noticed what he was doing and leaned forward in his saddle. "Are you afraid that I will charge the Prussian line single-handedly?"

His devoted aide stood stiffly to attention. "No sir, but should we not fall back to a safer vantage point? Your grenadiers fear for your life sir, especially since they are not here to protect you."

"Children worry," the Emperor said as he digested this concern from his Old Guard troops. They had always looked after him, his crusty veterans, and even now, after a hard fought campaign where so many men had fallen, they felt it necessary to protect him. Who could argue with such a sentiment? Besides, off to the west there was slightly higher ground which would give him an equal view. "Very well. We will move back to that mound over there so that my aides will be less afraid of stray cannon balls."

As the Emperor trotted away, Soult rode close to la Bedoyere and put a hand on his shoulder. Compliments were never easy for the irascible chief of staff but he did his best. "Well done, Bedoyere. If I had asked, he would have grown roots here."

*   *   *

The troops of the French line were really beginning to come alive as more and more of them became engaged with the Prussians; firing could be discerned from the banks of the Ohain brook all the way through the Bois de Paris. Several regimental bands were playing patriotic songs and the whole scene was coming close to resembling the field of Friedland in 1807. With every passing minute, French morale was inching higher as the whole army came together and brought Blucher's men under ever increasing pressure. Viewed from the middle ground of the battle line, even the privates could see the activity of their emperor and the great mass of heavy cavalry formed up to strike the enemy center. This indeed was the old magic at work again. Aides scampered to and fro, artillery massed itself wheel to wheel to pulverize the enemy line and masses of infantry waited patiently to give the final blow to an opponent who had been fighting all morning. A definite feeling of impending victory was in the air.

One group that was just getting into the act was Jerome's division which had taken the route north of the Bois de Ohain to assault the Prussian far right. Accompanied by Pire's ever alert cavalry, Napoleon's younger brother was in position and waiting for Foy's division to reorganize and emerge from the sanctuary of the trees. Prussian cannon were still thundering from across the brook and Jerome, irritated with the delay, was getting a bit temperamental when he felt that his chance to share in the heavy fighting was going to pass him by.

Perhaps the trait of impatience in the former King of Westphalia could be blamed for the next misfortune to befall the French army, certainly the last significant one of the battle of Ohain. General Reille, commander of the II Corps, had ridden into the forest to help Foy get his division together and had left Jerome with orders telling him not to initiate any attacks unless the enemy was in full retreat. He should have told him something else. Leaving Jerome alone in front of the enemy was comparable to leaving the fox in the hen house under strict orders not to eat anything; the young Bonaparte was just begging for more action and was determined to get it.

Jerome Bonaparte was not the sort of commander one really wanted to have in a battle of brains over brawn. There was no doubting his bravery, certainly, as his exposure under fire at Hougoumont and subsequent wounding proved, but never once did he show exactly how he was related to Napoleon in terms of military ability. Lecherous, spoilt and, admittedly, young, he possessed the ability of an illiterate lieutenant and probably would have remained that sort had he not been the brother of the Emperor. To the detriment of all, Napoleon felt that he had to be kind to his siblings (as always remembering his supporters) and thus the already once disgraced (or twice if you count the American fiasco) Jerome was given command of one of the best divisions in the army. Ironically, he did well at Quatre Bras but completely lost his head at Mont St. Jean. After the victory, he dragged his feet leaving the Hougoumont area as he wanted the garrison to surrender to him and now, much to everyone's misfortune, he had his men poised to strike against the Prussian town of Ohain. Close reconnaissance at the town showed it to be well defended with barricades and loop holed walls while its flank was protected by artillery on one side and a cavalry brigade on the other. Reille understood that only a full assault by the two divisions of his corps would carry the vital town and that it had to be a fully organized effort. Jerome, of course, did not understand any of this.

Mounted on his third horse of the campaign, General of Division Bonaparte watched the Prussians through his telescope, actually one belonging to an aide as his had broken, and tried to figure what they were up to. Steinmetz, busy shifting his men around in the town to face the French threat from the northwest, had his reserves marching to new positions and messengers racing off to confirm with Roder, again, that he would support his flank. Jerome, for all the world looking like a real commander, had his heart set in one direction though his mind told him to do something else. Reille had instructed him, slowly and right to the point, that he was to wait for Foy's men to arrive and then, on his command, to launch a coordinated attack against the town. The commander of the II Corps was no fool and, having once had his unruly subordinate ruin his orders, he was not about to have another fiasco take hold of the corps. Unfortunately, he would have no part in the decision about to be made.

Jerome gazed at the Prussians as they marched to and fro and his heart told him that they were in fact being heavily reinforced. Hard as this may be to believe, it is a fact that people will see what they want to if they are obsessed enough in that direction. Headstrong Jerome qualified completely in this category and as he lowered his telescope he knew what he had to do.

"They are being reinforced!" he exclaimed to General Count Guilleminot, his second in command and nominal mentor.

Guilleminot, considered one of the finest tacticians in the army, had been appointed to look over Jerome's shoulder and guide his actions with a firm but nurturing hand. At first, at Quatre Bras, the shotgun marriage of capable staff officer and rash imperial brother had actually worked well and both men had come away impressed. Unfortunately, the impressions went wildly in opposite directions. Guilleminot began to think that perhaps Jerome could have some ability if taught correctly but Jerome began to think he didn't need anyone to teach what he already knew so well! His subsequent debacle at Hougoumont was to be expected given Jerome's attitude and by now he had completely moved away from any possible intrusion upon his command by the more professional soldier.

The whole staff of the division rankled when Jerome made his abrupt comment and every telescope that could was raised to see if

Jerome was correct; no one believed it. Guilleminot, scanning the area repeatedly, shrugged his shoulders and was the first to lower his glass. "Sir, the Prussians are simply juggling their reserves to meet the threat from our front, nothing more."

"Are you blind, sir?" Jerome said, careful not to take another look. "We must attack them before they become too strong!"

"I would advise against such a move, sir," Guilleminot continued in a vain effort to get his charge to listen; perhaps it was the head wound that was stirring him up. "General Reille has given you orders to stay put and await the division of General Foy. Together you will be able to take the town."

"It will be too late!" Jerome continued, his hot head throwing away all reason. "Another brigade may arrive and bolster them. How will we take the town then? Even two divisions will not be able to!"

Guilleminot shook his head. "There are no other troops!" he yelled, losing his temper. "Against the Emperor's attacks the Prussians dare not move anything away to defend this place against a single division of ours!"

"You believe that because you are a staff officer!" said an indignant Jerome. "What do you know of these affairs? Stay out of mine!"

Guilleminot reeled in frustrated anger; his first impulse was to strike the impudent young general across the face with his glove. Controlling himself only with difficulty, he sat back and said nothing as Jerome whistled over Adjutant commandant Hortode, his chief of staff, to draw up orders to begin the attack.

The 6th Infantry Division of the II Corps numbered almost five thousand men at the moment of their attack and confidence was high. The soldiers could hear the rumble of the guns to the south and, like their leader, they too were eager to enter the battle and contribute to the impending victory. They did, however, think it odd that they were not waiting for Foy's division whose first units were now beginning to emerge from the forest. Jerome would wait no longer. Fearing that the experienced general would somehow steal away his glory when he took Ohain, it seems clear that Jerome, like the immature little dolt that he was, did not want to share the success with anyone and that the snub at Hougoumont in the morning may have prodded him in this direction. Napoleon and his army were about to pay the price of brotherly love.

Both brigades of the division had been equally battered up to this point in the campaign and so Jerome arbitrarily chose Soye's second brigade to lead the attack on Ohain. Oddly enough, Jerome asked Guilleminot whether or not he would like to take command of the first brigade as its commander, Baron Bauduin, had been killed the day before at Mont St. Jean. The general, wanting to put as much distance as he could between himself and the little upstart, accepted and rode off to join his new command; this would be Jerome's best decision of the campaign. Hortode reminded Jerome to send a rider to General Pire and ask for his support as well.

General Reille, ensconced in the forest with General Foy, heard the roll of the drums of the 6th Division and genuinely, if naively, wondered what was happening. Foy was under no illusions. This leader, bruised by a musket shot in the shoulder the day before, didn't need anyone to tell him what was happening with Jerome. Having served in Spain, he knew of only one Bonaparte worth his weight and that man was the Emperor. "That fool Jerome is attacking again!" he said caustically. He patted his forehead. "It's that hole in his head he received yesterday, pity the English were not better shots."

Jerome's division, deployed already for so long, hopped to it and swept ahead to attack the enemy held town. Prussian officers in Ohain yelled for their men to be ready and what cannon could reach fired at the advancing French columns. Steinmetz, watching from behind one of the barricades, actually said that it must be a mistake on the part of the enemy as another force had been seen marching out of the forest. This first unit, however, was not waiting for it. "Hold your fire!" he yelled as a jager near him fired off a long distance shot. "Wait until you know you won't miss!"

The front rankers of the division, the 1st and 2nd Ligne regiments, walked mechanically uphill across the fields towards Ohain in assault columns. Skirmishers raced out ahead in little clouds and the first puffs of smoke appeared like cotton balls in the distance. French artillery fire, a potent fire support weapon, was largely quiet as the whole affair was about as disjointed as one could possibly be. The Prussian guns, however, were not slow in finding the range of the advancing infantry and they took clear advantage of the situation. Even before it was under full swing, the attack by Jerome's men appeared to be in trouble.

Reille raced out of the forest as fast as his horse could carry him but arrived too late. Jerome's division was far enough up the hill that there was absolutely nothing he could do to stop it. Swearing aloud, he watched for a moment before telling his chief of staff to send a messenger over to Pire to order him to watch over the 6th Division. This time, Bonaparte would not receive any support; Reille was finally at the end of his rope and could be pushed no farther even if the commander was the Emperor's brother. General Lacroix, to his credit, did mention the lack of supporting guns, an odd oversight, and this was hastily corrected.

Cannon balls ripped through the tight formations of the 6th Division's second brigade and at about two hundred yards away from the Prussian positions, Soye was forced to halt his men and redress their formation. That done, they marched forward again. Seconds later, Colonel Trippe, commander of the 2nd Ligne, was hit and badly wounded by a Prussian jager and his command thrown into temporary confusion. Colonel Chevalier Cornebise of the 1st Ligne pushed on past thinking that perhaps the fire would lessen the closer they got to the town itself. He was wrong. As the 2nd sagged behind them, the 1st entered a tornado of shots from cannon and muskets that tore up the ranks of the regiment. The 1st, forty yards from the main Prussian defensive line, ground to a halt.

"Close ranks!"

"Cavalry!"

The terrible pounding the French lead brigade was taking was not lost on Steinmetz or General Roder who had his cavalry posted near the French left flank. The Prussian 1st Cavalry Brigade, consisting of all regular troops, was amongst the best in the army and had been waiting all day for an opportunity to charge an enemy division in trouble. Leading with two dragoon regiments, the 2nd and 5th, the Prussians charged out of the drifting smoke and headed right for the struggling pieces of the 6th Division's second brigade. Soye, the French commander, was on foot now trying to hold his men together in the midst of the carnage. Bodies were falling everywhere. Like others, he heard the call that horsemen were approaching and he yelled for his men to form squares. It was too late. Before he knew it, hundreds of Prussian dragoons were on his men attacking and riding over anyone in their path. The eagle bearer of the 1st fell and his flag was taken by one dragoon who immediately turned tail and raced for the rear. As the cavalry poured through the gaps in the formations the regiments began to come apart though the veteran cadres of the units floated like islands amidst the debris. Of the six battalions in the first wave, only two formed squares and both of these were from the 2nd Ligne. Disaster seemed in the offing. It was now, however, that Jerome's decision to hand over command of the first brigade to Guilleminot saved his division. The latter, seeing the cavalry advance, had immediately formed his new regiments into their protective squares and, being a theoretical tactician as well, called on them to advance to the aide of the 2nd Brigade. Given time, the battalions of the 1st Brigade paused, shook themselves into four sided defensive packs and slowly started to march ahead.

The confusion in front of Guilleminot's men was tremendous as foot soldier and horseman chased one another across the lower slopes of the hill. For the men of the 1st Brigade, all dark blue clad light infantry, it was difficult choosing targets as the swirling mass of humanity made it difficult to aim and not hit a comrade. Thankfully, the horses made far larger targets and most of the soldiers availed themselves of the opportunity to let fly with a frustration releasing shot or two. The Prussians, seeing the newcomers, wheeled their mounts to engage them and this alone helped many of the fugitives of the 2nd Brigade to reach the relative safety of these squares or to simply hoof it right off the field. About the only good thing going for the French now was the lack of Prussian artillery fire which was held to avoid hitting their own men.

"Here they come!" yelled Colonel Maigros of the 2nd Legere riding his horse inside the square of his fourth battalion. "Aim at the horses!"

The regiments of the 1st Brigade ground to a halt and immediately they were enshrouded in smoke as the soldiers fired at the charging cavalry. Several dragoons fell to the ground but still more came to surround and strike at the bristling squares. One horse fell dead alongside the 2nd Battalion of the 2nd Legere which caused a large hole to appear in the formation and force many men to scramble for their lives. Two Prussian troopers, seeing the calamity, leapt into the square thinking that more comrades would follow but no one did as the concentration of force simply wasn't there. The French, recovering from this stroke of fate, sealed the opening and then turned inward; the Prussian cavalrymen, chagrined, surrendered without a fight.

The Prussian dragoons were blown by now and what had started as a very successful charge was degenerating quickly into a mess especially as trumpets other than Prussian ones began to sing in the distance. The instruments belonged to the 2nd Brigade troopers of Pire's 2nd Cavalry Division which were now fulfilling their orders from General Reille to watch out for Jerome's men; Pire knew he was too late to save the 2nd Brigade but he could rescue the 1st. The French cavalry, all lancers, swept like a tidal wave onto the worn Prussian dragoons and turned their charge into a debacle. The chase scene of a few minutes before was now replayed except that the dragoons were on the other end of the point. Roder, watching the developments, ordered the rest of his 1st Brigade into the fight to stabilize the situation while instructing his smaller 2nd Brigade, uneasy Kurmark Landwehr troopers, to be ready for action.

General Reille observed from atop the hill and shook his head in a mixture of sadness and disgust. Part of this disaster had been his fault and he knew it well. If he had been able to control the upstart none of this would have happened and they would be attacking with two full divisions right now. He shook off the thoughts. At the moment he had a division to retrieve and a real attack to launch; what was more, he had grounds to do something else as well.

Pire's cavalry chased off the Prussian dragoons before being engaged by two more Prussians regiments and being pushed back in turn. Committing his 1st Brigade, Pire cleared the area again and forced the Prussians to retire with their eagle and the honors of the fight thus far. Ahead he could see yet another line of cavalry and on the ground were the bodies of hundreds who would no longer have a part to play anywhere. The remnants of the 2nd Brigade of the 6th Division streamed in from all angles covered by the troopers of Pire and the well organized and barely touched 1st Brigade regiments. In the distance, the Prussian guns finally began to open fire again. Reille, waiting for the 6th, gathered his breath and approached the downtrodden Jerome who looked as if his favorite toy had been broken.

"You disobeyed my orders," he started quietly, "and have cost the lives of many men."

Jerome looked up at his corps commander. "It was Soye's fault! He should have formed square! He should have . . . ."

"Silence!" Reille yelled, an action that shocked the entire II Corps staff. "You ordered the attack! It was your fault." He paused, biting his lip but otherwise remaining calm. "It is mine as well. The good general is responsible for the actions of his men," he continued, "I am relieving you of your command!"

"You cannot!" Jerome cried. "I command the sixth!"

Reille, for the first time in the campaign, felt a confidence surge through him like he had not experienced in years. This corps was his responsibility and he would do what he had to in order to ensure the safety and continued success of his command. Having been present at Wagram when Napoleon had relieved Marshal Bernadotte from command, Reille was no stranger to the necessity of replacing senior commanders in action; he just never thought that he would have to do it, especially to Napoleon's brother.

"Go, sir," he said growled, "before I have the gendarmes remove you."

Jerome began to walk his horse away. "You have no right! My brother will hear of this, rest assured!"

Reille shook his head. "Lacroix, send an aide to report to the Emperor what I have done," he said with a thoughtful smile on his face, "and make sure he rides faster than our misfit child."

Chief of staff Baron Lacroix grinned as everyone was quite pleased at this change of events. "I have just the man sir!"

As the broken general trotted away, Reille received Guilleminot who reported on the condition of the 6th Division. The 1st Brigade's commander actually had more positive things to say about the division than Reille would have thought as the men had naturally headed for the haven of the trees where Foy's troops offered them security and a quick route back to their own regiments. The 1st Ligne was in sorry shape as it had taken the brunt of the cavalry attack and had lost its eagle; their officers reported about a battalion of troops ready for action but no more. The 2nd was better off, almost three battalions strong but the 6th Division had effectively been cut in half and Steinmetz's men had only barely been touched.

The French needed time to reorganize and Reille took the steps to get them that time. The guns of the II Corps, back up to its full strength of 38 cannon due to the use of its spare carriages and the determination of its commander, Baron Pelletier, were finally assembling along the heights to bring the Prussians in the town under concentrated fire. Pelletier, acting under Reille's orders to exercise haste, grouped all of his howitzers into one battery with the intention of setting fire to the buildings under their observation and forcing the Prussians to seek safer havens.

In order to effectively rally and reorganize his infantry, Reille gave command of the 6th Division to General Guilleminot who thus completed one of the oddest routes up the chain of authority any man in the French army had ever experienced since the founding of the Empire. This officer had come to the Army of the North without a command and had been given over as an advisor to Jerome before the campaign started. Therefore, he had moved from an observer to a brigade commander and now to a divisional commander in the space of one hour! Pleased immeasurably at the chance to lead a division and with the removal of Jerome, Guilleminot intended to shine as much as he could.

Jerome's aborted attack at Ohain was a costly failure for the French but it would have one entirely unintentional side effect. When Steinmetz reported his success to Blucher and Gneisenau, they were very pleased and both expressed the feeling that the force defending the town would be sufficient when the time came to fall back. Prussian plans were well advanced by now and just a little more time would be necessary for them to begin the withdrawal.

*　　*　　*

All along the entire front the battle suddenly flared up again; Napoleon's orders had reached the commanders of the I, II and VI Corps. What had begun in the morning and continued on and off during the intervening hours once more became reality and the smoke and noise of battle reached the highest crescendo it had during the entire fight. Lobau's men, tired and worn out, rose to their feet and engaged Bulow's equally exhausted troops but failed to really notice in the haze that the Prussians had secretly fallen back during the lull to new positions some yards away. Now Bulow's men had to stop and fight. The crackle of musketry echoed through the dim shade of the trees. The divisions of Simmer, Jeanin and Donzelot all attacked again in the blood covered forest where they were barely held by the faltering Prussians troops. French infantry, using the trunks for cover, slipped forward by ones and twos as they infiltrated ahead in order to gain surprise. Bounding out again at the last moment, some of the Prussians were actually engaged in a bayonet fight. Though the cold steel fight was brief, the men of Losthin's 15th Infantry Brigade were very nearly blown over by the eagleless 5th Legere who were fanatical, to say the least, to retrieve their honor. Bulow himself had to ride the lines behind his men to encourage them to hold on. Like Archduke Charles at Aspern-Essling, there is an unsubstantiated story that he grabbed the flag of Infantry Regiment #18 and rallied the troops around it. Whatever the truth, the Prussians launched a limited counterattack which at least stopped the marauding French and allowed them to hang on to their trophy.

On the current French left flank, General Durutte, his command hidden in the small forest flanking part of the Prussian gun line, prepared to renew the attack from his quarter of the battlefield. Durutte, a canny and aggressive commander, knew what was about to happen. Waving his sword in the air, he ordered his men to their feet. In just a few moments the great arm of decision was about to reach out and their job would be to hold the enemy in place so that he would not be able to get away. Skirmishers slinked their way through the fields to close with the Prussian line which had fallen back in accordance to their orders. The cannons to his right shrouded the whole French center in smoke.

The sound of the impending great stroke was not discernible at first. A low rumble of hooves somewhere behind the French gun line could be heard by those close by but the Prussian high command did not notice anything out of the ordinary as yet. Couriers rode up, reported, received new orders and then galloped off in haste. Gneisenau, his hands full with the paper work of the withdrawal, was too busy to pay attention to the battle and thus only Blucher and a few aides remained to keep an active and keen eye on the French.

Major Huser, one of Blucher's aides, winced as he witnessed a series of cannon balls slice their way through Krafft's brigade in the front lines. Casualties had been mounting steadily and those units committed to the center had been entering nothing less than a terrible meat grinder. Bodies of brave Prussian soldiers littered the field marking every position they had taken up during the day; it was high time that the army fell back. What were they waiting for? The French were attacking all along the whole front except, for the moment, at Ohain but he had no doubt that they would begin there as well before long. The French guns had utterly ripped apart the opposing Prussian battery and left the ground covered with shattered carriages, dismounted guns and torn corpses of both men and horses. It was almost incomprehensible. Huser compared it to a child spilling his toys from a bucket and leaving them haphazardly along the ground. About the only thing favoring them was certain parts of the local terrain that hid units from the ferocious fire of the enemy guns. More and more Prussian guns were thrown into the zone of death if only to keep the French honest but it was quite clear that they had achieved complete artillery superiority in the center and were not likely to surrender it.

"We need more guns in the center!" Blucher demanded.

Gneisenau looked up from his work. "We haven't any more to commit without losing the cannon necessary to cover the retreat."

Blucher swore quietly, realizing that there was nothing they could do as yet until the army began to retreat. Bitter frustration assailed him from every corner but his head jerked up when he determined he had to do something, if only to inspire the men. With a quick snap of his reins, he rode ahead to visit the men in Krafft's brigade who were the most exposed to the French cannon fire. Gneisenau watched him leave but could do nothing as he and his staff continued preparing the orders to retreat; he had thought that they would be good at this by now. In a sense, it was with a certain relief that he saw his chief depart because it gave him the control over the army that he needed to allow for its withdrawal from the field of Ohain.

In the center, Krafft's brigade was in desperate straits. At the apex of the Prussian line, his men were bravely standing the heavy fire of the massed enemy cannon and dutifully filling the thinning ranks as every round that bounced through them took its terrible toll. The men, so strong and enduring for so long, were wavering and ready to run especially since French infantry, infantry of the so far unbeatable division of Durutte, was reappearing from the trees ahead of them. The bombardment coupled with the threat of the professional and well led enemy was becoming too much to bear.

Field Marshal Blucher arrived amidst the struggling brigade and saw with his own eyes the devastation being wreaked upon his men. Staring at anxious eyes, he called to them. This regiment, Infantry Regiment #9, was named after one of Blucher's favorite towns as it had played a small but significant role in the debacle of 1806. "Men of Colberg! The French are in the wood! Who will follow me in the attack against them?"

The troops, despite their poor condition but as could be expected, cheered him. Pushing in around their flag, they forgot their woes and were instantly ready to charge the French. Marshal Forward was with them! How could they fail? Fortunately or unfortunately, another event intervened and they would not get the chance to prove if they could have retaken the woods from Durutte.

"Sir! Look!" cried Major Huser who had accompanied his commander. "Look!"

Blucher had to stop at the insistence of his subordinate. Swinging around in his saddle, he could make out trumpets in the distance along with a new and growing thunder of noise. The French guns had fallen silent suddenly and through the smoke and haze he could make out a long dark body of troops sweeping ahead in magnificent order.

"Form square!"

Trumpet blasts were now audible as the great mass of French heavy horse surged past their own guns and picked up speed. The sight was spectacular to all those who witnessed it but probably less so than it had appeared on the eighteenth. The French reserve cavalry corps were badly under strength after the beating they had taken at Mont St. Jean and many of the horse were jaded from the exertions in the mud the day before. Still, enough men, some wounded, and horses, some captured, were in the lines of cavalry to inspire the greatest awe in the enemy. These men were the flower of the French horse and the finest troopers, regiment for regiment, in the world. Leading the whole magnificent pack was Kellermann's III Reserve Cavalry Corps, much used and thoroughly worn, while behind it was Milhaud's IV Reserve Cavalry Corps. Kellermann had formed his men into three lines; the first two were composed of the carabiniers and cuirassiers while the third line was brought up by his dragoons. All regiments of the corps were badly under strength. Milhaud's men, every one of them a cuirassier, formed two brigade strength lines behind the III Corps with Milhaud himself riding between the two corps.

Kellermann's and Milhaud's objective was simple: break the enemy center. Napoleon, remembering his experience at the battle of Eylau in 1807 where Murat's men had so savaged the Russians that they were no longer able to launch coordinated attacks, had decided that the most perfect and rapid solution to his problem of the Prussian retreat lay in a sudden and devastating strike to halt their movement. With the cavalry fight in the center taking up their time and attention, the French emperor knew that at the very least he would cut Bulow's men to pieces. If all went well, the whole Prussian army could be routed.

Napoleon's commitment of the heavy cavalry corps at Ohain amply displays the difference in the fighting techniques of a healthy Napoleon and an excited Marshal Ney. At Mont St. Jean, the French marshal had sent in the cavalry based on his belief that the enemy was retreating, an idea that was not substantiated by any of his subordinates. Additionally, few coordinating French infantry attacks were launched and those that were had already been in progress when the charge began. Here at Ohain, Napoleon had made sure of the intentions of the Prussians, confirmed by reports from experienced officers, and, in close conjunction with the latest assault by both I and VI Corps, sent in the reserve horse to break the enemy line and prevent him from withdrawing from the field. The difference in command between the two leaders is obvious and would play a crucial role in the fighting to come.

As the Emperor watched, rank upon rank of horse filed by his position to begin the attack on the Prussian center. Behind them marched forward Marcognet's division to fill the gap in the French center and await Napoleon's order to follow up the offensive and complete the expected victory. De la Bedoyere, sitting next to the Emperor on his horse, was a bit more composed now than he had been at Mont St. Jean. Using the tip of his telescope, Napoleon tapped him on the thigh and leaned over in his saddle. "You see, Kellermann and Milhaud will trample Blucher's center and the infantry of Marcognet and Quiot will break their position open. No half measures this time."

The imperial aide de camp nodded vigorously as he digested this ultimate lesson in battlefield tactics. "Yes, sire, but what about support for the cavalry?"

The Emperor abruptly pulled back as if in surprise. "You think my preparations unsound?"

De la Bedoyere shook his head. "No, sire, I just . . . ."

"You think well," Napoleon said, a little chuckle in his voice. "Domon's men and the Guard light cavalry are there to make sure nothing goes wrong this time."

Marshal Soult, sitting behind the pair, sighed in relief. At least those orders he had been able to both send out and receive back confirmations.

As Milhaud's men trotted forward, the commander of the

IV Reserve Cavalry Corps looked about his men in the space that separated the corps. Since the day before, he was a bitter man. At Mont St. Jean, his men had charged without any tangible infantry support and, though they had become masters of the Anglo-Dutch position, they could not hold the ridge because Marshal Ney had neglected to order any of the waiting divisions of Reille or d'Erlon to force the issue and rupture the enemy center. As his battered and abused men had returned from that debacle, he had felt a frustration that ran so deep that when he saw the waiting division of Quiot deployed and ready to march he could not suppress a triumphant cry that was immediately echoed by the troopers of each succeeding regiment in his entire corps. By the time it had reached the last regiment in the last wave few of the troopers really knew why they cheered but they did it nonetheless. On the hill behind them, Napoleon noted their good spirits but could only guess at what the cause of the cries were.

Milhaud's lead regiment, the arrogant 1st Cuirassiers, really epitomized the essence of the French heavy cavalry units. In an army grounded in bravado, these men were considered so cocksure of themselves that they had declared that their entry into the battle signaled the defeat of the enemy. This boast was not to be considered too lightly as the regiment had very impressive credentials having taken part in all of the prerequisite famous battles of the Empire including the mighty charge at Eylau. It was here that a regimental tradition began that earned them their cocksure reputation despite the fact that it began with an accident. The regiment had been deployed in the snow behind the remnants of Augereau's corps when the order came for them to charge the enemy with the rest of Marshal Murat's cavalry reserve. Their colonel, draped in his cape and wearing heavier gauntlets than usual, had waved them forward with his hand and then, while they trotted, attempted to pull his long sword out of its scabbard. Whether the sword had partially frozen in its sheath or he simply had trouble grasping it with his heavy gauntlets will never be known but the fact remained that the regiment had not drawn their swords until well after the rest of the regiments had. Just before they had encountered the shattered Russian infantry did the colonel at last order them to draw their swords and ever since then they had continued this curious and potentially dangerous tradition of not drawing their swords until the last moment. In the French army, this fact was greeted with respect and put down as more evidence that the 1st Cuirassiers were the most arrogant, next to the Guard heavy cavalry, in the whole army! Naturally, this was considered a very high honor.

The Prussian gunners were shocked by the huge amount of cavalry pouring their way and found it difficult to focus on the problem at hand of recovering from the French bombardment. Depressions in the ground marked the initial bounce hits of the enemy cannon balls and they were all around the light blue gun carriages of Blucher's army along with the debris of those same carriages that they had struck. Major Bardeleben, commanding the Prussian IV Corps cannon, had been struck badly by splinters and eventually carried off the field by his men which forced Colonel Lehmann to assume temporary responsibility for the gun line of the Prussian army. Lehmann was not in the highest spirits. Ever since the massing of the Imperial Guard cannon against his own, what had been a fight that could be contested quickly turned into a battle of steady destruction as the guns that were fed into the fight were knocked out one by one or, on at least one occasion, struck as they approached their firing position. He had never seen such well directed fire before and the destruction wreaked on his crews was even worse than he could have ever anticipated. Some guns stood stoically facing the enemy without men to crew them and some artillerists had just plain run away. Then, the French had ceased firing which gave him the idea that they might have a respite but this was quickly dashed with the appearance of the cavalry. He knew as he watched them that he could not even begin to slow them down.

"Canister!" he yelled, preferring duty over reality.

Such crews that were still on the firing line raced to find their personnel killing rounds while others were busy ramming home the deadly cartridges; speed was essential. Only a volley at near point blank range could possibly slow or stop the moving French regiments, Lehmann convinced himself, and he kept himself busy encouraging his men and extolling them to hurry.

The damage the Prussian gun line had taken was such that not even a perfect blast by every available gun could have stopped the French horse who by now had shifted from a trot into a gallop. In a suicidal movement, some of Pirch's gun teams were just now reaching the line and unlimbering, obviously under the orders of someone who had no clear view of what was happening in the center. Lehmann, surprised at this stupidity, waved them off in the vain hope that they could escape; the French were far too close to contacting them for such a move but it did give the men some hope rather than none at all. Riding back from that brief errand, Lehmann found the French to be less than one hundred yards away. All around him, the crews were still working their guns and only a few were ready to fire. Resigning himself to the inevitable, he raised his sword and yelled, "Fire at will!"

Almost as soon as he finished the last word, two cannon burst into life and then fell silent as the crews took off for the safety of the woods to the south. The rumble of so many hooves shook the ground and headed for his line like a great thunder storm; from where he sat he could make out the red crests of the lead troopers and the brave leader riding ahead of the whole force. The shots of canister, he knew, had barely touched them. Shifting his gaze, he noticed more and more men running away. "Back to your posts!"

Colonel Roge of the 1st Carabiniers, leading his regiment despite being wounded the day before, raised his sword and lowered it over the head of his horse. "With the point!" he cried over the tumult around him. "The point!"

Ahead of this regiment, General Kellermann rode and a faint

smile crossed his weather-beaten face as he somehow heard Roge over all the other noises including his own body riding his leather saddle. Solid puffs of smoke burst from the Prussian guns but not as many as he had feared. Fear came back to him in a hurry when something forcibly removed his hat and left him bareheaded. Behind him, two carabiniers went down when their horses were perforated and several others either were struck by or heard the metallic thump of the little enemy cannon balls that made up a canister round ricocheting off their armored breastplates; those that were hit probably gained a little religion after the battle as well. Nevertheless, though a few men went down against the erratic firing of the battered Prussian guns, the charge itself didn't lose a step. The neatly angled French line, leading with the right and declining by squadron to the left, swept forward with exquisite order and decisive purpose.

The failure of the Prussian guns to slow down the attacking French should not be attributed to any lack of courage on the part of Blucher's men. It is true that the French service saw higher levels of efficiency but that was grown from years of practical experience coupled with a tradition of excellence that went back many a campaign. Here at Ohain, the Prussians had been punished by the aforementioned efficiency and the sheer mass of heavy cannon thrown against them. Engaged by an enemy who could serve a twelve pounder almost as quickly as they could a six pounder, it was only a matter of time before the French would gain the upper hand. That the Prussian ran for their lives was only a culmination of all the previous actions during the day and not simply attributable to the charge of the French heavy horse.

"They have passed the guns, sire!" called out General Count Ruty, commander of the Army of the North's artillery, who had recently rejoined the Imperial staff on their small hill.

Napoleon, speaking with Soult, looked up from the map he and the marshal held and pointed to the charging horse. "And how is their order?"

Ruty lowered his glass. "Excellent, sire!"

"Send word to Marcognet and Quiot to be ready to advance. The first obstacle had been passed," the Emperor said to Soult who reached for his order note book and pen. "You sent word to Domon and Lefebvre-Desnouettes?"

Soult nodded. "Yes, sire, they have been informed and are awaiting your command."

"This staff work agrees with you Soult? I am afraid you are getting good at it," Napoleon continued, his headache now gone and his spirits higher. Even if all went wrong from here on, they appeared to be over the hump of the battle with everything inexorably moving their way.

"I fear that as well, sire," Soult replied with the same sarcasm while waving forward four more aides. Up ahead, another aide had just ridden up.

While Napoleon remounted La Desiree to watch the beginning of the cavalry action, the lead regiments of his great mounted arm were just reaching the almost abandoned Prussian gun line. One crew still was madly trying to stem the tide by themselves as they rammed home a shot with the French horse practically on top of them. One officer of the 1st Carabiniers could not bring himself to kill such a foolhardy but brave bunch of gunners and so he just pushed his horse past the left wheel of the carriage and continued on. Unfortunately, the men behind him had no such compunctions or simply had not been able to see what the Prussians were doing. Except for one man who hid underneath the piece, the crew was cut down completely.

General Kellermann, leading at the very center of the French line but still ahead of the rightmost carabinier squadron, leapt over a broken gun carriage in an unnecessary flamboyant display that almost ended in disaster when his horse slipped slightly on the edge of a fallen cannon ball. Recovering, he forged ahead towards the primary target of the charge: the Prussian center and its defending cavalry.

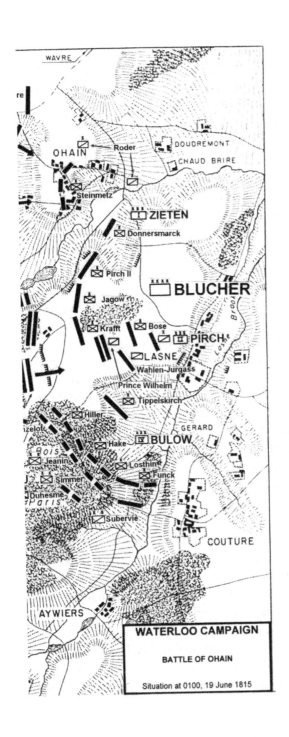

WAVRE

OHAIN ← Roder

DOUDREMONT

CHAUD BRIRE

Steinmetz

ZIETEN

Donnersmarck

Pirch II

Jagow

BLUCHER

Krafft   Bose

PIRCH

LASNE

Wahlen-Jurgass

Prince Wilhelm

Tippelskirch

Hiller

GERARD

Hake   BULOW

Jeanin

Losthin

Simmer   Funck

Duhesme
Paris

Subervie

COUTURE

AYWIERS

WATERLOO CAMPAIGN

BATTLE OF OHAIN

Situation at 0100, 19 June 1815

The center of Blucher's army was covered at this moment by two strong brigades of Prussian cavalry from the IV Corps, two more brigades of horse from II Corps along with one brigade of infantry quietly in the rear of the whole and intended to be the solid rearguard of the army. The two corps cavalry reserves, one under Prince Wilhelm of Prussia from IV Corps and the other under General Wahlen-Jurgass of II Corps, were deployed one behind the other in lines of brigades. Both units, whether by design or chance, positioned their entire Landwehr 3rd brigades in their last lines; these last units were regarded as the least reliable in the army as some barely were capable of controlling their mounts at anything faster than a trot. Wahlen-Jurgass, however, still was without his 2nd Brigade which was riding hard from the north of Lasne to join in the coming fight.

Prince Wilhelm unsheathed his sword and nodded to an aide by his side. "Prepare to charge!"

The Prussian 1st Brigade of Colonel Eicke, was fully reorganized by now and pretty much back in fighting trim after the messy fight against the French horse earlier in the day; the 1st Neumark regiment had now been brigaded with his unit. Leading with his hussar and Landwehr regiments against an opponent who was obviously armored, Eicke attempted to even the odds by refusing his last regiment, the 1st West Prussian Uhlans, on his left and using it to strike the French flank as the latter became engaged. It was a good plan but one that would not last contact with the enemy.

"Charge!"

The French heavy horse at last threw itself into a dead run, its third such mighty thrust in four days. Riding high on emotion and the hoped for victory, it was a wonder to all of the generals involved that they were able to sustain such a charge. It is high testament to the courage of the officers and men of the regiments that after so much pain and trial that they could again behave as the powerful instruments of decision as they had been on many other battlefields. Their one problem was that there were simply a good deal fewer of those instruments to deal with what was coming up on them. Including only the men actually in the charge, around 4,000 French cavalry were closing in on perhaps 6,000 Prussian cavalrymen who were far less fatigued and mounted on fresher horses.

The charge of the French heavy horse was spectacular to those that were able to watch it from a safe distance. Prussian jagers, hidden in the tip of the Bois de Paris, observed and took the occasional sniper shot at the passing regiments and wondered what could stop such a force. The dust kicked up by so many horses and the tremendous pounding of the animal's hooves made the whole seem grander as wave after wave surged past the trees. Thanks to the French formation of stepped squadrons in the leading brigade and columns thereafter, the lines looked like great unbroken massive sweeps of horse flesh mounted by thousands of armored troopers.

Prussian trumpets sounded the charge. The 6th Hussars kicked in its heels and pushed for the enemy but the 1st Neumark, very much still smarting from the earlier fight, wavered in the face of the mighty French assault and then, suddenly and without any warning, crumbled and made a dash for the rear. This unexpected disaster left the Prussian uhlans in a very poor position unless they did something quickly and to their credit they angled to the right and accelerated speedily to give support to the 6th Hussars.

There were few instances in the Napoleonic Wars when light horse, in an even face to face cavalry fight was able to defeat their heavier opponents. This was not one of those rare cases. The two leading French regiments, the 1st and 2nd Carabiniers, had been waiting a good long time to cross swords with an enemy at full tilt and now that chance presented itself in the form of a hussar and lancer regiment of the enemy. The armored fist closed up boot to boot, the sun reflecting off the brightly polished brass breast plates and helmets, all at once a magnificent and deadly sight.

The 2nd Carabiniers had the honor of beginning the biggest cavalry fight of the campaign. Coming up on the lively 6th Hussars, they slammed into this brave regiment which immediately found itself totally outclassed and out muscled. The ensuing sword fight between the two regiments was held for a moment by the bold

Prussians but the weight of the French attack and the fact that they wore armor dictated against Blucher's men and, having taken enough, they tried to fall back from the melee. In cavalry fights casualties are generally fairly low until one side or the other turns to get away and it was the same here. With only their speed to help them, the hussars were overturned and lost a great many men to the point wielding French horsemen. The 2nd pushed ahead to pursue the retreating enemy.

Cavalry corps commanders do not belong riding with their leading regiments and Kellermann, to his embarrassment, had momentarily lost control of his situation. Charging with the 1st Carabiniers, he had gotten himself engrossed in their movements and now found it impossible to do anything but go with the general direction of his men. Their target, the Prussian uhlans, had already lowered their lances and was approaching rapidly and so he had no place to go but forward. Luckily for him, and his luck during the campaign had already been quite good, his one lancer opponent was a bad aim.

The 1st Carabiniers were attacking a force almost twice as large as their own but their own confidence and elan only propelled them faster at the enemy. The bristling front of lances gave the enemy an initial advantage but, once they were engaged closely, the lance was more a nuisance than an asset. Credit must be given to both Prussian regiments for charging the French heavy horse as it was a most difficult proposition to take on the elite of the enemy's cavalry at the best of times and especially when your horses were only light ones. What they did not know was that the horses of the regiments they were attacking were in many cases worn out or completely jaded from the fatigues of the campaign. At least one French horse fell over and died during the charge from over exertion and many others were slowing even before the regiments were able to close. Consequently, the French formation was becoming wider and more uneven as the charge came on.

A lance point went slicing past his boot as Kellermann penetrated the enemy formation and parried the lance aimed at his chest. The first two ranks of the Prussians were armed with lances but the next had simple swords and these clashed all the rest of the way. Screaming horses and wounded men littered the ground but here again the heavy armored troopers of the carabiniers held the upper hand and the fewer numbers of them held their own against the more numerous enemy. One squadron of lancers wrapped around the French flank and pushed itself home, causing considerable disorder before it too was ejected and pushed away from French line. However, Blancard, the brigade commander, was sufficiently alarmed to have the recall sounded as he saw his troopers become far too loose and disorganized to sustain another direct charge. The French horse, hearing the retort, stopped their pursuits and raced to reform.

Blancard's order to recall his first brigade was just what both sides needed. The spearhead of Kellermann's corps had beaten two enemy regiments but had found itself badly outnumbered and weakened by worn horses and simple confusion. The Prussians of Prince Wilhelm, on the other hand, were able to reform the two regiments and rally the third while the second line maneuvered to join the fight. Given the aggressive French attitude during the campaign thus far, this recall order so early in the attack can be viewed at first glance as almost a defeatist move but closer examination reveals probably what Blancard knew better than any historian later. Like it or not, the French heavy horse was virtually a spent force. Having not been given orders early in the campaign by one of Soult's oversights, they were forced to stage rapidly forward to be in time for the opening shots of the campaign. Then, both cavalry corps had been engaged in a heavy fight at the battles of the sixteenth and then again on the eighteenth where the severe mud on the field sapped the energy of most every man and horse. Without any great amount of rest, they had now been committed again to a charge over firm ground against fresh enemy cavalry when really they had no business even being engaged at all. However, the French emperor simply had no choice and both Kellermann and Milhaud knew it. The Prussian army, if allowed to escape, would provide the rallying point of all the allied armies on the frontiers and bolster their spirits at an most inopportune time. Napoleon was willing to sacrifice his men now to pin Blucher's army in place and give his troops the chance to crush him and perhaps end the war in an afternoon.

The cavalry fight quickly entered into its second phase. Having seen the enemy upping the ante, Kellermann, regaining his position, ordered up the second brigade of the 12th Cavalry Division to support the 1st. These men had suffered considerably at Mont St. Jean and currently every ranking leader in the brigade was either badly wounded or dead. Consequently, Baron d'Hurbal himself, the division commander, repaired to their side and waved to Kellermann to show him that he was leading them in.

The Prussians returned to the fray with a fanatic urge to wipe out the small French force ahead of them. The 1st Neumark, brow beaten back into line with the 6th, were still a bit skeptical but remained under the watchful eye of every man in the unit including Prince Wilhelm himself. Fearing their own friends more than the enemy, the three regiments returned to the attack with the 1st Neumark safely squeezed in between the other units. The renewed charge was successful at first. Striking the exhausted French horse before they could completely reform, they pushed back the Carabiniers and threatened to envelop them when the lancers, now mostly without their lances, slipped along their flank and appeared in their rear. The menace did not last long. The French 2nd Brigade, led by General Baron d'Hurbal, parried this Prussian thrust and once more the enemy light horse found themselves manhandled by the heavier cuirassiers and then broken back to their own lines. D'Hurbal did not wait to reform this time and swung his men out to chase the enemy off the field and allow the battered carabiniers to fall back through the other regiments and reform. The Prussians dashed away in a fright and thanks to their swifter horses managed to outdistance the French who still smelled victory in the offing. The fight was just beginning, however, as help for the Prussians was on the way.

Prince Wilhelm of Prussia watched with concern the plight of his light horse and he cursed the fact that no heavy horse was with them to counter the armored spearhead of the French. However, an experienced aide had noted the lack of decisiveness on the part of the French and guessed, correctly, that they were fatigued and therefore could be overwhelmed. Pointing this out to the prince, the latter decided to push his advantage in numbers as far as he could by committing still more horse to the fight and inviting the cavalry of the II Corps to join in along his left flank. Shifting his third line troopers to the right, the prince was pleased to see the cavalrymen of Wahlen-Jurgass smartly filing into position; the latter commander was anxious for a little revenge against the French horse and now seemed to be the perfect moment to get it.

The opportunity was possibly greater than any man on the Prussian side quite realized. Kellermann's primary claim to fame was his perfectly timed charge against the Austrian center at the battle of Marengo in 1800 which had tipped the scales of battle and helped First Consul Bonaparte win the day. The Emperor Napoleon, never forgetting the favor from Kellermann, had gone out of his way to protect the mischievous but excellent cavalry general for many years from the problems he frequently got into. While Marengo was a famous victory, it was also over fifteen years ago and a new feather in the cap of General Kellermann now seemed like good thing to acquire. It was now that Kellermann overextended himself in his new bid to break an enemy center position. Probably confident because Milhaud was behind him, even though he would never admit as much, the general wanted more than just to defeat the enemy cavalry and secure the Prussian center: he wanted to blow it wide open. To do this, he would need a suitable formation of infantry to attack and the poor brigade of General Krafft appeared to be the most likely target. Krafft, having had to cancel his impending attack because of the French cavalry threat, had pulled his exposed brigade back during the confusion of the first cavalry attacks but, realizing he was just a spectator at the moment and since he was waiting for his withdrawal orders in the face of the division of Durutte, he failed to put his men into protective squares. Kellermann's eagle eye saw this and he determined to do something about it. Riding over to General Baron Guiton, commander of the 2nd Brigade in the 11th Cavalry Division, he ordered him to attack the Prussians and drive them from the field. Guiton found the order exhilarating and, more importantly, possible as the enemy was simply watching and was out of formation. Within a matter of minutes, the cuirassiers began to move ahead along with a company of horse artillery.

*　*　*

The French cavalry attack, though really only about twenty minutes old, had bitten deep into the Prussian position and had paralyzed all movement by the Prussian infantry as the horsemen of both sides attempted to throw the other back. This inactivity by the Prussian army was eagerly set upon by the French. While the fighting continued apace in the Bois de Paris, Durutte's men were emerging from the trees and cautiously pushing their way ahead towards Krafft's line which had remained in formation to face their attack. Some voltigeurs from this division, sweeping out ahead like always, wandered over to the Prussian guns to spike them just in case things went wrong.

For the Prussians, everything hung in the balance. Blucher had by now left Krafft to his own devices and had taken up a position with the remaining regiments of the IV Corps cavalry where he could observe the fighting and maybe even join in again like he had at Ligny. Prince Wilhelm, directing his men coolly, had already sent in most of his good regiments, despite the fact that this left him with a reserve of only Landwehr cavalry though it must be admitted that even some of these militia units were proving to be decent soldiers. One thing he made sure of, however, was that he saved the absolute worst trained regiments for last. The prince, perhaps realizing just what he was up against, wanted a heavy anvil of horse to throw the French back at last and finally break their momentum. With Wahlen-Jurgass' men forming up alongside the last remaining regiments of Prince Wilhelm's cavalry, there was a real chance that they might be able to do just that.

As the cavalry fight developed, Count Gneisenau, frantic with concern and having at last finished his orders for the withdrawal, remounted and rode ahead to view what was the ruin of all his plans. The French commander had obviously been able to sense the shift in the battle and had released his heavy horse to prevent them from leaving the field. He stared into the sky, covering his eyes with his right hand. Unlike the day before, there was no darkness available to come and protect them and he knew as his heart sank that they must win or be destroyed on the field of Ohain. Gerard, he knew positively, had taken Chapelle St. Lambert and, more importantly, had seized the bridges over the still swollen Lasne brook and placed cannon on the heights to the east to discourage Prussian counterattacks. If Gerard led an attack across the brook from that town, he would have to strip off desperately needed troops from the front lines to oppose him and thus weaken the overall effort. Courageously, he decided to leave the orders he had given intact rather than react to something that had yet to happen. As a result, he took limited measures. First, he allowed Pirch's little battle group of guns and regiment of cavalry to continue on their way to the bridges at Chapelle St. Lambert to give the impression of Prussian strength and keep the French general honest. Second, he ordered Bose's covering brigade in the Prussian rear center into square, a very wise move it turned out, and, finally, he ordered Bulow to pull his men back out of the Bois de Paris if he considered it practicable. The commander of the IV Corps, however, was disinclined to pull back while his main line was engaged and so he didn't budge an inch except along Funck's front which was less under the attention of the French than the other brigades. Napoleon's pinning battle, Gneisenau could see, was working.

Bulow's refusal to retreat while under attack would have appeared rather ironic to the French attackers had they known why he could not. Fighting under the concept that they must cut their way to daylight, the French soldiers had actually postponed their hard fought victory but, in the end, provided just what the Army of the North needed to attempt a mighty defeat of the enemy. Bulow simply could not fall back because the pressure against him was too great. The time was half past one and the battle was clearly at its climax. French artillery continued firing fast and furious though their ready ammunition was just about out. Only on Reille's front was there any respite and here only because of Jerome's stupidity. Exhaustion was gripping both sides but more so the French as this was their second pitched battle in as many days. If the battle was to be decided, it would be decided in the next hour.

*   *   *

Success, it is said, follows the bold. Kellermann's troopers believed this and their faith turned quickly into the slaughter of the enemy when Baron Guiton's brigade of cuirassiers surprised the Prussian infantry out of the dust cloud around the swirling horse fight. Seeing the cavalry wheel and charge a moment too late, Krafft's battered regiments attempted to form squares but only a few succeeded. Infantry Regiment #9, so recently exhorted by Blucher, retained that magical moment and performed the tricky maneuver with expertise, calmly shooting down several horsemen from the 11th Cuirassiers who, incidentally, were without their iron breastplates. The Elbe Landwehr troops were less lucky. Fatally delayed, the militiamen bravely tried to follow the example of the 9th but the rapidly maneuvering columns of French heavy horse burst in amongst them and quickly ruined their formation and dispersed them in a fury of trampling hooves and sharp pointed swords. Seeing this, the shaky squares of Infantry Regiment #26 wavered until two of the three battalions cracked and ran for their lives. The cuirassiers rode on, thrusting and knocking over anyone in their path as they chased after the broken infantry scattering towards the safety of the trees. In the distance, Jagow's men, thoroughly frightened at the spectacle, hastily formed squares as well. French horse artillery, positioned for just such an opportunity, zeroed in on the densely packed squares and began to take them under fire.

While Krafft's brigade died, Prince Wilhelm's planned cavalry burst started to become reality. Holding back only his third line of Landwehr cavalry, the prince threw into the fray five regiments, four of hussars and one of lancers. To this was added Wahlen-Jurgass' first brigade of two dragoon regiments and one of lancers; the field was getting quite crowded. The Prussians, aligning themselves briefly, moved forth in a great wave of horseflesh.

When General Kellermann saw what the enemy was about to do, he quickly realized he had made a mistake in sending away Guiton's brigade to savage the infantry. Left with only his third line brigade, two regiments of dragoons, he had no option than to commit them and ask Milhaud for support. The latter, however, had already foreseen what would happen and his first line was on its way to stabilize the situation. This line, including the famously arrogant 1st Cuirassiers, bore up gallantly and without any hesitation charged forth against the advancing Prussians. As usual, the 1st Cuirassiers had not yet drawn their swords.

Kellermann's lead brigade was in deep straits now and Colonel Roge had no other recourse than to order his men to retire back towards their own lines to reform while he still had the chance to do so in peace. The horses, badly treated for so long, simply could not go on but at least he knew that his colleagues in the cuirassiers would be able to cover the retreat of his blown regiment. The Prussians, however, had other ideas and their attack forced him to stop and face them without the benefit of a countercharge. To their high credit, they stood their ground and received the shock of the vengeful enemy full on. The savage sword fight resumed but the enemy was so numerous and his waves so great that eventually the regiments could only dissolve into pockets and try as best they could to get away. "Hold them!" he yelled across the fight to his men.

The carabiniers' salvation, as Colonel Roge had prayed for, was not slow in coming. Caught in the middle of yet another fight, they recognized their own dragoons as the latter slammed into the Prussians and gradually began to force them back. Still, the Prussians came on and it was only superior French leadership and sword play that held the balance. Almost surrounded, the troopers of Kellermann's corps fought like madmen and finally were relieved by Milhaud's men as the cuirassier brigade of General

Dubois shifted the tide of the fight back to the French. Bending at first, the Prussian regiments at last fell back and, for the moment, gave up their onslaught to reform and attack again soon. Under the cover of Milhaud's regiments, the carabiniers fell back as best they could proudly boasting their own eagle and the flag of the Prussian 6th Hussars, a standard that was later claimed by the 2nd Dragoons and only grudgingly given up.

Guiton's jubilant brigade reformed off to the left of the fight and Kellermann lost no time in redirecting this unit to support his battered troopers in the front line. D'Hurbal rode up to his commander, his left sleeve dark from the blood that he was losing. "My second brigade needs to be pulled back to reform."

Kellermann agreed and told him to go with them. Milhaud now rode up. "Take your men back behind my columns and reform. I'll take the fight from here."

The former, biting his pride, could do nothing but nod. The Prussians had proved good opponents and Milhaud's men would be the ones to win the great prize this time. The taste in his mouth was not entirely bitter, however, for as he sat there sweating in his uniform, he realized, after so many years of fighting, that he was doing exactly what had to be done to win a battle. It was not terribly glorious but a new appreciation for the Emperor fomented itself and gave him at least a slight bit of comfort.

The commander of the IV Reserve Cavalry Corps lost no time in taking complete control of the situation he found the heavy cavalry in. Prussian attacks were growing in size and intensity and, with the retreat of half of Kellermann's blown squadrons, it was going to be difficult to achieve the decisive success he hoped for unless some support could be thrown together to break the Prussian regiments. His biggest problem was the same as Kellermann's had been: horse fatigue slowing down his regiments. But, thankfully, his troopers had at least the decisive victory at Ligny under their belts rather than the unsuccessful attacks against the Anglo-Dutch that Kellermann had been forced into. In this sense, Milhaud's men were a bit fresher than Kellermann's but certainly not by much. He, too, had to watch out for exhaustion while the fight continued. Sending back two messengers, he asked Domon's light cavalry to move in support and gave word to the Emperor that his men had engaged. That done, he rode ahead to ascertain the Prussian position.

*　　*　　*

Not very far away from the swirling cavalry fight, one man shut his telescope with a snap and placed it down on the table by his legs. The French emperor, tired but growing increasingly confident, sensed that his plan was working and found that his headache was almost entirely gone. Being a realist, he decided that it had dissipated due to his concentration and he could look forward to its return later that night. Neither Doctor Yvan or Larrey had been seen as of late and he did not want to interrupt the tasks of these worthies just because he was now rolling on adrenaline. The crash, he feared, would be a hard one.

Napoleon sat in his combat chair with Soult pouring over the maps of the area. "Gerard has taken Chapelle St. Lambert which cuts off that line of retreat. Reille will soon attack Ohain. It appears that Blucher only has one option. He will try and push north through Doudremont."

Soult nodded as he pulled one end of the map over to see for himself. "With our men positioned as they are, they have to unless Thielemann evades Grouchy as well and marches west to relieve them."

"They are beaten," Napoleon replied shaking his head. "This time I would bet that they are heading towards Berlin rather than Brussels."

The chief of staff had to agree. The guns to the east had fallen silent some hours before and this suggested that a fight was over though he knew the silence could be deceiving as Ney had done nothing on the morning of the sixteenth and that had told Napoleon that his marshal's battle was already over! Still, at this point in the battle, the positive spirit of the Emperor was infectious and he gave the Emperor's statement more credence than he had before. Count d'Erlon rode up along with several other officers who all seemed to converge on the imperial headquarters at once. A cavalry aide, one of Milhaud's men he recognized, slipped past the slowly walking d'Erlon and saluted smartly.

Napoleon noted the initiative with approval. Looking at the man, his eyes squinting in the bright sunshine, he asked, "What news have you?"

"Sire," the young officer began, "General Milhaud sends his respects and states that his first line has entered into action."

"In what strength?" Napoleon asked in his usual rapid fire manner.

"A brigade of cuirassiers, sire."

"What is the enemy strength?"

"The general estimates around 4,000 men, sire."

"And General Kellermann? Where is he?"

"Rallying his men, sire. I last saw him with the carabiniers."

"The fight, it goes well?"

"We have repulsed every charge."

Napoleon stood up out of his chair and it fell backwards behind him. Walking over to the aide, he clasped his hand on the man's ear and gave it a fearful tug along with a friendly smile. Turning to Soult and nodding to d'Erlon, he said, "General d'Erlon's I Corps will attack the enemy center."

General d'Erlon, having waited for those words all morning, saluted smartly and ran over to remount his horse. He knew what he had to do. Three divisions, those of Durutte, Quiot and Marcognet must now advance against the enemy center and complete the victory just as Soult had done ten years before at Austerlitz. To be given such an honor was a vindication of sorts for his dismal showing the day before and a sure sign of confidence from the Emperor. The battle was his to win.

The similarity of situations between Austerlitz and Ohain was not lost on the quiet chief of staff either. Ten years before he had been thirty six and a brand new marshal in his first campaign at that exalted rank. He remembered vividly how nervous and eager he had felt on that cold morning in December just as he remembered the sharp rebuff he received more than once when he asked if he could launch the main attack against the Austro-Russian center. That day he had learned a page in the art of war from a true master and gained an enduring memory that he would carry with him always. Austerlitz had practically ended a war on its own that day and he fervently hoped for France, and Europe in general, that Ohain would do the same.

Unfortunately, in the midst of such confidence and good will, there was still one sour point to take care of. As the Emperor watched d'Erlon ride off with his staff in full tilt, another face and uniform he recognized rode into view; he scowled as his eyes registered his wayward sibling Jerome. A few minutes before, one of Reille's aides had relayed the story of what had happened at Ohain and he knew he would have to relive the whole thing again as soon as Jerome came over to complain. Generals he could handle with a curt order but what could be said to a brother who had rallied to him as soon as he had landed? Was that not why he gave him command of the 6th Infantry Division? Without appearing anxious, Napoleon gathered himself and thanked the heavens above that it wasn't Pauline, his favorite sister, who was complaining. That event he might not be able to handle.

Jerome scampered up, his sword hanging limply at his side. "Something terrible has happened! General Reille, the scamp, has relieved me of my command!"

Napoleon played calm. "You did not follow your orders."

Shocked at this lack of support, Jerome was taken aback slightly. "But, the enemy, they were being reinforced."

"That is not what Reille has told me," the Emperor replied a little harder as he sat back down on his chair which an aide had stood up again for him. "You compromised the men of your division for a second time."

"It was not my fault!" Jerome yelled.

That did it. Napoleon could handle men who recognized their mistakes but would not tolerate those who tried to shift the blame onto another commander. Jerome had spoiled the feint at Mont St. Jean by actually assaulting the great chateau and causing heavy casualties on his division against the advise of Guilleminot. Here at Ohain he had done it again.

Standing up violently and knocking his chair over, again, he growled, "Do not make things worse on yourself, general! You have played the imbecile and I will not have it! Be gone!"

Stunned, Jerome fell silent and stood quietly for a moment before backing away to his horse. Napoleon, incensed and rigid, waved off his aide de camp and picked up his own chair. Sitting down as Jerome rode away to sulk somewhere, he noticed Soult staring at him. "My sisters are intriguers and my brothers fools and cowards. Why was I cursed with such a selection?"

Soult shrugged. "It was excellent foresight to have General Guilleminot there to take over when he departed, sire. In Russia, our right floundered for days after he rode off."

The Emperor's smile returned. "Maybe I should have left him in the navy."

Sarcasm in his blood, Soult offered a final solution. "Or in the United States with Miss Patterson."

$*$ $*$ $*$

As Kellermann's men retired to rally and reform, Milhaud's troopers were carrying the fight in the Prussian center. After the initial clash of his first wave with the enemy, the commander of the IV Reserve Cavalry Corps had made a special effort to regroup with speed and catch the opposing horse disorganized. The unit he chose for this task was Travers' 2nd Brigade of the 13th Cavalry Division to be followed by the 1st Brigade and supported by 14th Cavalry Division. Using his men as an armored battering ram, he hoped to pierce the thick lines of Prussian light horse and affect the rupture of the center that would cause their retreat. If his men could instill enough panic amongst the enemy, the battle could be won there and then.

Travers' brigade was the tip of the attack but nothing more than that. Very much under strength at the start of the campaign, they were committed as the cutting apex of a large wedge-like formation that would successively hit the Prussian horse and attempt to drive them from the field. The formation, made in haste but well done for all that, placed Travers' 2nd Brigade in the small first line of two regiments followed by Dubois' 1st Brigade who would support his left with one regiment in line and one in column. On the right, Baron Farine's 1st Brigade of the 14th would do the same and the whole would be backed up by Vial's two regiments in columns in the rear. Horse artillery formed up on either side of Vial's troopers.

With Kellermann's corps able to offer only limited support, Milhaud was gambling on using the last reserves of energy he and his men had to shatter the Prussian cavalry and win their center. However, what might seem a rash action was not so in light of the supports available and asked for by that experienced commander. Even as both sides rearranged their lines for the next strike, Domon's light cavalry division was maneuvering around the grand battery and nearing the scene of the fight. Behind them, Lefebvre-Desnoettes and the Imperial Guard light cavalry walked forward though, to be sure this time, only Napoleon's direct command could get them to engage in the fight. Thankfully for the French, the Napoleon of old had regained the field of battle and was keeping a watchful eye on events as they unfolded.

Riding around to make sure everything was perfect, Milhaud, satisfied, ordered his men to advance. Here again was a major difference in the way the armies of France and Prussia operated. The Prussians were without many good cavalry officers and even fewer had as much practical experience as Napoleon's men; the days of Seydlitz and his mighty squadrons were but a dusty memory. Organizationally, cavalry units were tied to their infantry corps and interaction between the corps reserves was shaky at best. Consequently, it was never up to the striking power of the cavalry in a large reserve to directly influence the course of a battle. More often than not, the cavalry brigades of the infantry corps were spread out across the field to cover the infantry. It is perhaps ironic that for this struggle, the Prussians did in fact end up having a mass of cavalry at just the right spot purely through position and accident. The French, on the other hand, had found that proper use of the reserve cavalry corps could be a decisive element in their fighting methods. Detaching divisions of light cavalry to directly support the infantry corps, the French massed their elite heavy cavalry regiments into the reserve corps to be committed as the Emperor saw fit. Thus, if part of the army's main line was shaky or broken, as at Eylau, and the enemy were advancing, Napoleon could throw his reserve corps into a massed attack that could, at the very least, stop the enemy and gain him time to reorganize his line and prepare it for defense. Likewise, and more recently, Milhaud's cavalry corps had been used at Ligny to support the attack of the Imperial Guard and break the enemy center. Despite overall Prussian superiority in numbers, the heavy cavalry smashed the Prussians and was never in serious danger of being overwhelmed by the enemy horse as they were scattered across the field by brigades with never more than two anywhere in the vicinity of Milhaud. Here at Ohain, Milhaud was again engaging the Prussians, although this time, because of the terrain and chance, the enemy was able to mass two of his three reserve cavalry units to face him and to try and prevent a repeat of Ligny.

Fighting armored cavalrymen was having a demoralizing effect on both Prince Wilhelm's and Wahlen-Jurgass' men but both commanders felt that if enough of their troopers could be brought to bear against the enemy then they would have a chance to overwhelm the French with their sheer numbers. They knew the French were exhausted but they also knew the taste of long straight cuirassier swords and any attempt on the French had to be made carefully and with as much order as possible. Currently, as the light dust settled across the field, they could see that the force ahead of them was not very strong in numbers but always formidable in fighting strength. Consequently, they planned to use their greater numbers to fall on the flanks of the French and surround them thus depriving the heavy squadrons of the impetus they needed to flatten everything in their path. Prussian officers dashed back and forth aligning their regiments and preparing for the attack.

The Prussian high command was getting very nervous with

the threatening situation that Milhaud had placed them in. Occupying the heart of the Prussian center, the presence of the French cavalry had excited orders from Blucher and Gneisenau to sweep them away so that the army could fall back in one piece. Blucher's aides had already held the old marshal back once from charging and Prince Wilhelm knew he had to move quickly lest the French follow up their positional advantage with heavy infantry support.

While a battery of artillery unlimbered near him, Count Gneisenau watched the battle from the right of Bose's static brigade surrounded by his staff. Unnecessary quiet chatter was being exchanged and it was clear that they were all getting a bit edgy at the thought of French cavalry in control of the center of their position. With the enemy horse there, all movement was at a halt.

A rider from the IV Corps raced up and dismounted. "Sir! General Bulow reports infantry advancing in the enemy center."

What Gneisenau had feared was fast becoming reality. If the French were allowed to march their infantry right up behind the cavalry, there would be no holding them. Bulow's men, engaged to their front, would be trapped and destroyed and only what remained of Pirch's and Zieten's corps would be able to escape to the north. The French heavy cavalry had to be pushed back at any cost.

A few hundred yards away, another man was having similar thoughts. Field Marshal Blucher, mounted on his horse on a rise behind the 2nd Pommeranian Landwehr Cavalry Regiment, had been observing the cavalry fight for all of its short but violent life and he felt powerless to do anything. At the moment, everything was in the hands of the cavalry officers in the center. The French were clearly organizing for another attack and he felt the urge to simply join in the assault he knew his own troopers were getting ready for. Major Huser, having witnessed Blucher's literal trampling at Ligny, managed to talk him out of it when he pointed out Durutte's men marching to attack the remnants of Krafft's shattered brigade which was still under fire from one of Kellermann's horse artillery companies. Blucher, concerned and distracted, was determined to hold the line and he rode over to give moral support to the men at the same time that Milhaud gave the order to advance.

Trumpets sounded across the French battle line as the troopers of the IV Reserve Cavalry Corps began to walk their mounts forward. Officers ahead of the ranks, each line tightly packed boot to boot and the whole acting like the precision instrument it had grown to be, the sight was awesome to all who saw it. Easily better than any trained cavalry force in the world, the French horse maneuvered as one unit, their evolutions perfectly timed and executed. As they approached the halted Prussian troops, they increased to a trot, their iron scabbards clanging restlessly against their legs and their heavy swords drawn but mostly at the resting position; the cuirassier main weapon was a long and heavy sword and was not intended to be held point out for extended rides. The rumble of so many hooves in close proximity shook the earth and Milhaud, riding with his men, hoped that the force would shake the Prussians as well.

The Prussians had almost finished their plans when the French began to advance and both the prince and Wahlen-Jurgass knew quickly why the French had been so dominate before the Russian campaign had killed so many of Napoleon's horses and men. A cavalry strike force as the one now closing in on them had not been seen since Borodino but, with the peace, the French had been given a little time to rebuild their forces and remount many of their regiments. As the two commanders now saw, to their dismay, the French cavalry leaders were still very much alive. The enemy line, despite the fighting over the course of the campaign, was aligned beautifully and gaining the speed of danger to their forces. Whatever complete plan they had would now have to be discarded in favor of a more impromptu version but, without another thought, they dutifully undertook to do their best; there was no one sided bravery here.

Caught unready, the Prussian horse had to launch their counterstroke without the forces they wanted in the places they wished to have them. Given the fact that they planned to surround the French horse, Prince Wilhelm had wanted to shift his second brigade to his right to replace his third brigade, the Landwehr troopers, in the vital flanking spot. He had been unable to do this. Wahlen-Jurgass on the other hand, had done so by moving Lieutenant colonel Sohr's recently arrived 2nd Brigade of two hussar regiments to his left flank and keeping the remnants of his 3rd Brigade behind the first line. At this point, however, halfway was good enough and they would have to gamble with what they had at hand.

The French advance had gathered momentum properly but, again because of the horses, was already becoming a bit ragged. While the troopers did they best they could, the officers knew that after the first contact there would be little they could do to get the tired mounts to rally and be ready to charge again. Nevertheless, for perhaps this last time, they pushed, prodded and spurred their mounts into a frenzy as they never had before. Like the Prussians, they had to attack with what they had.

"Charge!"

One last trumpet call and the French heavy troopers raised a great cry as they inexorably closed with the advancing Prussian host. Once more, the oncoming tidal wave of cuirassiers was too much for some of the prince's men. This time, two hussar regiments faltered at the last moment and began to retire in confusion as Travers' brigade, the spearhead of the attack, galloped into the gap in the Prussian first line and chased the enemy towards his second echelon troopers.

"Advance! Keep moving!" yelled divisional commander Watier to his men as he followed Travers' brigade into the hole. He knew that their momentum had to be kept up for if they allowed the horses to catch their breath, there would be no getting them to give more than a trot later.

"Draw swords!" yelled Colonel Ordener of the 1st Cuirassiers as was their fashion just before contact was made. "With the point!" he added, as was his fashion as their commander.

Prince Wilhelm's second line, made up of the 8th Hussars and two of his better Landwehr regiments, the 2nd Neumarck and 1st

Silesian, were dismayed by the two brother regiments, the rough handled 6th and 1st Neumark, as the latter bolted for the rear in a panic. Thankfully, Major von Colomb had set up in such a way that the regiments, aligned in columns of squadrons, had plenty of room available for the "retiring" friendly troops so that they would not disturb his own horse too badly (unbeknownst to him, several Saxon soldiers pressed into the 8th Hussars took the opportunity to "disengage" as well). Unfortunately, the French were pursuing so quickly that there was no time to form into a line of battle. Hesitating for only a moment, he ordered the charge sounded with the thought that the columns would be able to penetrate the armored wedge and stand a better chance of surviving the contest. The Prussians advanced.

The French line finally struck a few seconds after Prince Wilhelm's first line all but vanished. The 1st West Prussian Lancer Regiment, minus their lances, collided with part of Travers' leading brigade and then swept onto Baron Farin's 1st Brigade where a sword fight broke out and the squadrons became intermixed; Farin's first regiment began to lose its momentum. To the left of the Prussian line, Wahlen-Jurgass' dragoons tangled with the other regiment of cuirassiers but broke under the impact of that force. That did not matter to the Prussian commander, however. Posted with his flanking brigade, Wahlen-Jurgass, anxious to avenge the pounding he had received the day before from Gerard's men, had carefully watched the French flank regiment swing out and engage his dragoons; that they broke only helped his position. With them out of the way, his men could sweep into the French rear.

"No prisoners!" he yelled as he gave the order to attack. "For the Fatherland!"

The hussars of the 2nd Brigade gave a cheer and started to round the French flank. To their front only the remnants of one fight remained and the two regiments of reserves that Milhaud had kept in columns in the French rear. The latter, seeing the jaws of the trap closing, took a look over his shoulder and saw more cavalry on its way to attack his left flank. There was just too many of them to deal with at once.

"Vial! Action flanks! Move!" he yelled to the brigade commander nearby.

"Fire!"

The retort of two horse guns startled Milhaud to the bone; an enterprising officer, probably sensing as well what was going to happen, had unlimbered a section just to get in a shot to help before the enemy closed. The general, taking a last look behind himself as he rode off to join his men, mentally promised his own sword to that brave soul who had thought to engage the enemy horse with the guns.

The brave man was Captain Lenette, commander of the 4th Company of the 3rd Horse Artillery Regiment. A veteran of many a campaign, the intelligent and suave commander of the French guns had waited for just such a situation and had detailed the two best crews in the company to be ready to dismount and prepare a section of cannon to welcome the enemy should they manage to flank the attack. If nothing else, the Prussian would be in for a surprise when they attempted to get into the French rear. The smoke from the two just fired guns obscured his view but their job was done.

"Limber!"

Milhaud had been right. The two blasts of canister had surprised the enemy hussars and slowed the advance of the right-hand regiment to a suspicious crawl. The other, however, knew no such problem. Fired by certain victory, they ignored the cannon and concentrated on the regiment of cuirassiers working up to speed ahead of them; they knew they would meet the enemy at the trot only.

Vial's two regiments, the 6th and 9th Cuirassiers, formed in parallel columns in the rear of the strike force, faced about to their respective flanks and prepared to charge. Not wanting to waste precious time, Vial simply ordered them to draw their swords and charge; the enemy was just too close.

The fight in the Prussian center was becoming very confused. Travers' brigade had penetrated through the first enemy line like it wasn't there (which in a way was true) and had moved on to the second which was coming up in columns. Farin's brigade had been split into halves with one regiment fighting a slow moving sword fight and the other gleefully chasing Prussian dragoons. Dubois' men were following Travers but their commander had seen the Prussian flanking attempt and was preparing to shed at least one regiment to stop that threat. In the rear, Vial's men were completely split and charging in opposite directions to protect the French flanks. Milhaud, finding himself almost alone, decided to find the nearest intact formation and so he rushed ahead to find Delort.

Travers' men galloped ahead without pause. The Prussians, driven by desperation, did the same. The impact of the two forces was a terrible jumble of horses as the mighty cuirassiers broke through the ranks of enemy horse only to be met by more and more troopers as the columns bit deep and penetrated the armored wedge. Men fell by the score, horses collapsed but as quickly as it began it was over and Travers found himself completely on the other side of the cavalry fight with two battered but essentially intact regiments of cuirassiers. Just as he was about to give the order to sound the reform, he spotted Bose's infantry brigade and a large group of officers riding hard for the protection of the squares. Aggressive by nature, Travers decided not to reform and instead use his last energies on the Prussian infantry.

"Enemy cavalry!" yelled a sergeant in the square.

Count Gneisenau excitedly pointed out the cuirassiers to an aide. "Hold them, men!"

Flashes from Prussian model 1809 muskets rippled from the thick ranks of the square as the cuirassiers thundered by in clumps and tried to break open the infantry. Almost inevitably, one square collapsed in fear and the French horse hunted them down mercilessly as the foot soldiers ran for their lives. The Prussian gun battery supporting the infantry shattered the front line of the 12th Cuirassiers with a blast of canister but soon found itself flanked and cut to pieces by the Farin's wayward regiment that had failed to hear the recall sounded and had kept on chasing the Prussian dragoons. Another Prussian battery behind the infantry brigade neatly cut down their own men with more canister thinking that the routed dragoons were attacking Frenchmen.

Colonel Lahuberdiere, commander of the 10th Cuirassiers, found himself the deepest into the Prussian position as his troopers veered to the right after savaging the gun battery and receiving some warm shots from the infantry squares. It had been a wild ride already. Having cut apart an unsteady Prussian dragoon regiment, they had followed so closely upon it that they routed the second line of Landwehr cavalry with barely a fight and scattered it across the field as well. After that brief episode in which both sides burst through the Landwehr, the cuirassiers found themselves almost alone and the Prussian guns became a tempting target to engage from the flank. Trying to stay clear of the battery behind the infantry, the colonel sounded for his men to reform in an almost quiet sector of the Prussian rear. Around him, camp followers, train troops and others who were not where they were supposed to be scrambled at the sight of French cavalry and dashed about in all directions. Lahuberdiere ignored all of them and calmly set about reforming his disorganized regiment back into proper squadrons and contemplating how he was going to get out of his predicament. Still, the rear of the enemy army he found to be surprisingly quiet.

Travers brigade was completely blown and as they, too, tried to reform they found themselves coming under fire from artillery and infantry fire. The horses would barely move and from experience he knew that they wouldn't be able to force more than a trot out of the heavy mounts. Looking about for help, he spotted the 10th reforming in seeming peace across the way and so he made the decision to move there while he still had the chance and while the horses felt inclined to move. Just as he thought, the animals protested and simply bounced along at a maddeningly casual gait as the normally fearsome armored troopers swung around the rear of Bose's brigade. Travers himself had his already wounded horse hit again by a musket ball and he had to be carried on another mount by his trumpeter who, like all the trumpeters, did not wear a heavy cuirass and whose horse seemed to still be in fine spirits.

Elsewhere on the field, Prussian numbers were making

themselves felt. The 5th Cuirassiers, engaged hand to hand with the 1st West Prussian Uhlan Regiment, put up a stiff fight against the fanatical Prussians until the 1st Dragoons slammed into their flank and completely disrupted the regiment. The French got the worst of the fighting and had to retreat right into the teeth of the surrounding Prussian hussars who also did their best to crush them between the two forces. This desperate moment intermixed all four regiments and brought everyone except the fleeing French to a halt. The routed cuirassiers, faced with life or death, fought with the single minded determination to get away but, even so, left a good many saddles empty when at last the remnants did in fact get free. From then on, the men of the 5th would never again complain about the weight of their cuirasses which saved quite a few from certain death.

The French right had been compromised. Some Prussian regiments reformed while others kept pushing ahead in a wild frenzy to kill anything French on the field. Victory looked as if it was swinging in the favor of the Prussians. Milhaud and Delort, separated from their men, were chased by a large group of hussars. But perhaps the most unusual waste of horse flesh was the squadron of hussars that pursued Captain Lenette's horse artillery company which was racing for the French lines at full gallop. These overeager Prussians were so intent on their prey that were quickly brought up short by French chasseurs and sent flying to the four winds. A new player had entered the deadly game: Domon.

*   *   *

Napoleon watched coldly from atop his horse the progress of the fighting in the Prussian center. Kellermann's spent troops were streaming back in pieces to the French lines while Milhaud and his men were apparently being swallowed by the mass of enemy horse. Domon's chasseurs were moving to engage but without Kellermann would their attack be enough?

Dismounting awkwardly, the Emperor kicked a rock across the ground as he struggled to decide what to do. Despite the fact that the Guard cavalry had been involved in the fighting the day before, he was still loath to deploy it lest some other calamity made him regret his decision. In the back of his mind was that nagging reminder of the battle of Mont St. Jean when suddenly he had no cavalry whatsoever left to deal with the enemy and his position could have been easily ruined had it not been for Gerard's fortuitous march on Lasne.

"Soult!" he burst out as the thought of the IV Corps commander made itself known. "Be sure that we have a baton for our new marshal of France, Gerard."

The chief of staff smiled disinterestedly. Gerard had been lucky. "Yes, sire."

Napoleon caught the slightly disgruntled voice but ignored it; there were more important things to do. Telescope in hand, he watched the swirling fight and the growing number of troops streaming back to their own lines. "Guyot, what do you see?"

General Guyot, commander of the Imperial Guard Heavy Cavalry, sat mounted near the Emperor; after the "incident" the day before, the Emperor was taking no chances that his own guard troops would be swept away without his orders. Guyot, like many of the officers, was watching the fight through his telescope. "Domon is moving to engage, sire, but Kellermann is blown."

The situation was as he had seen it. The heavy cavalry, thoroughly worn out, was having a hard time fending off the Prussian masses. Nevertheless, the infantry of d'Erlon's corps was on the move and if they could hold out long enough then the battle was won anyway and the cavalry could be sacrificed. He paused. Practicality aside, could he let his men, his friends, be crushed by the enemy mounted onslaught? Would his conscience allow him? Whether he liked it or not, the die was cast and the Emperor knew his hand had been forced. Nodding unnoticed to himself, he said quietly, "Send in Lefebvre-Desnoettes."

"The Guard cavalry, sire?" Soult asked as he tried to pin down the Emperor with his eyes but the latter continued to ignore him. Picking up the previously written commands to that general to join in the fight with a free hand, he waved over one very brightly clad cavalry aide de camp. "Immediately. Verkaik! Carry these orders to General Lefebvre-Desnoettes with all dispatch."

*   *   *

General of Division Baron Domon was very much in the mold of the other light cavalry officers of the Army of the North. Very experienced, cool headed and superb leaders of men, these commanders had proven critical to the successes of the Grande Armee over the years and now at Ohain they had already played a vital role. Domon himself was a veteran of many years though he had only been a cavalryman since 1799. However, a quick learner and with an eye for light cavalry work, he had worked his way up the ladder of promotion quickly and he participated in many of the great cavalry actions of the early empire including the battle of Eylau. However, an association with Marshal Murat which proved lucrative at first but then very definitely soured, tripped him up and almost put a stop to his career. However, the lack of available good leaders gave him a chance and he had used it to his advantage. Now, in the midst of the most desperate cavalry fight of his life, he had been thrust center stage to influence the course of the battle with his three regiments of chasseurs. Having fought a good deal already, Domon was nevertheless ready to accept that there was one more role to be acted out by his troopers in green.

Domon's division had been alerted by General Milhaud of the latter's impending charge against the Prussian horse and, alert and ready as always, the chasseurs of the three regiments comprising the division had slowly moved up in a deliberate fashion so as to retain complete control and not tire out their mounts. The general himself, having ridden over the same ground he had helped to defend the day before, was confident and positively radiated this strength to his staff.

"We will break them like we did yesterday," he said, waving his hand gracefully. "Rest assured."

By now, Milhaud's corps was in a desperate situation. Effectively sliced in half, three battered regiments were retiring in confusion to a position near the Prussian infantry line and the other regiments were nowhere to be seen. The Prussian cavalry, completely disorganized but at least partially successful, was striving to reform and also to pursue the routed troops into the ground. Prince Wilhelm and General Wahlen-Jurgass sounded the recall but enjoyed only limited success; they had to reorganize before the French could bring in reinforcements or rally themselves sufficiently to fight back with affect.

A quick glance over the field was enough to tell Domon exactly what he had to do. Drawing his saber and placing it carefully on his right shoulder, he ordered his division, formed in three lines of regiments, to draw their weapons and increase to a trot. Any attack he made would be completely controlled and made to maximum effect.

In naval warfare during the age of sail, the best way to do damage to an enemy fleet was to lay your ship alongside the nearest enemy, open fire low and proceed to batter her into submission. While clearly Domon was no naval officer, this was exactly what he did. Routing a pursuing Prussian hussar squadron without much ado, he looked for and found the nearest sizeable enemy force and launched his men at them with the sharp speed and agility that light cavalry was known for.

The lead regiment of the 3rd Cavalry Division was the 4th Chasseurs and their Colonel, Desmichels, knew an enemy out of position when he saw one. The Prussian 5th Hussars, bloodied but victorious, were about to experience the cost of being caught unawares by fresh and revenge-minded enemy mounted troops. Without waiting for any orders, Desmichels, a trusted subordinate of Domon, ordered an immediate charge against the reforming hussars despite their greater numerical strength; he knew that their manpower would not count for anything once he had struck and strike he did. Whether it was dust or simply a case of not paying attention to an ever changing situation was academic; the 4th Chasseurs hit the 5th Hussars so hard and in such perfect order that they never stood a chance. In a flash, their commander, Major von Arnim, was killed, their standard taken and the regiment blown off the face of the battlefield. The slaughter, and it was that, was savage as the French cut down the bewildered hussars before most could get away. Truly, when their own troops were in danger, the soldiers of France moved heaven and earth to save them.

The cavalry fight, still a continuing affair in the process of evolving, was barely an hour old. The entry of Domon's men was just the right application of strength the French needed to even the balance of the struggle and the former was the right commander they needed on the spot. Light cavalry has to be dynamic to win mounted actions using speed, guile and agility to keep the enemy off balance and unready. So far, Domon had used speed; it was now the turn of agility.

The charge of the 4th Chasseurs made the 9th Chasseurs, the next regiment in line, the ready attack force. Moving up the two remaining regiments at a trot to initially support the 4th in case they needed it, Domon instead reacted to a move by the Prussians. The 3rd Hussars and the 1st Neumarck Landwehr Cavalry Regiment were engaged in a harrying pursuit against a regiment of cuirassiers who were trying to reform. Angling off his second regiment, Domon ordered them to charge to the support of the cuirassiers in order to extricate them and give them time to rally while he and the third regiment, the 12th Chasseurs, waded in the middle of these two fights to lend a hand to his men in the case that either was beaten. Domon twisted the tip of his mustache as he watched like a hawk from his saddle. Cavalry fights are touch and go affairs with the victors one moment becoming the vanquished the next and it was imperative to be the one who sees rather than the one who was seen.

The persecuted cuirassiers were from Vial's brigade, victims of the maxim mentioned above. Successful in their primary fight against the 5th Hussars whom they were able to meet at a trot and hold to a standstill, the 9th Cuirassiers had been flanked and rolled up by a mass of dragoons and more hussars when their left had become exposed during the fight. Retreating, they had met up with their sister regiment, the 6th, who, after smashing the Landwehr cavalry to their front, had performed the tricky maneuver of reversing direction after a charge and reengaging to their rear. Protected by a bold front put up by the 6th, the 9th had started to rally their blown mounts when the Prussians attacked again and put the 6th to flight by enveloping it from both flanks. It was at this moment that the 9th Chasseurs arrived to relieve their miseries. In a flash, the intermingled French were joined by friends and together they succeeded in driving off the attacking Prussians. However, for these two regiments, this charge was their last one and, like Kellermann's troops, they proceeded to fall back from the enemy center and retire from the fight.

Fugitives, both Prussian and French, were everywhere. Broken regiments could be seen running away, attacking and reforming as if in a continuous motion with the advantage not going to any one side. Riderless horses meandered around looking for stable mates and wounded soldiers dragged themselves if they could to any shelter nearby so that they would not be trampled; horses generally avoid objects on the ground but in a massed charge they don't always see where they are running. It was in this environment that Domon's division played its last but most brilliant card. This time, guile was their ally.

Domon had remained with the 12th Chasseurs as the rest of his division took care of business on either flank of the regiment. Both of the sister regiments of the division had been successful at the first attack and that left him in the middle with the 12th looking for more trouble. It was not long in coming. Freshly reformed, the Prussian 1st Dragoons, now under the command of Major von Pfeiffer after their colonel had been badly wounded, wheeled around to face off against the feisty chasseurs of Domon and for a full two minutes both sides faced one another without budging an inch. This was a game of wits and nerves for the side that flinched first would be the recipient of a devastating charge. Domon's troops, unlike the cuirassiers, were fresh and eager. Pfeiffer made an abortive first move, a feigned charge, but against the experienced eye of General Domon, it quickly went for not when the French ignored it. A moment later, the general played his hand by quietly turning and nodding to an officer behind him. While the Prussians watched with suspicion, the colonel of the 12th gave a near invisible hand signal to his trumpeter who stiffly sat up and played a series of notes that caused a single squadron of the regiment to shift to its right very rapidly and place itself into a position to flank the enemy unit while the rest of the squadrons suddenly tensed up in their saddles. Thoroughly alarmed, the Prussian reaction was to begin to turn to attack the detached chasseur squadron so that it would not lead the assault on them.

"Charge!"

Just as the Prussians were fully involved with their shift to face and attack the detached squadron, the colonel of the 12th gave the order to charge and catch them while they were out of position. Following the lead of the trumpet blast, the chasseurs raised a great cheer and dashed upon the Prussian dragoons who were dumbfounded as to what was happening. Caught moving in the wrong direction, their officers didn't know what to do and the whole regiment lost its cohesion. Worse, the detached chasseur squadron also attacked and quickly placed the 1st Dragoons in an impossible spot. Bending at first, their formation rapidly degenerated from a line into a blob as the troopers tried to push their way clear of the oncoming French, an act that only served to worsen their debacle. Fumbling for a moment, they finally cracked and fled from the oncoming chasseurs who found it difficult to catch them. Almost immediately, Domon ordered them to sound the rally and halt the attack.

The success of the 12th was short lived but the strikingly successful charges of Domon's division bought the exhausted French horse valuable time. As the enemy milled around in confusion patching up his formations, the French heavy horse that had been broken were able to withdraw to the west without further molestation. Indeed, quite a few dismounted troopers could be seen as well making their escape.

The Prussian commanders, seeing this new entry into the arena, directed what intact reserves they had to attack the chasseurs instead of going after the worn out cuirassiers. Wahlen-Jurgass, busy rallying what he could of his brigades, directed the fresh 2nd Uhlan

Regiment to throw back the 4th Chasseurs as they pursued the broken 5th Hussars while Prince Wilhelm reformed two regiments to attack from his flank.

It was at this point in the fight that Blucher suddenly made a reappearance. Not satisfied to simply sit back and watch the clash of the mounted regiments, he rode from where he had been encouraging Krafft's brigade to join up with the Landwehr cavalry regiments of Prince Wilhelm's third line, some of which as yet had not charged. Blucher arrived to find the battle shifting to favor the French once again. Another of their divisions had emerged onto the field and had made short work of the scattered Prussian regiments they had met. Snorting in disgust, he swore and rode out in front of the mounted regiments; it was time the French met a real force of cavalry.

"Now, my children! Now!" Blucher cried out, once more becoming the hussar of old.

Collected around the Prussian commander in chief were the elements of four regiments of light cavalry and their morale now soared to fever pitch. One regiment of the third line was left behind, the 2nd Pommeranian regiment, and it was instructed to wait until Blucher himself returned to lead them in. This latter regiment, newly formed and filled with raw recruits, was Prince Wilhelm's weakest unit and it was important that it be led competently if it was going to be effective at all in the battle. Despite its rather timid background, it was to become legendary.

As more and more French cavalry streamed back to their own lines they were met by cheers from the advancing infantry of d'Erlon's corps. Feeling vindicated, they returned the compliment with gusto knowing that their sacrifice had not been in vain as it had the day before. Durutte's men were already well ahead, though clearly they could do little more than rough up Krafft's remnants until a decision had been reached in the cavalry fight or the rest of the corps arrived to break open the Prussian center. To their right, Marcognet's men had just passed the French gun line and were steadily moving up in the mixed order while Quiot's division had come forward in columns on their left. Into the gap between the divisions walked the exhausted cavalry who could not manage any faster pace. Lefebvre-Desnoettes' Guard light cavalry filed past the right of Marcognet in columns. The crisis of the Prussian army had been reached and victory, it was clear, hung in the balance. If Blucher and Gneisenau could defeat the French cavalry and bring d'Erlon to a halt with their own, they would be able to pull Bulow out of the woods and conduct a withdrawal from the battlefield as the French, more than likely, would be too tired to pursue them closely. By this point in the battle of Ohain, it was clear that the Prussians could not win it but they could avoid losing and that in itself would deprive the French of the victory they so desperately needed. If, on the other hand, Napoleon was successful, the Prussian army would be split in two with Bulow's men almost certainly being taken prisoner and the rest of the army being hard pressed to get away.

Blucher's presence galvanized the remaining Prussian forces and he led the four regiments into a powerful charge aimed at Dubois' brigade of cuirassiers which had become separated from the rest of the rallying horsemen and largely forgotten. Dubois, isolated to the northwest of Bose's brigade but successfully reorganized, had been entertaining the thought of joining Travers and Lahuberdiere when he spotted the beginning of Blucher's charge against him. Deciding then and there what to do, he ordered his regiments into a single column of squadrons that he himself would lead in a counterstroke through the Prussian line. If they could maintain at least some speed, his men could avoid being flanked and instead they would be able to blast through the enemy and achieve what he desired: escape back to their own lines. Dubois knew his men had little fight left in their mounts and any further hanging on without sizeable support was just asking to be annihilated.

Despite the protesting of their mounts, the French troopers formed their single squadron front column and advanced to meet Blucher and his hard moving soldiers. Barely achieving a trot, the two regiments struggled manfully to maintain their ranks with many of the men using a good deal more spur than they ever had before. However, there was a definite feeling among the cuirassiers that, as musket balls and the occasional cannon shot bounced through their ranks, could only be described as desperate bravery. A charge by heavy cavalry can only be successful if it has mass, speed and proper support. Dubois' men, in the condition they were, had none of these qualities.

General Domon, taking the 12th Chasseurs back into hand, had his hands full protecting the withdrawing heavy cavalry. The 4th Chasseurs, chased back by the Prussian uhlans, had to be relieved by the 12th which quickly turned the tables while the 9th Chasseurs returned to rally as well. For a while it seemed that Domon alone was holding the French foothold in the Prussian center. Thankfully, it only seemed that way for there was yet another force that had a part to play in the struggle.

Conflicting trumpet sounds marked the clash of Blucher and Dubois. Charging forth like great unstoppable forces, the meeting of the two sides was as violent as any in the fight thus far, that special brutality that marked the more recent battles between the French and Prussians. General Dubois, leading his men in the breakout attempt, immediately received a cut to his face that caused him to fall backwards off his horse. The rest of the horse, however, madly prodding their snorting and maddened mounts, pushed through the Prussian ranks and blew a hole in the enemy line that could be followed by the rest of the brigade. Prussian flanking regiments desperately wheeled to strike them but the speed of the terrible charge was too fast for them to react to and they failed to catch even the tail of Dubois' men. Blucher, exhilarated with the vitality of the short battle but frustrated in his attempt to crush the French cavalry, located Travers' brigade on the far side of Bose's brigade and instead decided to lead his men at them.

"They have spotted us, sir," said one officer to General Travers as the latter arrived back from placing his squadrons of horse into proper order. Given the time to reform, he had taken advantage of it to rest his men, continued to scare the enemy infantry and take command of the wayward 10th Cuirassiers as well. Massed together, they were the most formidable force of cavalry the French had on the field.

The Prussian cavalry commanders rode like madmen trying to reorganize and revive their battered regiments. Like two punch drunk fighters, the French and Prussians were teetering in place with the fight to be won by the fighter who could land the last great fist. Wahlen-Jurgass and Prince Wilhelm strove to do this by gathering all of the remaining regiments they could and forming them back into a semblance of the brigades from which they had come. The hussars were badly mauled but reforming what men they could, the lancers, all without lances now, were in fairly good shape but not a single dragoon squadron could be culled together from the two shattered regiments. Landwehr cavalry prevailed in the forces being assembled but some of these men had not proved so bad after all and the mass taken together was far more horse than the French could face them with.

Here again, as the forces rallied for the last throw, the differences in the organization and professionalism of the two forces could be seen. Both Prince Wilhelm and General Wahlen-Jurgass had trouble assembling the men especially after Blucher started to lead charges. Not unnaturally, the rallying troopers had fallen in with him rather than heed the sound of their own recall trumpets. Thus, the regiments were fragmented and their corresponding striking power lessened. The French, on the other hand, stuck strictly to their proper parent formations and rallied very quickly though this latter must also be attributed to the fine officers they possessed as well. Nevertheless, the serious exhaustion gripping the French horse and the still formidable mass of enemy cavalry was gradually tipping the balance of the fight towards Blucher's Prussians.

*   *   *

While the cavalry engagement entered into its last throes, the infantry of both sides were still fiercely engaging one another all along the line. Durutte's division was trading volleys with both Krafft's and Jagow's brigades and was making both of them even shakier than before. These commanders, becoming increasingly desperate, called to their leader, Zieten, for reinforcements but he could only deploy Pirch II's intact brigade to help. This deployment left only Donnersmarck and his single battalion as the I Corps reserve. Along the entire Prussian line, there were no sizeable reserves left except for Tippelskirch's brigade behind Bulow's tree covered front.

The forest continued to be an open sore. Lobau's men were busy in the trees as always with Subervie's cavalry helping to blunt and turn back a desperate counterattack by Bulow's men who had attempted to turn the right flank of the army and thereby relieve pressure for the whole of Bulow's line. A few good volleys and two feigned cavalry charges cooled their ardor, however, and when they retreated they left quite a few casualties on the ground but the situation stayed pretty much where it had begun. In the meantime, a vivandiere could be seen working her way through one regiment with free drinks for the exhausted men in the ranks. Somehow or another, Lobau's men were still very much in the fight though it is true that Morand's battalions of the Old Guard had been advanced to more visibly back them up with their daunting presence.

On the French far left, however, events were happening again. Reille, angry and frustrated, was about to contribute to the battle for the first time in the day (that is if the relieving of Jerome is not counted). Assembling his men outside the Bois de Ohain, he was depressed to see that so many of Jerome's men had not returned to the ranks, a common ailment when infantry get swarmed on by cavalry. The 6th Infantry Division, amongst the finest in the whole army, was only a shadow of its former self but for all that still ready to march again. The men, he knew, were suspicious of Guilleminot for the simple reason that Jerome had exposed himself more than once and had been wounded; despite his incompetence, bravery was always respected. Guilleminot, though a veteran, was new to the division and viewed only as a replacement. Like people everywhere, the substitute is almost never treated the same as the one replaced until that person proves himself. For this reason, Reille had already determined to stick close to the 6th and allow Foy to attack on his own while he bolstered Guilleminot should he need it.

Their task was not an easy one. Steinmetz had proved an able commander already in the campaign though his troops had been beaten and badly disorganized after the battle of Ligny. Here at Ohain, his troops were behind barricades of kegs and overturned wagons with more men massed in the buildings of the town. His overall position was a good one as well. One flank of the brigade rested on the Ohain brook while the other was protected by Roder's cavalry leaving only a direct frontal assault or a tricky combined arms attack the only options open to the commander of the II Corps. Reille, smarting from the repulse of Jerome's men but more confident due to his firing of the commander, was thinking more clearly than he had during the entire campaign. Unlike the day before, manpower was at a premium and therefore could not be wasted, he thought, calmly forgetting that trained manpower never should be wasted. To be fair, his poor conduct the day before was eating at him and he responded with probably the best plan he could devise under the circumstances. Having massed his howitzers already, he had prepared for the attack by setting alight the western end of Ohain and forcing the Prussians back into town or out into the open. The rest of his guns, massed together between the infantry divisions, were busy with a general bombardment of Ohain designed to keep the enemy honest and off balance.

"You will have to keep them off of us," Reille said to General Pire, "I intend to press our attack across the open ground."

Pire nodded. "I would suggest alerting your flank regiment of the certain possibility of being charged by enemy cavalry. My men will do the rest."

"Agreed," Reille replied as he watched the smoke rising from the town. "I do not intend to lose any more men to their horse."

The light cavalry general managed a weary smile. "With brother Jerome gone, our chances of success have increased tenfold."

With the thought of Jerome's repulse fresh and burning in his mind, Reille rode over to that commander's former charges who were busy putting their battered ranks back into order. After the beatings they had taken over the last few days, it was a wonder that any men at all returned to the colors but yet they were here all the same. To the normally impassive general, this was a sobering moment, one of those few unexpected times when a brief second comes to a man to reflect upon everything that he had done in his life. These men were his responsibility and their lives depended on his ability to exercise that often terrible job. His own lack of control at Mont St. Jean and even here had compromised that trust and he cursed himself for it; as a general he had to command, not be commanded. With his orders clear (after receiving yet another command from the Emperor to attack with no mention of Jerome), he was firmly set in his way to take Ohain and hold it.

As Reille walked his horse slowly through the assembling ranks of soldiers, he came across a very preoccupied Sergeant Demimor of the 1st Ligne who was busy mounting an eagle on the end of his musket by tying it down with a piece of rope. Knowing that the regiment had lost its regimental eagle to the Prussian cavalry attack, he was at a loss as to where this second eagle had come from.

"Sergent!" he called out as he dismounted amongst the troops. "Come here at once."

Demimor straightened out like a child caught stealing and carefully slid the musket behind his body as if the general had not seen it. "Sir!"

"Bring the bird!" Reille said, shaking his head. Had the sergeant stolen the emblem from another regiment? That shameful act would be the last of him.

As the sergeant approached, literally shaking in his shoes, several officers could be seen dismounting and jogging over to the potential confrontation. But Reille was closer and faster. Taking the musket mounted eagle from the sergeant, he turned it towards himself and was surprised to find that its base bore the number one. Holding it close, he looked for discoloration around the digit, a sure sign that another had been removed, but found nothing. At this point, the officers of the 1st arrived to the great relief of the embarrassed sergeant who had only been acting under their orders to mount the "cuckoo."

"General Reille!" said Colonel Chevalier Cornebise as he stood at attention while his other officers saluted; Chevalier Cornebise's arm was in a makeshift sling.

"What is this?" Reille asked, his curiosity aroused. Having been a commander for many years, he knew how the men responded to the plight of their eagles and would gladly risk death to see them safely away from the enemy. This standard, he was sure from his examination, belonged to the 1st but he had to be certain. "Do you know the penalty for stealing the eagle of another regiment?"

Colonel Chevalier Cornebise knew the game was up. "Sir, we, I . . . the eagle is ours sir!"

The general waggled a finger in front of his face. "Your eagle was taken by the enemy an hour ago. Where did this one come from?"

"Our second battalion, sir."

"Your second battalion?" Reille questioned, his suspicions confirmed. In the early years of the Empire, each regiment had one eagle per battalion. After the campaign of 1809, with eagle administration in chaos, the Emperor had decided to do something about the multitude of eagles; but so bad was the confusion that his orders only came down in 1811! That year, he ordered all but one of the eagles in each regiment returned because it was too easy for the battalions to lose the expensive emblems and they provided excellent propaganda for the enemy when they were captured. Many regiments did not like this order one bit but Reille had thought that most of them had in fact done what they were told to do. Apparently, from what he held before him in his hands, some had not.

Reille scratched the accumulating stubble on his chin; the inappropriate and absurd thought went through his mind that he needed a shave. "You defied the Emperor's orders did you not colonel?"

Colonel Chevalier Cornebise, legion of honor winner and with the marks of at least two wounds visible on his face, looked down at his feet. "Yes, sir."

Other officers gathered round. "Sir! The men wish to be led

by their eagle. Let us attack the town behind our symbol," begged Captain Gran as he removed his cut open shako. "We can muster but a single battalion anyway, sir."

Reille relented. Unlike some men, this general knew the power of such sentiments and he was only too happy to have his men actually eager to attack the strongly held town. "Very well then, gentlemen, I propose to you a challenge. I will allow you to keep your abducted eagle if your men are the first into Ohain."

Chevalier Cornebise bit his lip. He knew from bitter experience how strong the Prussian defenses were and how difficult it would be to fulfill the general's wish for them breach the town first. Nevertheless, the men of the regiment, he knew, would want to give it a shot. For some reason, despite disasters like they had suffered before, it was not uncommon for soldiers to want to try again. This time, because of the concentrated artillery pieces and the presence of Pire's alert cavalry division, their chances were far better than they were when Jerome had launched the first attack. However, he still didn't like the odds. "We accept, sir."

The other officers of the regiment were pleased but apprehensive at the same time. Pride should be restored but would they be able to survive long enough to enjoy it? In the distance, a loud explosion could be heard in the town.

*   *   *

The French might have been a bit more confident had they been able to see into Steinmetz's mind. The Prussian commander did have a strong position but the pressure being exerted on the rest of the corps was such that his own level of confidence was fast dwindling. His greatest fear was that the French would break through the center and strike north before the army could withdraw from its position. His placement at Ohain therefore became even more critical but if reserves were drawn in from Pirch II's brigade then his own brigade could be in danger of being cut off. He had other problems as well. French howitzer fire had not only set the western part of the town on fire but had managed to strike an ammunition caisson that, when it exploded, caused a stampede of men and horses and set fire to another part of Ohain. Smoke threaded through the streets of the stricken town while the drifting smoke was obscuring the assembling French divisions. Perhaps his worst problem was the fact that many of his supporting guns were running low on ammunition, a problem aggravated by the French control of Chapelle St. Lambert and the ongoing cavalry fight in the army's center. Morale, on the other hand, was still high even though the infantry regiments had to evacuate parts of the barricades and buildings they had used to thwart Jerome's ill fated attack.

An aide rode up from General Zieten with bad news: Pirch II's brigade, the last large unit of the corps as yet unengaged, had been moved south to help sustain the Prussian line as Jagow's and Krafft's men lost their will to fight and began to fall back. This commitment stabilized the front but further isolated Steinmetz's men at Ohain. The general knew that the only infantry unit left to support him was Donnersmarck's single battalion and certainly that would do him no good at all. As for his own reserves, he held in hand sixteen guns to aid in counterattacks or to cover his own retreat.

Shaking his head, Steinmetz took another look through the smoke towards the west. In his veins he knew that the French would be back and this time with a vengeance. His men were already taking a heavy pounding from the massed French guns and most of his first positions had been burned or simply shattered by cannon balls. Despite all this, however, he knew his job and was determined to do it. If and when the French came, he would do his absolute best to turn them back again.

The wait was not a long one. Under the cover of madly firing artillery pieces which effectively made the Prussians wish they were somewhere else, the French divisions of Foy and Guilleminot began to advance down the hill. For the men of the 6th Division, the march brought back the very recent bad memories of their previous attempt and the mangled bodies laying across their approach path did nothing good for their morale; when tough Sergeant Habet of the 2nd Ligne tripped over the leg of a dying horse and collapsed cursing, however, that event did wonders for their spirit!

At least one band materialized to accompany the infantry, discreetly of course, and Pire's troopers alertly walked along the flank of the division deliberately tempting the Prussian horse to charge. Roder's horse, however, destined to cover the retreat and still smarting from Pire's attention from the last attack, seemed content to hold onto its captured eagle and wait out events. Thus, by combining his arms properly and attacking in like fashion, Reille, though he did not know it, had neutralized the superior Prussian cavalry and given himself a free hand to attack Ohain.

Prussian guns once more targeted the French infantry. Working carefully to avoid wasting ammunition, the guns crews of the II Corps performed well but found that their efforts were being diluted or even countered by the French. Durutte's attack had opened up the area in which the French could deploy and Jacquinot's cavalry had moved into this gap in loose formations to scout the enemy positions and threaten his lined up guns. Because of the shakiness of Jagow and Krafft, guns were replacing infantry in the effort to hold the French and this meant that they were pulled out of the supporting batteries on the other side of the Ohain brook thus robbing him of their help.

The French guns at last fell silent though the howitzers simply shifted their aim a bit higher and let fly farther east (one of the reasons artillerists are never trusted by infantry is that they hate having projectiles flying over their heads in case one should fall short). The French infantry divisions now came under artillery fire but, with the objective so tantalizingly close, they pushed ahead regardless towards the burning buildings. Practicality was indeed mixed with courage here; the commanders knew that the sooner they came into close contact with the enemy, the sooner the artillery would have to cease firing to avoid hitting their own men! Ignoring casualties which clearly were far less than before, the infantry gained momentum even if their columns became a little ragged in the process. This time, at forty yards there was no blinding volley or cavalry charge to stop them and, except for the occasional jager, the leading voltigeurs, of the 1st Ligne incidentally, pressed through the smoke and cleared the first broken barricades. Prussian troops, lined up behind a second obstacle, opened fire.

As expected, the Prussian guns also had to cease firing as the French entered the town in force and pushed down every street and alley they could find. With their ardor high, no enemy position was safe and Steinmetz found himself staring at his troops as they were ejected from most of the town in the first rush. Only in the northern and eastern sections did the fusilier battalion of Infantry Regiment #12 hang on and turn back every French attempt to throw them out. Steinmetz, shocked to say the least, was a little slow in reacting but once he did he moved decisively. Taking his intact second line, Infantry Regiment #24, he ordered them to attack the disorganized French while he set about getting his men into formation again.

Infantry Regiment #24 had been posted on the reverse slope that formed the center of Steinmetz's position. The town of Ohain, more or less a forward leaning "L" shaped group of buildings, was built along the ridge with open fields along the slopes leading towards the brook. The Prussian commander cleverly positioned his second line and his reserve artillery here to keep them out of view and therefore out of harm's way. In perfect order, the 24th felt out the French penetration and poured in strength ahead and around it.

The French had managed nothing more than a precarious toehold. Led by the suddenly fanatic 1st Ligne, they had penetrated deep into the heart of the Prussian position, catching units in the flank and generally dislodging the two defending regiments more from threat than fact. Getting confused in the town, at one point they fired on each other and actually headed in the wrong direction briefly before officers came to set them straight. With the billowing smoke and the normal frenzy of battle, this confusion was not uncommon. Additionally, the 6th Division had outstripped the 9th and assaulted on its own. Naturally, this disorganization did leave them open for a counter stroke and the Prussians were determined not to disappoint.

Led by the loose order fusilier battalion, the men of Infantry

Regiment #24 under Major von Laurens swiftly covered the ground to the town and caught the French milling about with no direction. Pouring forward in numbers, they proceeded to return the compliment to the 6th Division and force them to relinquish their hold on the town. The savagery of the contest could be seen during this counterattack as the Prussians gave no quarter to the repulsed French and bayoneted everyone they came across. The cry "No prisoners!" could be heard from a great many mouths. Advancing through the streets with speed, the Prussians harried the French out but then were stopped in turn by Colonel Tissot's 92nd Ligne as the latter covered the sudden retreat of Soye's brigade.

Like the Prussians the first time around, the French barely knew what had happened to them when they found themselves on the other side of the town again with their own officers cursing them and trying hard to get them back into a semblance of a formation before the enemy cavalry charged. The threat was a keen one and the infantry obeyed with speed but the Prussian cavalry did nothing to justify the fear and continued to watch Pire who was quite satisfied to watch right back. Guilleminot rode through his reforming troops and praised their courage but mentally noted that the 1st Brigade would need to lead the next assault with the help of Foy's first brigade which had not even come to grips when the French were thrown out. At least the smoke and general confusion did not clue in the Prussian artillery and draw their fire.

Just a bare fifteen minutes after the defeat of the first attack, the French were ready again; that they rallied so quickly was not only a testament to their discipline but also to the lack of any pursuit. Leading the way for the 6th Division was the 1st Legere which was entirely deployed in a skirmish formation to bring the enemy under fire and allow the assault columns to approach without molestation. Scampering ahead at a dead run, the light infantry, working in pairs where they could, got as close as possible to the smoldering ruins of the nearest houses and fought their way ahead. Their actions had the intended effect. Prussian fire was aimed at them and the defenders completely lost touch with the situation and the strength of the French divisions closing on the town. One group of light troops situated behind a low wall sighted a mounted Prussian officer doing a reconnaissance, Lieutenant colonel von Kleist of the 1st Westphalian Landwehr Regiment, and promptly killed him with a bullet to his breast. Others traded shots with their Prussian counterparts who were hiding mainly in the upper stories of the buildings to get a better angle for firing. Colonel Despans-Cubieres, encouraging his men in the line, was struck in the thigh by one such jager and had to be carried off the field.

Gauthier's 1st Brigade formed Foy's first line and his two regiments struck the Prussians hard and in very strong numbers. Concentrated and well led, the troops threw themselves at the hastily prepared defenses and breached them with speed and violence; sappers had been directly attached to the leading companies to help clear the way. Riding the tide of momentum that always shifts from the first attacker to the next in village fighting, the French swept the southern section of town with little effort but became fiercely engaged with the enemy for the rest. It was here that the men of Reille's corps came across the brutality that was such a trademark of the fighting thus far between the French and the Prussians. One problem for Blucher's men, however, was that Foy's and Guilleminot's men had not yet experienced this new formality of warfare and were consequently appalled at the murder of their comrades in the streets. Just as they were building a fervor, Steinmetz's latest though slightly delayed counterattack struck.

The Prussians, shaken and losing heart, took longer to reorganize this time around. Steinmetz showed his courage here amongst the battalions of Landwehr as he rode over and rallied the wavering regiment and brought it up to proper spirits. Supported by cannon fire from the two reserve batteries that had been held back, the reformed 1st Westphalian Landwehr Regiment, now commanded by Major von Lobenau, attacked up the slope towards the southern edge of town. Once more, the attackers were able to catch the defenders disorganized and, with the help of a pointed bayonet, they began to push them back. However, the French congealed. Using the opposite sides of the recently broken barricades, they volleyed back down the street and brought the Westphalians to a sudden and unexpected halt. All at once, a grenadier company was pouring down the lane and it was the Prussian turn to run. Elsewhere, the Prussians had made gains but this time the French had hung on and were holding fast to what they had captured. More buildings caught fire, the smoke became very thick and the fighting became confused.

Reille watched the battle with some concern but he hid it from his staff as the battle progressed. Thrown out once, his troops had recovered and counterattacked and now a seesaw battle was going on in the town itself. Feeling uneasy, he dispatched a message to Pire to aggressively cover any French withdrawal that might spark a major enemy counteroffensive. II Corps was gambling on taking Ohain in this attack and its corresponding reserves were not strong in number.

The commander of the French II Corps need not have worried, at least not as much. General Guilleminot, becoming more and more confident that the Prussian cavalry had no intention of interfering, ordered the 1st Ligne out of the reserve and back into the attack in an effort to catch the defenders between two fires. The single battalion regiment, second battalion eagle and all, attacked practically under the noses of Roder's men but the latter did nothing save to continue observing the approaching Pire. The inactivity of the enemy horse allowed this unit to slip along the Prussian right and strike where the defenders thought they were strong but in reality were not.

The 1st Ligne drove the fusilier battalion of Infantry Regiment #12 out of the corner of town and quickly occupied what buildings they could. Nearby, a roof of a house collapsed in flames causing the evacuation of several Prussian jagers who were quickly given new jobs as prisoners of war. The other prong of the 6th Division's attack, led by the 2nd Legere neatly cut off a house loaded with Prussians but found itself at a loss as to what to do with them. The Prussian counterattack told them to concentrate on matters at hand. With a line formed in the street and their men firing from open windows and doorways, the light infantry made the Prussian attack costly but the latter, driven by desperation, still managed to retake some buildings and bring the rest under a heavy if badly aimed fire. In some areas, visibility had fallen to a mere few yards and because of this Colonel Maigros of the 2nd Legere found himself standing in front of a group of Prussians one moment and running as fast as he could the next. Prussian and French alike were dressed in dark blue tunics or gray overcoats and the subsequent misidentifications just added to the odd nature of the fight. French infantry resorted to calling insults in French to neighboring units if any question was in doubt which helped to locate friendly troops who would almost always return the compliment with gusto.

General Gauthier reorganized his men as best he could under the circumstances and launched a series of local counterattacks against the Westphalians which succeeded in ejecting them again from the southern end of town. That done, he consolidated his position and waited for the next attack by the Prussians as he was convinced they would come back again to try and throw them out. In the center, the 6th Division was holding fast but it was the 1st Ligne, tucked away to the north that caused the most concern to the Prussians and soon enough unhinged their line. Fearing for their rear, the battalions of Infantry Regiment #12 fell back to do something about the flanking enemy when Maigros and the 2nd Legere advanced right after them to occupy the abandoned houses. That was the last straw. Convinced the French were in great numbers, the 12th retreated clear out of town and clustered amongst the artillery pieces along the slope.

Steinmetz knew the game was up. The Westphalians were broken, the 12th was demoralized and the 24th, reformed but weak, was not in any shape to attack again. French light infantry fire began to whistle around him while he made his last meaningful decision of the campaign. Gathering his thoughts, he ordered his men to pull back to a position at Doudremont with orders to reform and hold the area. Ohain had fallen.

CHAPTER 16

DEATH OF A PRUSSIAN ARMY

GÉNÉRAL de Division Mouton, Comte de Lobau and commander of the French VI Corps, recounts the final moments of the struggle in the woods at the end of the battle of Ohain.

By the beginning of the afternoon, my men were all but exhausted. Having fought for over six hours against a more numerous and determined enemy, I could not help but marvel at the fact that they were able to keep up their attacks and maintain their high morale. I was proud of my men and the role they had played in this famous victory.

At two in the afternoon, the troops of my opponent, General Bulow, were being pulled back out of the forest after the failure of their last counterattack in which General Simmer and General Subervie displayed such excellent judgment and courage. The soldiers of the VI Corps were too worn to pursue at first and I had to rely on General Donzelot's division from I Corps, a division that the Emperor had detached from that corps to give to me, to initiate the pursuit and support the cavalry attack in the center. Donzelot met with immediate success as General Hiller and his brigade were surrounded and forced to surrender. What a moment! After all the time we had spent on edge during the morning, we now had the greatest satisfaction imaginable and the thought entered my head that perhaps we could collect more prisoners since at least four Prussian brigades had been facing us in the forest.

I will always remember the struggle in that forest, the Bois de Paris, and know that it played such a vital role in the course of the battle. I will also remember that amongst the trees both sides waged a brave and honorable battle where the excesses of Ligny or Ohain did not occur. I lost one eagle during the fight, that of the 5th Legere, but I did have the immense satisfaction of being able to give it back to them when Bulow's corps laid down its arms. Like so many of my regiments, the 5th never gave up.

The French capture of Ohain made a bad situation worse for the Prussians. With enemy troops there and at Chapelle St. Lambert, only one escape route was available to them and this was quite a precarious one. Steinmetz, taking it upon himself to secure the area, sent his infantry to Doudremont and Chaud Brire while he asked Roder to send a brigade of cavalry to secure the crossing over the brook for the rest of the army, something the cavalry commander had already done. If nothing else, he would at least hold a bridgehead for the withdrawal.

It is a general rule that good news travels slowly but bad news moves like lightning. Almost before Steinmetz had assembled his rearguard, Pirch II, commander of the 2nd Infantry Brigade of the I Corps, got wind of what had happened and had informed General Zieten, something Steinmetz had not thought to do yet before he had organized his men. Naturally, Zieten was appalled at the disaster and sent rather original orders to retake the town. Ten minutes later, thinking a bit more realistically, he ordered Donnersmarck's battalion to the brook crossing sight to support Steinmetz's bridgehead and prepared to pull back his own battered brigades. Steinmetz, disgusted and busy, ignored the order to attack.

Gneisenau was the next ranking general to receive the news and, to his credit, he decided the battle was lost then and there. Clearly, with the town of Ohain taken by the enemy, the practicality of pulling back became more and more problematical and the sooner they could move the better things would go. Safe now from French cavalry roaming in their rear, he took action. First, he ordered Bose's intact brigade to be ready to march in order to cover the withdrawal from whichever direction they had to go. Second, he sent his fastest couriers to General Bulow with instructions to immediately pull back from the battle line every unit he could. Unfortunately, his third move could not be completed with a similar alacrity. Because of the swirling nature of the cavalry fight and the fact that Blucher was leading the horse, he could not locate the field marshal to tell him what was happening. The latter, involved in one charge or another and exhilarated with all of it, was difficult to spot in the mass of horse and thus the message was delayed. Courageous as the man was, the army as a whole was partly crippled as a result of his actions. Thankfully for Prussia, she possessed a man in the person of Gneisenau who would do his duty first before playing soldier and he continued controlling the army as the cavalry fight continued. Although both sides were exhausted, the struggle was not over yet.

The center of the Prussian army was thoroughly flattened and dusty as the hooves of so many thousands of horses crushed all plant life and pressed them into the dirt. In lower lying areas, water that had not yet drained could be seen again. Across this barren tapestry, the two sides gathered for the final attacks. A precarious balance had been reached between the veteran and skilled French and the more numerous and fanatic Prussian horse. Behind the lines, the blown pieces of both sides were attempting to rally but these troops would be too late to affect the decision that was about to be reached. As in most cavalry fights, the last side to receive timely reinforcements would almost certainly win the action.

Travers' brigade, swelled by the inclusion of the 10th Cuirassiers, had taken advantage of the enemy's confusion to canter quietly back to their own side of the lines and escape a possible trap; though worn, Travers' was not a man to leave his comrades in need. Indeed, he was ready to engage again if need be though it must be stated that his formation was probably in far better shape any of the other cuirassier units. Even so, both Kellermann and Milhaud were busy rallying their men behind the advancing infantry divisions just in case. As the French general looked around, he saw small clumps of enemy horse reorganizing across the field, especially around one leader, while the active French were showing a bold front with only a brigade of chasseurs. Near the forest, a large Prussian infantry brigade sat quietly in square just begging to be charged by his men and for a brief second he pondered if he should attack them. Coming to his senses, he called on his men to halt and face to the right. Domon needed their help, no matter how little or large that might be. What Travers could not see as he rode to align his men was the last force of cavalry from either side to reach the field.

General Lefebvre-Desnoettes, commander of the Imperial Guard Light Cavalry, rode at the head of his trotting regiments much like he had the day before. Splendidly dressed in his second uniform of the campaign, he felt that the Emperor was entrusting him with the victory they all so desperately needed. Coming up behind Domon's chasseurs, he saw them begin to move forward to engage the enemy. Immediately sensing an opportunity, he angled his lead regiment, the Guard Chasseurs, to the left in order to circle around the fight, flank it and then roll the whole thing up. In reserve, he left General Baron Colbert-Chabanais, commander of the Guard Lancers, behind Domon to shore up the line in case the chasseurs could not hold. Colbert, wearing the uniform of the "Red" Lancers, had his arm in a sling and a frown on his face; already wounded twice in the campaign, the old war-horse wanted to finish the business they had all started.

Blucher had by now rallied the pieces of a great many regiments but the horses of his troopers were nearly as blown as those of the French and the repeated repulses they had taken were very damaging to their morale. Still, he was able to put together a sizeable force and, after being tracked down and told of the disaster at Ohain, he gave these regiments to Prince Wilhelm and General Wahlen-Jurgass to lead against the French while he determined what could be done to stave off anything worse.

"The coward!" Blucher yelled about the smart Steinmetz. "Why did he abandon the town? Why does he not attack and recapture it?"

"I don't know, sir," was the quiet response. In this sort of mood none of the staff questioned the field marshal and they stayed respectfully out of the way. Major Huser, however, was different. Sticking like glue to Blucher's side, he watched with increasing concern as the old man's face contorted in a mixture of rage and sorrow. According to his commander's expression, he began to realize that they were losing the battle.

Trumpets sounded nearby and everyone in the small command group looked up to see what they indicated. To the west, the last great charge of the Prussian horse had begun against the French with the fate of the Prussian center riding on its outcome. The Prussian regiments, though numerous, were also very intermixed and it is difficult to say for certain exactly which units actually took part in more than squadron strength. Be that as it may, the first line force was a considerable one and Domon's troopers had their hands full as they met them halfway and forced a sword engagement. In short order, the chasseurs, outnumbered and nearly overwhelmed, fell back as the reserve regiment, the 4th Chasseurs, charged to help them out. For a moment the Prussians were held as Domon's troopers simply would not give ground. Wahlen-Jurgass, feeling the fight go stagnant, shifted a relatively intact uhlan regiment, the 2nd, to his left flank with orders to wheel against the French right and roll them up while his Landwehr regiments engaged from the front. Things went wrong from there. The battered 4th Kurmarck regiment broke and headed for the rear which forced Prince Wilhelm to commit another of his regiments, the questionable 1st Pommeranian, to fill the gap. Just as he did so, the 2nd Neumarck decided they had had enough as well and they fell back. Prussian morale, especially without Blucher in the ranks, was cracking. Sounding the recall, both sides fell back as Prince Wilhelm and General Wahlen-Jurgass redressed their unsteady ranks and prepared to renew the effort.

Domon, his division not only fighting splendidly but also for its life, knew that help was at hand. Seeing the arrival of more French horse, he had the word spread amongst his men that the time had come to defeat the enemy and drive them from the field. Exhausted but fortified, they cheered. What he had not counted on, however, was that one more force was about to make itself felt as well.

The last cavalry charge of the great fight began. With both sides moving at a trot only, it was as if the whole world had gone into slow motion. However, once cold steel was crossed, the fighting was especially savage. The 2nd Uhlans, ordered to flank the line again, moved out but stopped when their commander, Lieutenant colonel von Schmiedeberg, spotted a French flank attack in the distance and informed the general of what he had seen. Shocked, Wahlen-Jurgass ordered his only other recognizable regiment, the 3rd Hussars, to face off to the south while Prince Wilhelm attempted the flank attack on his end of the field. The chasseurs were spared for the moment.

The force that the Prussian colonel had seen was Travers' brigade. Despite the fact that his big horses were worn out, the aggressive commander of the unit had deemed it appropriate to support his fellow comrades by mounting whatever sort of attack he could muster from his regiments. In truth, Travers had the supreme luxury of being the only cuirassiers brigade that had been given time to rest and reorganize after he had sliced deep into the Prussian rear areas. Now that respite was paying off handsomely. Careful not to tire the already panting mounts, he gingerly led his regiments towards the Prussian flank knowing full well that the enemy commander would have to detach part of his force to face them or be rolled up by an armored fist. The 10th Cuirassiers, gallantly led by Colonel Lahuberdiere, formed the right of the line while the two smaller regiments, the 7th and 12th, formed the left in a strike force that appeared to be no larger than the size of one normal regiment! Nevertheless, the appearance of cuirassiers in attack formation on the flank of their attack was enough to draw notice and that would suffice for both sides.

Over on the opposite flank, the decision was about to be forced. Prince Wilhelm, having only barely consulted his colleague over tactics, did in fact attempt to attack the left of the French line. Shifting his own uhlan regiment, the 1st West Prussian, to the right of the line in a column of squadrons, he ordered them to wheel into the French rear and trap them between their two forces. Despite their alacrity, it was not to be. As the lancers followed their lead squadron around the Prussian right, the shock of their life was there to greet them.

The Guard Chasseurs of General Lefebvre-Desnoettes had arrived on to the scene. Sweeping wide around the left flank of Domon's hard fighting chasseurs at a dead run, they materialized on the field like a sudden apparition and threw the disconcerted Prussian uhlans into complete confusion. Penetrating their ranks with skill and speed, the elite French horse overwhelmed the enemy regiment, crushed its lead squadrons and chased the rest right off the field of battle.

The commander of this fine French regiment, General of division Baron Lallemand, not the same man as the artillery officer, was known for his reckless bravery and his cunning when given a chance. In Spain, he had seduced and trapped two British heavy cavalry regiments and smashed them in one fight, an action that had brought him great acclaim. Now, with his reputation stained the day before at Mont St. Jean, he was eager to get things right.

"Follow me! Follow me!" he yelled, waving his sword as the regiment burst through the lancers. Using the mighty momentum gathered from the rout of the lancers, Lallemand led the lead squadrons at the flank of the 1st Neumarck Landwehr Cavalry Regiment in the Prussian second line while his rear squadrons struck the flank of the 8th Hussars. Chasing right after the routed lancers, the chasseurs were able to catch the next Prussian formations as they reeled from their own routing comrades. In a moment, the whole Prussian right had collapsed with mounted fugitives riding like the devil to get away. One after the other, the right-hand regiments faltered in their fight and then broke for the rear as the Guard Chasseurs got behind them or even in their midst.

"Sound the charge!" yelled Travers as he saw the guard cavalry sweeping for the opposite flank. Even if they could only manage a trot, they had to reengage the enemy to help the other regiments. Spurring madly, the cuirassiers started to increase their speed from a walk all the way to a near gallop. Something special was in the air, a feeling that beckoned to both trooper and horse. It was if one last charge might not only win the battle but the whole campaign as well.

The Prussians that stood in the face of the onslaught fought fiercely but without support. Time and placement were not on their side. Whichever way they faced, French cavalry appeared on their flank or in their rear and it simply became too much for them to bear. Holding for a few moments, the last of the regular regiments either broke or retreated to the east leaving the center of the Prussian army in the hands of the French. Yelling in triumph, the French regiments ground to an exhausted halt and sagged over their horses. The battle was won.

*   *   *

The end of the cavalry fight gave the Prussian position to Napoleon but to him the victory was not complete until the enemy had actually been routed off the field. Cavalry cannot hold ground on their own, especially worn out regiments, and it would have to be for the infantry to make success into triumph. Unlike the Anglo-Dutch, the effective pinning attacks of Napoleon's army had drawn away the infantry covering the center of Blucher's army because the latter had trouble holding these heavy assaults. Thus, not only had the cavalry driven away the Prussian horse, it had also opened a large hole in the enemy line that could be advanced into by any available infantry. For the French, the foot soldiers were already on their way and in fact deep into the Prussian line.

Durutte's division was once again in the thick of the fighting as the soldiers faced off against elements of two Prussian brigades and several pieces of artillery. Out in the open finally and expected to hold the enemy, the division actually took its heaviest casualties of the day mainly due to the cannon fire directed at them. However, by heavily engaging the Prussians here, they prevented any shift of troops to patch the hole in the center which another French force was about to widen into infinity. Since the French cavalry had won the mid section of Blucher's line, no infantry unit could march to plug the gap created by the shuffle of forces made to hold the French. In this way, success secured success.

Marcognet's and Quiot's divisions, cheered by the rallying cavalry, marched past in perfect order with skirmishers deployed and the troops in the former division deployed in the mixed order just in case something called for a sudden change to the defensive. Because of space and terrain restraints, Quiot's troops were formed in columns on a regimental frontage that nonetheless gave the impression of vast numbers of infantry closing on Blucher's line. There was nothing to stop them. Marching across the debris of the Prussian gun line and onto the flattened earth that the cavalry had given them, they swept north of the Bois de Paris and behind Bulow's corps, part of which was still fighting Lobau in the woods. The strains of the "Marche Consulaire" echoed across the battlefield amidst the moans of the dying on the ground.

General Bulow's corps was hopelessly trapped. When Tippelskirch's men tried to deploy and march quietly to the west, the Guard Lancers of Colbert stopped the movement cold by threatening a bloody charge. Funck, the least engaged of all the commanders in the corps, also attempted to fall back but the alert Subervie, picking his way through a break in the forest, always stayed close enough to retard his progress and feign more aggressive measures. Still, there was nothing else the Prussians could do. Ordering his men to retreat, Bulow did manage to pull some of his troops out of the Bois de Paris and found, to his surprise, only a handful of French infantry in pursuit; Hiller's brigade, rapidly outflanked, was stuck where it was. The truth of the matter was that Lobau's men could barely move at all as they had been attacking all day and were all used up. Unfortunately, with the center belonging to French cavalry, and the bridge at Lasne cut, it would take a miracle to escape and Blucher's army was all out of miracles. To Bulow's dismay, French infantry in the form of Donzelot's division launched another attack and forced Hiller out of the forest and into the arms of Marcognet's passing division. Caught between two fires, the brigade laid down its arms and surrendered.

In the north, Zieten's men pushed for the bridge over the Ohain brook east of Chaud Brire where Roder's men were holding the crossing. As Steinmetz held the ridge against Reille who was dormant in Ohain, Donnersmarck's little force, already on its way, crossed over and reinforced his position. Zieten himself, directing the retreat from the brigade of Pirch II, pushed his remaining artillery pieces into position against Durutte with orders to hold the French for as long as possible so that the brigade of Jagow could fall back along with the remnants of Krafft's. Though the French did not know it, this threat was hollow in that the Prussians had very little ammunition left. The courageous artillerymen did as they were told and prepared to sacrifice their guns to gain time for their comrades. However, desertions began to increase at an alarming rate.

General Gneisenau, caught up in the growing rout, kept his head about him and did what he could to conduct as orderly a retreat as was possible under the circumstances. Around Chapelle St. Lambert, Prussian guns were in action against Gerard as the latter began to realize that his lack of orders was clearly a mistake and sought to change that by attacking across the brook. Along the Ohain, at least one usable ford was found, a deep one to be sure, just south of Chaud Brire itself and many troops, denied crossing near Ohain and thinking that the French had already cut off the other route, forced their way over despite everything. Packs, muskets, and typical army refuse lay at any point along the line of retreat with the wounded abandoned to the mercy of the enemy.

Zieten's bluff worked. Standing by their guns, the artillerists managed to slow the French enough to allow the infantry to disengage and a last blast of canister did stop Jacquinot's probe along the slopes. Bose's brigade, warned in time by Gneisenau to fall back, was well ahead of the game when French cavalry appeared to slow them up. However, along the way they picked up a cavalry unit of their own, the rallied remnants of the 6th Dragoons, and a few guns which was enough to stop the exhausted French from trying any last minute stunts to stop them. It must be said that around every formed unit was a flood of broken troops whose only thought was of escape. Thankfully for the solid retreating units, most of them tried to head for the bridge at Ohain which the French closed up after actually repulsing one Prussian attempt to seize it.

The Prussian army was disintegrating and no one knew this better than Field Marshal Blucher himself. Everywhere he saw, his valiant soldiers were in full retreat. Worn down so long by French infantry and artillery, the Prussian troops had taken all that they could and simply were at the end of their tether. Desperately, he rode amongst them to rally one battalion or another but even his best regiments were falling back under the pressure of the French attack. To his front, two divisions of fresh enemy troops were muscling their way behind the cavalry and not a man stood in their way. Looking about to do something akin to his actions at Ligny, Blucher came across the 2nd Pommeranian Landwehr Cavalry Regiment, a unit that Prince Wilhelm had been holding in reserve to cover the retreat of the infantry from Zieten's corps. Riding to their head, he unsheathed his curved saber and harangued them in the language they had come to expect from their commander.

"Soldiers of Prussia! The enemy must be thrown back! Follow me!" he cried out at the end of his short speech. The troops cheered wildly.

"Sound the charge!"

Thus started one of the most courageous if useless acts of the battle of Ohain. In fairness, it did sum up the Prussian general's approach to warfare and the spirit he was able to instill in his men. The charge would go down in history as "Von Kameke's Death Ride" after the colonel of the regiment. The 2nd Pommeranian Landwehr Cavalry Regiment, a unit of three squadrons that had more men than it had horses, was not amongst the finest of Prussia's cavalry but their final charge would seal the French victory at Ohain in a glorious if tragic way.

Blucher led the small force of less than three hundred men but, unlike the previous charges he had made, he aimed this blow at Marcognet's infantry division which was putting the finishing touch on the breakthrough in the center. What his thoughts were shall never be known but perhaps he believed in his mind that if he could stop or rout this French division, maybe Bulow's corps could extricate itself. Of course, he might not have been thinking that at all and was simply looking for a glorious way to die. Either way, the tiny regiment did not charge the nearer reforming French cavalry regiments and instead headed straight toward the mass of French infantry rhythmically advancing to the west.

Marcognet had angled slightly to the southwest as he advanced in order to make room for Quiot and also to more quickly entrap Bulow's men in the woods. His division, battered from the day before but now well fed and in good spirits, was at just over half its original strength but, as Napoleon knew, this problem of numbers would not be a factor. War being as much if not more a matter of psychology as reality, the Emperor guessed correctly that a fresh infantry unit advancing would be enough to induce the demoralized Prussians to either break or surrender. That he was right became clear when Hiller's brigade gave up the fight and was seen to be stacking their arms in the presence of Marcognet's men as the latter dropped off his weakest regiment, the unfortunate 45th Ligne, to take care of the Prussians. Napoleon, anticipating or at the very least hoping that Blucher's men would break, had already told Guyot to allow the Gendarmes d'Elite of the Imperial Guard to deploy forward and more easily take care of the prisoner situation. These men, called sarcastically the "Immortals" by the other regiments of the Imperial Guard because they seldom entered into pitched battles, did not constitute as major a concession as their name might suggest. The force, a single company under Captain Dyonnet, numbered at most one hundred men and had been guarding Napoleon's baggage most of the campaign, a necessary but tedious duty when the rest of the heavy cavalry was busily engaged in winning the battle. Here again, as Dyonnet led them forward to another thankless task, they were not too excited to ride past the limbering guns and up behind the marching infantry. Soon, their surprise would be total but their professionalism would be greater.

Drums beat forward the advancing French infantry and the

strains of music filtered overhead instead of the rain of cannon balls an hour before. Crunching over the flattened soil, it became evident to the officers of the two divisions that no enemy troops save those engaged with Marcognet on the right faced them. In the distance, a group of cavalry flying the French flag could be seen harrying the retreating Prussians but these men were too far off to be any worry and it appeared that the enemy was clearly in retreat everywhere on the field. D'Erlon, riding in the interval between Quiot and Marcognet, had already decided to have the latter division and that of Donzelot attack to the southwest in order to finish the encirclement of Bulow while Quiot continued ahead to support Durutte as he pressured Zieten's men into a hastier retreat. Voltigeurs ranged far and wide ahead of their parent units in search of targets but these were hard to come by and so they mostly gave relief to yet another wounded comrade when they came across one still on the ground. Prussian and French wounded lay moaning in pain scattered amongst the many dead horses. Old campaigners in the French light infantry knew what a stench the bodies would give the next day as the corpses ripened. Hurrying past, they went in search of more wounded.

The approach of the charging Prussian cavalry was an event that wasn't a surprise to the French until it was realized that they were in fact enemy troops. Having been held back by the woods north of the actual cavalry fight, the 2nd Pommeranian had been able to watch everything without so much as losing a horse to a misplaced musket shot. When the French went into pursuit mode, their horse, including the Guard Lancers, had shifted to the south and west leaving the small Prussian regiment to its own devices. Prince Wilhelm, wounded but still mounted, had wanted to save just one regiment intact to cover his own troops or, at the least, Zieten's if they should have to retreat. Blucher sabotaged this plan when he took hold of the regiment and aimed it at the French I Corps as it advanced like a sword into the heart of the Army of the Lower Rhine. Riding hard and with many inexperienced hands in the saddle, the charge quickly became as uncontrollable as it was unstoppable.

Officers of Marcognet's left hand regiment, the 21st Ligne, beheld the dark mass of Prussian horse and at first thought it was one of Domon's chasseur regiments retiring to reform. Colonel Carre, however, pointed out that they were moving with too much speed and, wanting to default on the side of caution, ordered his men into battalion squares, an act that saved his unit from being caught out of formation by the Prussian cavalry. Hearing the signal, the bewildered infantry did as they were told and their skeptical officers looked about to see what the cause of all the anxiety was about. Since the 2nd Pommeranian was so small and it was charging in from the left in growing disorder, it was difficult to see but the troops mechanically went about their change of formation and waited. They were soon enlightened. Scrambling voltigeurs came dashing back to the nearest infantry squares yelling that enemy cavalry was approaching. Sure enough, an odd wedge shape of straggling horse was closing quickly on the regiment.

Colonel Carre, like so many officers was wounded already and still commanding his regiment. Taking refuge with the 1st Battalion, he watched the proceedings with an almost incredulous eye. The enemy unit attacking them appeared so small that he wondered for a moment if a square really was necessary. "Aim for the horses!"

"Death to the French!" yelled Blucher as he hurried at the squares of the 21st Ligne. All around him the crazed troopers of the 2nd Pommeranian tried their best to keep up or pass him and the frenzy caused them to lose all formation. The unit, at one point in a double squadron front, had degenerated into a loose wedge of sorts with no order whatsoever and quite ripe for a counterattack by the French horse. The latter were not to be seen, however, since the cavalry action had shifted south and east by now and left the infantry on their own.

Marcognet's regiments came to a halt. The sudden and unexpected threat by the Prussian horse caused a flurry of belated activity; the battalions of the second line had barely finished forming their squares when the Prussians arrived on the scene. Little by little, the furiously charging horsemen careened at the squares only to have them vanish in solid flashes of gray smoke as the Charleville muskets discharged into their ranks. Blucher, charging behind some of the faster troopers including Colonel Kameke, was struck by a musket ball attributed to voltigeur Sergeant Dumolin from the 21st Ligne as he fell off his horse and landed at the feet of the furiously reloading French infantry. They soon knew someone of importance had fallen amidst them. Prussian troopers, those who followed up the shattered leading horsemen, slowed when they saw their beloved leader fall and, in a vain attempt to stop the French from recovering the body, they fought hand to hand with the defending French. Horses piled up at the spot where Blucher had fallen as the French simply discharged their muskets and pistols without aiming at the stalled enemy cavalry. Eventually, the remaining troopers swept on by but the 21st Ligne had emptied a great many saddles.

Colonel Kameke was amongst the few in the first ranks that had not been hit by French fire and he waved his men ahead to have a go at the next regiment in squares beyond the 21st Ligne. To be honest, the cavalry was boxed in and had no other place to go. Charging the 25th Ligne was about as fruitless as the previous attempt but every bit as furious. Swirling around the porcupine like French squares, the Prussians bravely tried everything they could to break up the formations and saber some of their hated enemies. The French ranks, however, remained disciplined and solid. Their fire killed and wounded more and more of the small regiment but not a man would say that the enemy did not at least possess magnificent élan that day.

Probably the most remarkable thing about the charge was that after penetrating into Marcognet's division, the Prussians had the gall to keep going right at the limbering French artillery in the distance. This, in part, can be attributed to the uncontrollable nature of the charge itself in that many of the troopers were in a very real sense only along for the ride that their crazed mounts were giving them. Once again, Colonel Kameke survived the fire of the French infantry and burst out the other side of the infantry division with woefully few troopers left; about half of the regiment had fallen already and the rest were scattered across the rear of Marcognet's men trying to find any escape valve that they could.

"To the guns!" Kameke yelled even though most of his men were out of earshot.

The artillerists of the grand battery were caught dumbfounded by the appearance of enemy cavalry. So bad was their surprise that they simply watched when they should have been setting up their pieces again. Arranged in a haphazard jumble of caissons and limbers, the guard and line cannoneers drew their pistols and sabers to at least fire back before they were overrun. Artillery caught limbered and unmoving was little better than a sitting duck. Thankfully for them, another force of cavalry had reached the field and, intent on vindication, had set their sights on the charging Prussians. These men, of course, were the men of the half squadron company of the Guard's elite gendarmes.

Captain Dyonnet, adjusting the strap on his tall bearskin cap, had watched from his horse the infantry pause and then change formations with only slight interest; infantry always moved around to better fit the terrain. When he noticed they were forming squares, he immediately stood in his stirrups to try and see what was happening. Could they actually be under attack by enemy cavalry? Where was the Guard cavalry and the rest of the horse? Sitting back down, he realized that his questions were silly and that the moment was his and his alone.

Dyonnet raised his hand to catch the attention of his troopers and stop them in line. Motioning to his trumpeter, he said, "Draw saber!"

Notes of harsh music resounded against the ears of the gendarmes and what they had waited for so long suddenly was becoming reality. Drawing their heavy swords, they knew they were going to use the edge instead of the flat side this time and their excitement was high. Never mind the fact that they numbered only one hundred men, the chance was here to erase all jokes and ribbing. In a way, they had their own battle to win.

"There they are! Forward!" yelled Dyonnet.

As the gendarmes lurched ahead, the first recognizable sign that a Prussian force larger than their own was coming could be seen but the troopers just fixed their icy glares on their targets and edged forward in their saddles in anticipation. The Prussians grew in proportion after every gallop of the horses and loomed numerous if scattered across the field. The gendarmes, formed in a single line to cover the greatest frontage, moved like an anvil of cold steel.

The difference in the cavalry units was fundamental and could well have represented a microcosm of the entire mounted fight. The French, less numerous but very professional, faced a stronger but less organized and less well led force of Prussians troopers, the classic case of quality versus quantity. The gendarmes, big troopers mounted on heavy horses, were part of the Imperial Guard and, despite the ribbing, were all the stronger for it. The Prussians, newly organized and with indifferent morale, had to rely solely on the possibility of overwhelming the French though, given the dispersed nature of the regiment, that would not be possible here. Neither side could outdo the other on bravery, however.

Dyonnet led his men at the tip of the Prussian attack as the surviving troopers of the latter escaped the clutches of the infantry and chased after their leader. Kameke, well ahead and with little thought to his own safety, was surrounded by perhaps a half dozen men when the French line came into view and then and there they knew that the game was up. The huge looking gendarmes, for all the world looking like the Grenadiers a cheval regiment, gave the impression of far larger numbers simply because of their own size, their hat size and their perfect formation. Nevertheless, having chosen their method of death, the Prussians did not shirk from it. Raising a loud cry, they went right after the gendarmes.

None of the six Prussians survived the contact with the gendarmes though Dyonnet had his bearskin cut almost in half by a saber stroke. Kameke himself fell to the expert swordsman trumpeter. It seemed that the French had simply swallowed the Prussians whole as the formation of the gendarmes remained very much intact. More and more Prussians showed up but with their leaders dead and the horses tiring, they began to lose heart. A slight retrograde movement by the last remaining mounted officer precipitated a retreat that quickly became a rout and, finally, after a wild charge into the heart of the French army, the 2nd Pommeranian Landwehr Cavalry went to the four winds and ceased to exist.

*　　*　　*

Blucher's charge, while the height of gallantry, changed little if anything in regards to the battle. Bulow's corps was still trapped, the more so since Lobau's men were filtering out of the forest, and French cavalry, careful not to engage too seriously, held the movements of his brigades to an arduous crawl. French horse artillery, reappearing in the wake of the cavalry fight, now resumed their task and began to pulverize the squares with a withering fire of canister that only made things worse. Huddled in a great mass east of the forest, Bulow could only hope for some saving move or a miracle from God. Neither came. As Marcognet reformed, the French advance began again and soon infantry battalions were taking the places of the exhausted cavalry regiments and throwing forward the forever irritating voltigeurs. The Prussian IV Corps, cramped into shattered squares, could do little else than take the carnage as it was delivered; casualties mounted quickly.

In the center of the line, Quiot's men had passed Marcognet and were nearing the forest from where the 2nd Pommeranian had launched their futile attack. Just as at Austerlitz, there were simply no troops in the area to immediately deal with the French attack but unlike that battle there was no Russian guard division available to counterattack the breakthrough. Rounding Durutte's right flank, the lead brigade of the division entered the wood while the voltigeurs started picking off what remained of the artillerists of Zieten's I Corps. Quiot's advance forced Zieten to fall back again and in a greater hurry now than before because his men would potentially have had to cut across the front of the French division if he didn't move. This retreat spurred Durutte again and his men, already sensing victory, hard fought like the day before, began to press the

Prussians from the front while Quiot slipped towards their flank and rear. It took everything Zieten had to hold them together and in this he did a credible and brave job; the I Corps, battered and bruised, retreated in fairly good order towards the bridge, the last obstacle. Zieten himself, a veteran of the battle of Vauchamps in 1814, knew what it was to be trapped by the French and saw no future in it. Learning from bitter experience, he was to be instrumental in the moments to follow.

By 2:30, the entire Prussian army was in retreat or trapped. Steinmetz stopped Reille's halfhearted attempt to attack Doudremont and from then on was the master of the ridge. Roder sent another brigade to cover the northerly route of withdrawal while his men helped fight the French IV Corps and tried to keep it away from the bridge over the Ohain brook. Donnersmarck was over the brook as was Pirch II and Jagow. Bose's men were holding the French bridgehead in check and fighting for as much time as they could to allow not only themselves but the remnants of the cavalry, Krafft's brigade and any other troops who could make it to cross as well. The Prussian army was beaten and there lay safety only in flight.

*　　*　　*

"All reports indicate that the enemy is in full retreat, sire," said Soult as he walked up to the Emperor who was pouring over his operational maps.

"When Gerard attacks," Napoleon said as he rubbed his hands together, "we shall cut their army in half."

Soult's eyes widened but he made no comment to this. Instead, he opened his notebook and began madly scribbling some orders for the commander of the IV Corps. "Yes, sire."

"We have caught at least four brigades of Prussian infantry around the forest," Napoleon continued. He stared at his chief of staff. "Just make sure that they stay caught when you send off those orders to Gerard."

Soult bit his lip and stared at his feet. "It shall be done, sire."

Napoleon could afford to be charitable to his uncomfortable

comrade as he knew from the reports filtering in from Lobau and d'Erlon that Bulow was hopelessly encircled, his back to the brook, and Zieten's men were being hard pressed against where Gerard would soon intervene. The Emperor felt confident that his new marshal would act accordingly and sever the last line of retreat for Blucher's ruined army. He would not be disappointed.

*　　*　　*

The long and bloody struggle was not over yet and it was Gerard, the future Duke of Lasne, and his corps at Chapelle St. Lambert that turned a memorable victory into an outstanding triumph along the lines of the battle of Friedland. Since the fall of the former town, Gerard had been the trump card that Napoleon could now play to cut off the Prussian retreat and essentially destroy the Prussian Army of the Lower Rhine. This statement presupposes that the Prussians would be able to recover from the hammering they had taken on June 19th. Gerard, sitting quietly at Chapelle St. Lambert with his reorganizing corps, had waited patiently while patrols combed the area looking for more wayward Prussians. These busy hussars captured a Prussian dispatch rider who told them that Thielemann's men were in full retreat from Wavre though so far Grouchy had not yet mounted a pursuit. Gerard himself received a message from the marshal in which he was told that the right wing would march to join with the main army as soon as it was possible and that Exelmans corps of cavalry would be fanning out to the east and north to locate Thielemann so that they would know of his whereabouts. French commanders cared little for surprises.

Gerard waited for orders to attack the passing enemy but none ever came. Clearly the Prussian army had been beaten in battle and the fact that they were marching to safety bothered him greatly. His chief of staff, Loriere, urged him to attack them and, after watching Pirch II's brigade march away, he made up his mind. Ordering up every gun save one company, he ordered them to fire on the passing enemy troops to the south while he attacked from the more northerly crossing; this was his original plan but, like most plans, it quickly changed. Gerard had already formed bridgeheads over the brook, a wise move, and from these he was able to push in more infantry and a few cavalry to try and expand on his design and distract the Prussians long enough for him to cut them off. General Pecheux's division was given the honor of leading the attack and he accepted proudly. The troops, rested and with a meal in their stomachs, rushed to their ranks; lowly soldiers they might be but after the last two days they would follow Gerard anywhere.

Pushing ahead recklessly, the French infantry filed over the bridge in such solid ranks that any Prussian artillery piece would have had a field day with them. But no shots bounced through them though as the artillerists had long since limbered and tried to get their guns away in the panic to get over the brook before the French seized the bridge. Expanding their grip on the left bank, the 30th Ligne fired a volley into the mass of vehicles in front of them and watched as horses fell over and men were crushed in the rout. Advancing more slowly, they caused the fugitives to run from them and right at the formed troops beyond them. These soldiers were members of Bose's brigade who had been making good progress and probably would have made it to the bridge had not Gerard taken things into his own hands. Now, enemy infantry were within musket range and the Prussians were forced into an engagement to drive the French back before their numbers grew too large enough to be able to handle.

Major General Bose watched in disgust the rout of his own army. Cavalry troopers, train vehicles, artillery caissons and every type of foot soldier pressed for the bridge without regard for anyone's safety. In fact, the fugitives tried to press in amongst his formed troops but they were forcibly driven off with musket butts and sharp bayonets. These desperate men slowed down the movements of everyone and the bridge over the Ohain was packed with soldiers who could only be considered non-combatants now. French fire, supported by well served artillery, was cutting them all to pieces.

The bridge itself was a nightmare. Artillery drivers, always a breed unto themselves, were doing their best to get their precious pieces over the brook and were running over any infantry and dismounted cavalrymen who were unfortunate enough to get in their way. Frustrated, the foot soldiers became more aggressive and they drove one gun team into the water with a crash. Prussian officers attempted to establish some order but most were ignored and one was even beaten unconscious and left for dead. General Zieten, safe on the opposite bank, was pulling together as many of his men as possible around Steinmetz when he saw what was happening and he gave orders to continue the process while he went to sort out the men at the bridge. Reaching there as a gun team swept by, he ordered his escorting cavalry from Roder's brigade to advance onto the bridge and regulate the flow of traffic if they could. Sadly, while French artillery rained down cannon balls on them, it took a few shots and several dead men to stop the stampede and regain some order. Bose's men were holding the French and there was time enough to do things right. Zieten posted his cavalry on both sides and left three trusted officers to make sure that the operation went smoothly. A Prussian medical officer asked permission to cross over and attend to the wounded. Zieten agreed.

Just south of the bridge, the last of the formed Prussian infantry still able to operate continued to engage Gerard's men as they crossed the brook. Their commander, Bose, well remembered the bridge scenario from the day before but was not inclined to let it bother him. He was the rearguard and he must hold the line open for the rest even if they were just fugitives now.

"Get your guns into action!" Bose yelled to the commander of the II Corps artillery. French guns were dominating the crossing area from the high ground around Chapelle St. Lambert and were enjoying a rare respite from the enemy artillery fire. Bose knew that he had to distract the French guns and help along movement at the bridge approach. "Suppress their fire!"

Lieutenant colonel Rohl shook his head. "But sir! We will be trapped!"

"Do it!" he ordered again. "Or we will all be trapped!"

The Prussian guns, fifteen cannon in two six pounder batteries, were from the II Corps covering force around Lasne that had been bombarding the French "actor" engineers playing at the bridge over the Lasne brook. Hoping for a quick escape over the brook, they would be denied and instead deployed for action near the French bridgehead. Finding a suitable spot, they came to a stop and wildly ran to unlimber the guns.

Bose's precaution was well taken. The French guns, operating in close cooperation with the infantry, were ordered to shut down this threat to the infantry attack. Gerard himself, positioned near the guns, watched this new development and immediately lamented the fact that the Prussians had any guns left to shoot with. Shaking off the wishful thought, he sent an order to General Vallin to throw forward a few squadrons of cavalry in loose order to threaten the artillerists and upset their intentions. As he sat back on his saddle, he told himself that it was very nice having superior troops in both quality and number.

"Fire!"

The first six pounder cannon roared to life as the Prussians retaliated against the French guns on the hill. This was followed in quick succession by the rest of the line and the mad dash to reload began. The French, forced to readjust their cannon, could not reply for a few minutes and had the insult of one cannon actually being struck and dismounted by a Prussian cannon ball that lodged directly into its muzzle. That gun captain swore heartily while his crew looked on bewildered; in a few seconds they were helping other crews short on men.

The frightened mob of refugees at the bridge had calmed down and the ordered presence of the saber wielding cavalry stabilized a dangerous situation. Men who had been recently dumped into the brook picked themselves out of the water and even the artillery drivers were noted to be more patient. Still, the pace was brisk while the morale of the troops remained a bit on the jittery side.

"Hurry!"

Bose's regulars had stopped the French infantry attack momentarily with a savage bayonet charge that tumbled the enemy back into his bridgehead. Jagers from Infantry Regiment #21 made life hot for the slightly overconfident men of Pecheux's division and Colonel Ramaud of the 30th Ligne was hit in the ear and tumbled from his horse. This setback caused a revision of the French plan and, inevitably, their solution was to send out a mass of skirmishers to swamp the jagers and then follow this up with another, more structured attack on the Prussian infantry. In addition, General Pecheux, commander of the 12th Infantry Division, requested fire support from the guns which had switched their fire to crush the Prussian cannon firing at them.

From the eastern bank, Gerard still watched the proceedings. He saw the repulse of Pecheux's first attack and the gathering of Vallin's men to the south. The idea was to divert Prussian attention to every angle and stretch them too thin to effectively react anywhere; the attack was to be the proper use of superior numbers. To this end, he had changed the plan to include Vichery's division attacking from the south to follow up the cavalry.

An aide rode up and reported to Loriere. "Sir, Lieutenant Messier from General Pajol."

Loriere, like most chiefs of staff, was somewhat comfortably sitting down. Gerard, not taking any chances, had ordered Pajol's men to scout virtually everywhere, including the south, to see if any Prussian troops were in the vicinity. Also, he wished to make as early a contact with Grouchy as he could, almost as if he was feeling a vital need to rejoin the wing he had tried so desperately to avoid. While this might seem strange, it makes sense when Gerard is viewed objectively as a professional. In the moment of their great triumph, no one wanted another Kulm to sour the wine. "Make your report."

The young aide, obviously new at this, straightened up. "General Pajol says that the Prussians we engaged have withdrawn well to the north and that there are no other enemy troops to the south or east. We have made contact with Marshal Grouchy's forces near Limale."

Loriere, having anticipated the result, handed the aide some more orders and his receipt and dismissed him. Walking up behind the standing Gerard with his order register in hand, he cleared his throat to get his superior's attention. "Sir, Pajol has reported our flanks clear. I have told him to keep his scouts deployed just in case and to bring the rest back and to concentrate them east of Chapelle."

Gerard nodded. "Good. I want our reserve artillery company deployed against the bridge. It is time to force the issue."

The French IV Corps, so quiet for so long, was in full gear. Pecheux's division, pressuring the enemy with skirmishers, was under orders not to attack until the cavalry reported it was ready to move and that delay would allow for the last company of artillery to deploy and begin to fire on the bridge. Whether they knew it or not, Bose's men were doomed.

Gun captain Weismuller covered his head as a heavy round shot struck the wheel of a nearby limber and sent splinters in all directions. "Sir," he yelled to Lieutenant colonel Rohl, "we just lost our fifth gun! We cannot hold!"

The Prussian officer had his orders. "Keep firing!"

Vallin's cavalry was ready. Moving out in ones and twos with their carbines loaded and held in their right hands, the horsemen dashed across the bridge and, led by a fearless captain, raced south along the bank of the brook to skirt around the infantry posted to cover the bridge. The latter, seeing the cavalry, formed square in a natural reaction and at once received a greeting from the French guns. Hauptmann Eckard shook his head, there was no winning this situation.

Behind the horse came more infantry of the IV Corps, this time from Vichery's 13th Infantry Division, and they ran ahead leading with their grenadiers to catch the Prussians in square. Reaching the end of the bridge, the grenadiers were met with a volley that slowed them but they returned the fire and fought forward to allow the rest of the division to come into play. Some men jumped over the side of the bridge and into the shallows in an effort to get past while the rest just pushed from the back to get on with the attack; no one ever likes being stuck in the middle of a crowded bridge.

The Prussians had already redeployed in a battalion mass formation, an allied tactic that had originated with the Austrians. This formation, a cross between a column and a square, allowed for greater freedom of movement and wider frontage while retaining at least a few of the benefits of being in a solid block against cavalry. The fire of the blocking battalion held the French at bay and kept the west bank of the southern bridgehead free for the moment of enemy infantry. Unfortunately, the 6th Hussar Regiment was loose on the Prussian side of the brook and was now taking pot shots at the artillery from behind them as well as panicking the remaining fugitives who were now beginning to really overcrowd the bridge approaches. The gunners, already harried by the French artillery, believed that they were being fired on by their own men and they waved and swore to have the fire stop. Puzzlingly, it increased.

"Now 30th! Forward!" yelled Colonel Ramaud as he led his men on foot.

At the north bridge, the French attacked with renewed vigor and succeeded in pushing back the Prussian infantry. More troops of the IV Corps swept onto the western bank and began to deploy. Bose's men rallied and counterattacked but too many of the enemy had gotten across and the latter held the bayonet toting Prussians at bay and repulsed their attack. Watching the enemy pour more and more men across the bridge, Bose knew he was losing the contest. When the troops retreated, he immediately ordered another attack to be mounted at once. If the French could be held back by constant attacks then maybe the damage could be minimized.

The guns of the IV Corps were wreaking havoc on the defenders as almost every shot fell and bounced exactly where it was supposed to. Along both bridgeheads, the positioned guns chose their targets, of which there were many, and placed their deadly missiles square into the midst of them. About the only problem the French gunners faced was the dwindling ammunition supply but Gerard had told them to just keep firing away to support the attacks and the ammunition be damned. The opportunity was now and should not be lost.

"Tell Oberstleutnant von Wienskowski he must fall back on

the bridge!" Bose said to an aide next to him. An instant later, the man's horse had been struck in the head by a crossing shot that left the animal only a bloody stump. Jumping off as the corpse collapsed, the aide wiped the blood from his face and shook his head; that was too close. Remounting another horse, he saluted and, with great relief, rode away.

Infantry Regiment #23, deployed in battalion masses, received their new orders with relief and, in a very deliberate fashion, they began to fall back towards the rest of the brigade defending the northern bridge. This behavior, however, was not acceptable to the French and they took up the slack at once though the professionalism shown by the Prussian regulars was steady and strong. Step by step, they fell back down the road heading north all the while keeping up a fierce if not well aimed fire. The threat was good enough to keep the French from getting too close. Unlike some of the other troops, these men still had a lot of fight in them and the local French commander saw no need to press the issue, yet.

Despite the fact that they were holding, barely at times, but holding, time was clearly running out for the Prussian brigade. As the wave of fugitives at last began to thin, Bose finally gave serious thought to his escape. He had done well in his bid to cover the retreat but perhaps he had done it too well as his own escape was now becoming problematical. At the moment, his troops were holding the French away from the vital bridge but he needed time to concentrate and allow for his more distant regiment to take over from where his men were fighting; it is apparent from this decision that he had already decided to give up the guns.

Bose brought up the 3rd Elbe Landwehr Regiment from the center of his position and ordered them to help attack the 30th Ligne which at last was trying to flex its muscles and get out of the bridgehead. It was a moment too late. The French 6th Hussars, the regiment whose squadrons had raced over the bridge before Pecheux had attacked, had been watching intently the action thus far and, after finally collecting all of their men into one area, had decided to intervene. Rallying together, they could see both the artillery pieces being abandoned by the enemy and the retreat by the regiments towards the bridge over the Ohain. French infantry was still being held in check and it seemed likely that the enemy would get away. Colonel Prince de Savoie-Carignan decided to commit his men to an attack, one that would hopefully slow the Prussians and relieve pressure on the French bridgeheads.

On command, the 6th Hussars drew their curved sabers and began to advance, their colonel angling the regiment towards the bridge over the Ohain brook in order to stop the movements of the Prussians. On the French side of the brook, General Baltus de Pouilly recognized what was happening and ordered his men to cease fire; this was very much to his credit as no one had any idea that the 6th Hussars would mount an attack of any sort. When Gerard questioned the decision when he rode up, his artillery commander shrugged and pointed down the slope. The commander of the IV Corps didn't say anything either and both men simply watched to see what would happen.

The Prussian infantry abruptly came to a halt as the command to form squares was signaled between the regiments. With French horse controlling the whole Prussian center, it was not unreasonable to assume that a strong force of enemy cavalry might put in an appearance and they were taking no chances, not when they were so close to escaping. Roder's cavalry still had a squadron of troops on the south side but they remained idle in accordance to their orders to hold their position; Pire at this time was starting to threaten Roder's command and the latter had forbade any movement of horse south of the brook. This order would prove costly for the Prussians.

The battalion masses formed square easily but, as the cavalry approached, they were rooted to the ground and all retrograde movement ceased which was exactly what the French needed. Spared the blistering fire from these Prussian units, they now returned the favor on the enemy and mercilessly shot apart the defenders while at the same time slipping up the far bank of the brook to get around the enemy. Freed to move again, the French lost no time in pushing over the northern bridge and establishing a very strong presence between the bridge and the 21st. The race was lost.

French hussars came to the squares and, like their infantry predecessors, they were met by hot fire from the formations and were broken up. Individually racing between the solid hedgehogs, Vallin's cavalry could do nothing to break them and their casualties were fairly heavy. However, they had done their job. When at last they retreated, the French were between Bose and safety with the bridge over the Ohain in their hands. French artillery fire resumed and the infantry began to surround the enemy units. Pecheux's men continued to pour across the Lasne bridges while Vichery formed a semi circle from his bridge to the crossing site on the Ohain. There was nowhere to go.

*　　*　　*

For all intents and purposes, the battle of Ohain was over. Gerard's IV Corps sealed the final escape route available to the Prussians and, though many tried to escape by swimming over the brooks, the vast majority of the troops were compelled to lay down their arms and surrender. The last group left fighting on the field was from Bulow's command and he was completely surrounded by the French army. Lobau's men had him sealed off from the south and west, d'Erlon's troops and the cavalry covered the north, and the east was blocked by the Lasne brook. Even there, however, Pajol's light cavalry were watching and they certainly were not adverse to fish for swimming Prussians.

General Bulow, his head wounded by a voltigeurs bullet and wrapped in a bandage, was still in command of his men and he brought them together tighter and tighter as the French pressed them from every side. Like the Roman infantry at Adrianople in 379 A.D., they could still fight but they faced certain annihilation versus an enemy that was hurriedly hauling up guns to shatter their formations. Moreover, French cavalry was clearly moving between them and any form of safety that could be offered by the brook and this alone meant that even a mass charge to the water's edge would do him no good as the soldiers would be massacred on the spot by the charging horse. Faced with this dilemma but refusing to stop hoping for a miracle, he held on even though the bulk of his men were exhausted and desperately thirsty.

Napoleon had moved ahead after the Prussian death ride had finished and, after receiving a sudden battery of reports from every commander across the field, he knew that they had truly won the battle. The Prussians, split in two and trapped between the brooks, had been shattered and driven apart by his victorious army with the result that part of the army was retreating northwards and the other was trapped in a pocket just east of the Bois de Paris. Ordering forward every company of horse artillery still able to move, including that of the Imperial Guard, he instructed them to finish the job against Bulow's men just as the artillery had finished the battle against the Russians and Austrians at Austerlitz. Suddenly, he felt ten years younger.

"Sire," Soult was heard to say as they walked their horses forward towards the former Prussian gun line. Motioning towards the path of the brook in the distance that blocked the escape of the Prussian corps, he said, "It is a second Friedland."

The Emperor, barely able to resist a show of bravado, contented himself with a simple grunt and the comment, "It is a first Ohain."

The cannon of the French horse companies quickly deployed around the large Prussian pocket and added their special touch to the terrible actions taking place at this late point in the battle. Deploying in gaps between regiments, the artillery pieces quickly made a bad situation worse. Literally blowing holes in the opposition who could not effectively fire back, the Prussians at last began to crack and run away; sadly for them, there was nowhere to run to. Sighting some fugitives, a squadron of Subervie's cavalry simply moved forward and the entire group, perhaps a battalion worth, raised their arms and surrendered. Soon, whole formed units were seen by the French doing the same thing and no enemy officer doing anything to stop them. Locked in without a place to fight, the troops passed the word that the situation was hopeless.

"We are surrounded!"

"Blucher is dead!"

A trickle at first, the battered troops began to drop their fouled arms in place and cower on the ground. Whole ranks performed the same motion and the signal was unmistakable to the French who had cornered them. Victory.

"Hold your fire!" was the order passed down the French ranks. A last, unfortunate blast of canister ripped from an artillery company but surprisingly the retort of muskets seemed to fall away almost simultaneously across the entire front. The common soldiers, uncertain and apprehensive, stared at each other from musket range with their guns lowered but still at the ready. For both sides, it was an emotional moment. Having been locked in combat most of the day, the men could only behold their enemies and simply remain quiet. Bulow, having given the order at last, coaxed his horse forward to give up his own sword.

Cautiously, officers from the corps of d'Erlon and Lobau stepped out of their ranks holding pistols by their side and their swords in the air. Prussian officers and some sergeants did the same and soon more senior officers were making their way forward. Lobau, not wishing to miss the final act of the battle, had mounted for the first time that day and was sitting erect behind the men of the 5th Legere who were eager to see if their eagle was still amongst the troops of Bulow's corps.

An aide rode out from the Prussian ranks. Speaking in a harsh French, he asked where the commanding general of the VI Corps was. All eyes turned to Lobau and, despite his natural aversion to notoriety, he coaxed his horse forward between the silent lines of troops. General Bulow broke out of his own ranks and, sword in hand, approached his most worthy foe. Lobau's men had fought with exceptional dexterity and courage against his larger host and, in the Prussian commander's opinion, had won the day for Napoleon.

Without uttering a word, the grimy face of the Prussian general was enough to show his great if grudging respect to Lobau and, hopefully in return, receive good terms for his troops; the French could still crush them if they so wished. The Prussian army had fought savagely throughout the campaign and Bulow, though he himself had acted correctly, felt that certain feelings of animosity might yet surface and cause the French to return the brutality, an all too common reaction in war. Strangely, the fighting in the forest had been exceptionally clean and these tired but victorious French troops did not seem inclined to want to shoot them all but instead seemed relaxed and curious. Stopping his horse about a foot from Lobau, Bulow unsheathed his sword but the former aide de camp would have none of it. Instead, he raised his hand in a clear motion to stop the enemy general and said, "It would please me if you kept your sword, sir."

Bulow nodded slowly and thanked him. With a heavy heart, his head sagged to his chest but he was man enough to steel himself and look Lobau in the eye when he made his final command statement. "Let us end this slaughter, general. My men and I will accept any terms you wish to give."

Lobau nodded but remained surprisingly cool. "All that is required of you, sir, is the surrender of your arms and the continuance of your good will. I hope your internment will not be a long one."

Bulow bowed as best he could on his saddle. "You do me honor, sir."

*　　*　　*

The surrender of Bulow's forces marked the end of the battle of Ohain. The French, exhausted after two solid days of battle, fell to their feet at the spot where they had finished their advances and set about bivouacking on the battlefield. All around, the dead and dying lay in jumbled piles of twisted flesh and spilled blood, each body marking a distinct phase of the battle. Napoleon rode amongst his troops with his staff as he always did after a battle and ordered markers placed by the wounded and in general began the horrible process of saving whoever could be saved and saying good-bye to those that could not. Bodies of men and horses littered the ground everywhere and the debris of a defeated army, too, was scattered liberally across the battlefield. Shakos, 1809 muskets, backpacks, cartridge boxes and even whole uniforms were left on the ground in such large numbers that they appeared like trails of cloth leading to the bridge over the Ohain. Wrecked artillery pieces and abandoned caissons marked the various stages of the action while the growing pile of captured standards was becoming quite large.

Napoleon at first had only a vague idea as to how many of the enemy brigades had been captured but the colors taken by his men grew after every passing moment. Bulow's men, parading past the VI Corps, dropped off their muskets in neat piles and then, reluctantly, lowered their standards so that they could be gathered up by the victorious French army. Soult was heard to mumble that the Invalides did not have sufficient room for all the flags captured these last two days. The final Prussian standard bearer, a huge swarthy character with a large mustache, failed to produce the usual Prussian cross and black eagle standard. Instead, perhaps with even greater reluctance, he brought forth a shot torn French flag surmounted by a golden eagle.

"There it is!" cried the men of the 5th Legere as they saw their revered standard being handed over to a French officer. All at once, the light infantrymen collected around the bewildered major and quickly liberated the tricolor from him. Spreading the flag just in case, they could see that it had stitched on it the a very definite name: *L'EMPEREUR NAPOLEON AU 5me REGIMENT D'INFANTERIE LEGERE.* The men gave a great sigh of relief. Their eagle had come home.

The trophies captured by the Army of the North were numerous. Large numbers of prisoners, cannon, standards and other military paraphernalia were in their hands. Leaving with only their able bodied soldiers, the Prussian army left behind them thousands of wounded men and quite a few artillery pieces given up when their ammunition had run out. The French, too, had suffered, though obviously not as badly, but they were too battered and tired to even try and mount a major pursuit. Instead, Pire's virtually unengaged men were loosed to chase Zieten but Roder, in a rare display of strength and imagination, managed to slow them enough to let the infantry get on their way. Pire, not too concerned about his repulse, knew that more forces would be arriving to bolster him so he did not press the enemy too harshly; Grouchy himself would be conducting the operation before long and certainly he would know what to do. Thus settled, the cavalry general remained in contact but gave the weary Prussians a chance to march in peace; they would need the rest.

Napoleon's ambulances made their way over the field accompanied by the moans and gasps of the men dying on the ground. The battle of Ohain, fought on a constricted front with concentrated armies, demonstrated the disaster of armed conflict quite vividly as in such a narrow area there were piled thousands of wounded men many of whom would die soon right where they lay. As the sun set that day, the Emperor walked through the Bois de Paris and onto the center of the battlefield where he stood quietly for some minutes without speaking a word. Ultimately, this field of battle was the price Europe had to pay to see his return come to fruition and the thought saddened him greatly. After so many years of conflict, it was hard not to wish for peace.

*   *   *

French losses in the battle of Ohain totaled upwards of 9,000 men, a sizeable percentage given the weak strength of the Napoleonic army. Having engaged with approximately 56,000 men, the loss rate was just over 16%. These losses, coupled with the losses suffered the day before, clearly hurt the Army of the North in terms of strength but, more importantly, the two battles had restored the luster and pride of the French army. Ever since the dark days of 1814, the army had labored under the threat of treason from the high officers and a general lack of confidence amongst the private soldiers. During the campaign, despite glory won early on at Ligny, the specter of disaster had been with them until the light of victory at Mont St. Jean began to reverse the process and fix the damage already done. Ohain itself had provided the final framework for this recovery as for a few hours in the morning the situation had been very much touch and go; the fact that the army needed to march hard to rescue Lobau's endangered VI Corps just made the fighting that much more urgent and, since it was ultimately successful, that much more satisfying. However, for now, the soldiers of France were content to sleep on the field of honor and did not bother to worry about anything beyond that; good stories, some real some not, would emerge at a later date.

Blucher's Prussian Army of the Lower Rhine was quite a different story. Torn in half by the French cavalry and savaged all day by accurate French artillery, they had suffered terribly and their casualties prove the case. Blucher's army had not only lost their commanding general but had nearly 16,000 casualties and 22,000 men taken prisoner. Desertion as well would take its toll on this army and Prussia would find itself without a field force of any real strength left in western Europe. The Prussian army had fought stoutly but their poor choice of position and lack of real command control hurt them badly as they not only failed to use their initially overwhelming numbers to advantage but they also failed to move decisively when it became clear that the French were gathering strength and that the initial attack had been repulsed. Now, only a shattered fragment of Blucher's proud army was left and it was running for the east as fast as it could move.

In the end, the fundamental differences between the French and Prussian armies would weigh heavily in the outcome of the battle. The French infantry, fortified by their victory at Mont St. Jean and confident in their assumed superiority over the Prussians, had proven far more tactically flexible than their enemies on the field and had been able to turn back greater numbers on many occasions. The Prussians, having put together a sensible set of instructions that emphasized flexibility in combat, simply did not have the officers or noncoms to properly implement this relatively new manual of arms and even less money to complete their organizations. Prussian cavalry was used with little imagination, organized as they were along the lines of the French all arms divisions that had proven so cumbersome earlier during the wars. With their cavalry brigades tied to the infantry, no true strike force of horse was ever available or conceived; this was a decision that would put a greater emphasis on battles of attrition rather than one of concentrated aggression as exercised by Napoleon. That the Prussians were able to mass a number of their brigades at Ohain was simply a fortunate coincidence even though the battle of Ligny should have taught them better. The last major arm, the artillery, had not yet reached its true striking power yet and could be overcome by smaller numbers of exceptionally efficient French cannon. However, there is no real shame in not being able to match the French guns as the latter were the finest in the world and had been for many years. Thus, for Blucher's army to win battles, it had to either overwhelm its enemy or defeat him in a battle of position. At Ohain as at Ligny, this process would fail with heavy casualties.

The Napoleonic victory at Ohain had firmly reestablished the pride and confidence the French soldier looked for and expected in his superiors. Count Lobau, the one time aide de camp, had faced off a very large Prussian corps and had held it at bay like Lannes at Friedland in 1807 against the Russians. The Bois de Paris, his very own battleground, had so stalled and interfered with the Prussians that the latter were never able to fully deploy their heavy strength. The tenacity of he and his men thus made up for the lack of numbers of the French VI Corps. However, this explanation does not do justice to the excellent tactical handling of the French forces in and around the forest nor does it put at least some credit into the hands of the French command system. Napoleon expected his commanders to be aggressive and to take opportunities as they presented themselves. This tendency amongst his senior officers became so commonplace that when one commander failed to do these aggressive moves, like Bernadotte at Jena and Wagram, it showed up like a sore thumb. General Simmer's counterattack in the face of the mighty enemy assault seems so contrary to general sense at first sight that it is easy to overlook it. However, this timely strike, done in brilliant style, may well have saved the VI Corps from destruction and the Army of the North from a reverse early on. Likewise, General Donzelot's march across the field and into the gap in the French line finished the Prussians and forced them onto the defensive even as they still had numerical superiority. Just as at Ligny, the organizational structure of the French army would give them strength beyond mere numbers.

For the other senior officers of the French army, the battle of Ohain would provide the opportunity to make up for their mistakes at Mont St. Jean and allow their true competence to show through. General d'Erlon, his troops scattered from the British cavalry charge the previous day, had made certain that his men would be reorganized and ready for this battle. His advance into the center of the Prussian position with Durutte, Quiot and Marcognet was accomplished without a serious flaw and sealed the victory for the French army. Durutte, as usual, proved to be a very tough nut to crack and his division took the most casualties of all the divisions in the I Corps. During the fight, he had successfully engaged two enemy infantry brigades and their artillery, all troops that could have been better used to shore up the center of the enemy army. Even Marshal Soult, the lackluster and sarcastic chief of staff, had made a comeback of sorts as the seriousness of the situation the day before made him reevaluate his position and try to do what was expected of him. Thankfully, his few mistakes did not cost the French as badly as they had before and the opportunism of Gerard fixed the most crucial one before it could become worse. This latter commander, while not doing anything quite as spectacular as the day before, had carried out his orders with imagination and, in the end, capped off a brilliant performance by the whole French army. Truly, the battle of Ohain would be one for the record books.

In many ways, Ohain was a melting pot battle in that the French army had gone into it in separate parts and had come out of it as one whole. The regiments gained pride in themselves and their sometimes new officers while the talk of treason quieted down to something less than a murmur. About the only words spoken on that subject were about Count Bourmont and how any real Frenchman would shoot him on sight if he were stupid enough to come back to France. Around the bivouac fire that night, the soldiers sat and pondered the brilliance of being alive after an action before dozing off to sleep under the stars. Aside from scouts, spies and the occasional messenger, the French army fell into a deep slumber that night right on the battlefield. No one realized that they had just won the campaign.

The action at Ohain firmly reestablished the aura of invincibility that Napoleon had enjoyed for so long during the ten years since Austerlitz. Having put together a brilliant strategic plan in the repeated form of his first Italian campaign and then carrying it through like he had in 1796, he could feel the great surge in strength and pride that his accomplishment fully warranted. Paris would be morally fortified by the news of the great victories on the successive days and all of his political opponents would cower under their slimy rocks where they would have to hide until another time; he did, however, still have plans for the treasonous Fouche. Davout, the "Iron Marshal," would now be able to rest easier and, without looking over his shoulder so often, he could focus on the job he had at hand. At the moment, with conscripts pouring into the regimental depots of the army, he had 170,000 replacements available to make good the losses suffered by the army thus far. How times had changed! Just five days before, the outlook for France had appeared dark at best. Now, with night falling on the battlefield, the tremors of Mont St. Jean and Ohain began to radiate out to the capitals of all the monarchies involved in the Seventh Coalition. At least one government would not survive the month.

Napoleon's handling of the battle of Ohain, unlike Mont St. Jean, was firm and decisive. Never far away from the point of action, the Emperor had taken himself out of his exhausted stupor and had forced himself to follow through for his beloved France. On this day, the French army had started marching very early in the morning in response to the critical situation that Napoleon knew they were in. This recognition of the urgent situation would carry through for both the Emperor and his army the entire day of Ohain. Both would come out better for it.

Late that night, Napoleon sat on the floor of the farmhouse that he had made his headquarters. The battle over, he could afford to relax for a moment and ponder what the future held for him. Would his wishes come true? Would Austria make peace and, perhaps just as important personally, would they return his son to his arms? Taking in a deep breath, he listened as the Old Guard Grenadiers acting as his escort went quietly through the changing of the guard. The sounds gave him confidence and brought a smile to his face. In a very real way he was with his family and heaven only knew that these men would certainly not turn against him.

Napoleon slid the map of Alsace to his knee and leaned closer to it. Pouring over his maps was a favorite and relaxing activity and comparing them to the latest information gathered from the frontiers he was able to get a better grasp of time and distance. Making some mental notes, he began to formulate his next series of actions that would quickly remove the Army of the North from Belgium and place it in a matter of days in central France. The Austrians, he mused, would have a thing or two to worry about then if they crossed the border! However, Napoleon was fairly certain that once Schwarzenberg heard about the twin battles, he would think better of invading France. He heard a knock from outside.

Soult opened the door and entered as the Emperor grunted his assent. "General, er, Maréchal Gerard sends his compliments and requests orders for operations tomorrow."

Napoleon looked up, the weary bags under his eyes quite evident. He had made this deserving general the twenty seventh Marshal of France for his excellent service during the campaign. "Gerard, eh? He is a good soldier. Come here."

As the chief of staff approached, the Emperor motioned for him to come down to the floor. With a slight hesitation, he did, though only on one knee. "Do we begin the pursuit in the morning, sire?"

Napoleon rubbed his left eye with his finger and fished out something that was bothering him. He nodded as he blinked several times in a row. "Yes, Soult. Grouchy will take control of Exelmans directly and will block Blucher's remnants from joining Kleist's corps which is still near the Moselle. We'll let Thielemann go." He paused. "Old Blucher. The most implacable of my enemies and now he is dead. Be sure he is buried with honor."

Soult nodded in agreement. If there ever was someone who

had done everything in his power to challenge them, it was the Prussian commander. With his death, the greatest driving force aside from English gold was gone from the allied armies. "I have seen to it personally already, sire. General Bulow told me to give you his compliments and gratitude for the act."

Napoleon looked up at his marshal, a look of sarcasm on his face. "He thought I would chop him into small pieces and eat him perhaps?" He chuckled. "The monarchs of Europe always are surprised by my honor yet think nothing of violating their own peace treaties. I suppose they are above such laws."

"We are still considered the upstarts of the continent, sire," Soult said with a shrug. "They will probably continue to do as they please."

Napoleon shook his head. "Not this time. Think, Soult, both Blucher's and Wellington's armies have been destroyed. Belgium will join us again. England's government will fall shortly and then the payroll of this whole coalition against us will evaporate. The Austrians and Russians have no zeal when they are penniless. Without England, they are nothing I tell you, nothing! Who will stand against us now?"

The chief of staff considered. "Even if the English government does hang on, Schwarzenberg will not cross the Rhine if he hears about our victory and the Russians will be too weak to challenge us alone on our own soil." He stopped, his mind thinking the facts over. "We may have won the campaign, sire."

CHAPTER 17

THE AFTERMATH OF THE BATTLE

Baron Larrey, the man Napoleon called the most virtuous in the world, gives a picture of the end of the battle at Ohain through the eyes of a man of medicine rather than of a soldier.

What a tumult we had been through! To say that the last two days were anything but exciting and terrible for all of us would not give a true picture of what we had endured throughout this long fight. Our army had been victorious in two famous fights and I was as pleased about this as any man. However, because of the intensity of the fighting, my medical troops were overwhelmed in every respect despite the heroic presence of many medical staff of the English army. The Emperor had made it clear that all soldiers, regardless of which army, should be adequately cared for and this placed an enormous strain on the already limited resources we had to call upon within the army. After the battle on the eighteenth, I had practically taken over the village of Mont St. Jean which I garrisoned with wounded men from every army. All buildings in the area were stripped for mattresses, alcohol, food and any other form of comfort available but in the end the wounded were still far too numerous for our meager resources. Regrettably, many men were left without any aid on the field of battle itself though thankfully our gendarmes did their jobs dutifully and more than once chased off would be murderers and thieves. That night, many wounded men died from exposure and lack of care.

The morning of the nineteenth brought more of the same as the battle was renewed with vigor between ourselves and the Prussians. Wounded men began to stream back in large numbers and I had no place to put them. Our salvation that day came in the form of the residents of the local and neighboring villages who arrived to give succor and compassion to the multitude of wounded men. Their help was a true blessing and I fully credit them with the high rate of recovery we were able to give our patients, something I know would not have been possible otherwise. These people performed prodigies of service as they helped collect and then fed virtually every wounded man before the night had fallen. In war, the suffering is so great that many times one loses sight of normal human charity; when such an event occurs, it stays with you always. Such was the case here in Belgium in 1815.

Napoleon's victories at Mont St. Jean and Ohain shook the world of the allied Seventh Coalition and brought it to its knees. The Emperor's intention had been realized fully and his obvious foresight had borne excellent fruit. Whatever allied troops that had crossed the Rhine into France were found to be scuttling home when they heard the news and French nighttime guerrillas were harrying them every step of the way. Operations on the other fronts aside from Belgium quickly came to a head with resolution generally on the horizon.

The Vendee district of France, the traditional area in the country where savage small scale civil wars took place, had risen up to challenge the Emperor in the name of the Bourbons. However, years of fair Napoleonic rule and cowardly Bourbon presence had taken their toll and when the revolt began, it did not attract as many followers as it had during the beginning of the French revolution. Without a hundred thousand man army to protect him, no Bourbon prince would dare land on shore to march with his subjects against the veteran regulars waiting for them and this fact always did wonders, bad ones, to their morale. After a few small engagements, the French under Lamarque managed to mouse trap the Vendeen army and utterly destroy it in battle on June

16th. This action effectively ended all thought of insurrection and really made the leaders in the Vendee wonder why they kept spilling their blood for someone who never even bothered to come ashore. In quick manner, the revolt was over.

On Marshal Suchet's front, the Piedmont frontier, this commander of France found himself heavily outnumbered and certain to be overwhelmed if he sat tight where he was. Suchet's army, the Army of the Alps, was made up of regular and National Guard troops and numbered just over 23,000 men. His opponent, General Frimont, commanded over 60,000 men. In early June, Suchet sent off 7,000 men to General Lecourbe and his Jura army to help the odds there even though they placed him in an even tighter spot. Characteristically, Suchet, the only commander to have won his baton in Spain, decided to attack, the one sure way to pin General Frimont's Austro-Piedmontese army in place and force him to pay attention to the small French force. Striking at many places at once, Suchet successfully engaged the larger enemy force and produced shock waves all the way up their command structure. He was not victorious everywhere but then that had not been the point; Frimont would now proceed to tie up his troops against Suchet rather than sending them anywhere else. In this manner, the first few days of operations along the Alpine front began.

Learning of Napoleon's victory in Belgium, Suchet decided to gamble on his opponent's morale and dramatically change the state of affairs along the frontier. At Conflans on June 28th, Suchet engaged and seriously defeated Frimont's II Corps under General Bubna and drove it away with little loss. This battle frightened the Austrian general and, despite his numerical superiority, he fell back hurriedly, leaving the doorway to southern Switzerland and northern Italy wide open. Following up his success, Suchet pressed forward with his smaller force taking a rear guard near Geneva and in general preventing Frimont from gathering his battered troops together. Schwarzenberg, the allied commander in chief, shifted part of the Army of the Rhine south into Switzerland to compensate which had the happy effect of relieving at least some pressure elsewhere along the French frontier. When Napoleon advanced into Alsace, he would find the Piedmontese frontier calm and the French flag planted on allied soil instead of the other way around.

The only other active theater of war was along the Rhine where General Wrede and his Bavarian corps had crossed the frontier at Saarbrucken on June 10th and had marched in a southwestern direction with the vague target of the city of Nancy. Mont St. Jean and Ohain changed all that. Outside of Morhange, this brave but mediocre general received word that Napoleon had been victorious and suddenly all thought of advance disappeared into the mist. Halting just long enough to collect some supplies and harried all the way by bitter French peasants (Bavarians were especially brutal looters), he retraced his steps back to the river in an ultimately disorganized effort to escape back into the arms of Schwarzenberg's mighty host. Like the British at Lexington during the American Revolution, the French peasantry poured out to see them off with musket balls and pitch forks. The Bavarians were very happy to put most of France behind them.

General Schwarzenberg had planned for the concentric attacks to begin around June 27th but his natural caution and fear of Napoleon forced him to delay his object. Emperor Francis of Austria, keeping in constant touch with his field commander, had warned him before the campaign had started that the army was not something to be used without the utmost discretion. Austria was even more bankrupt than she had been before and no war in France was worth the possibility that the rest of the empire would collapse because a general had risked, and lost, the last viable army that the country could throw together. Working under such a restraint, Schwarzenberg was understandably hesitant to launch any form of attack that might trigger a full scale Napoleonic counterattack; he had seen the French emperor in action in 1814 with an army of 40,000 men. What would he do with 140,000 men? The thought wore on the Austrian general and he sent orders for Wrede to retreat (which he had already begun to do) and for the offensive to be postponed at least until a clearer picture became available of the extent of the allied loss and until the tardy Russians arrived.

The Russian army under General Barclay was a day out of Wurzburg when the first news of the battles of Mont St. Jean and Ohain were heard. Interestingly, the accounts of the battles were fairly accurate though a detailed description of the burning of Brussels was included also which, of course, had not happened. Unimpressed by rumors, Barclay kept moving west and at the same time making enemies wherever he went. Cossacks swarmed over the normally quiet German countryside and looted and pillaged as if they were in an enemy land. Here, too, stragglers began to vanish during the night and a few reprisals took place that only served to make relations worse. Two days later, the rumors of Mont St. Jean and Ohain were confirmed as true and Barclay halted his strung out army to concentrate and await further orders. News of Napoleon marching for Alsace had brought the entire allied war machine to a crashing halt.

Though large, the Russian army probably scared more allies than Frenchmen. This is not to say that the troops were not good because they were. The real problem many of the allies, including Schwarzenberg, knew was that the Russian command structure was in pain at the moment and not likely to recover soon. Barclay was the commander and he was a good general. However, his officers hated him because they thought of him as a foreigner in their midst. His unpopularity hampered operations and led to the Russian army moving at a crawl during their marches. Still, he was the best Russia had available. The finest Russian leader, Bagration, had been killed at Borodino, Kutusov, the hero of the retreat from Moscow, was also dead and Bennigsen, the leader who had been crushed at Friedland, was a broken man. The Russians simply had no choice of leader but they could and did interfere with Barclay and delay or even ignore his plans. The rift in the Russian army was serious enough to disrupt the campaign and this fact made many reluctant to fight with them.

*   *   *

For most of the French army, the twentieth of June was a day of leisure. Bruised but proud, the Army of the North at Ohain had earned a rest and Napoleon was more than pleased to let them have it. At the moment, the only troops running around were mounted and these were kept busy chasing the Prussian rearguard while General Exelmans of the right wing moved north to head them off. Grouchy was in full communication with his commander now, no doubt due to the chastising he had taken from the various dispatches the Emperor had sent him. However, Napoleon in victory was a generous Napoleon and in the end he simply told Grouchy to take control of the cavalry and some infantry and keep the pursuit of the Prussian army going. The right wing commander, relieved at this new assignment, returned to his more normal command and took control with vigor. Capably organizing the efforts of the chasing cavalry corps, he directed the pursuers to press more on the Prussian right flank than on the left in order to shift their axis of retreat to the south and into the arms of Exelmans. A sharp encounter south of Louvain indicated where the Prussians were (the French, in time honored fashion, having lost them in the night) and Grouchy reported the action immediately to Napoleon who instructed him to head them off farther east. Thus began the French pursuit.

On the morning of the 21st, the Army of the North moved east leaving the battlefields of its fame behind. Marching for Liege, Napoleon hoped to block the Prussian escape route and force the rest of the army to surrender before he moved south to meet the expected attack from the army of Schwarzenberg and his German allies. At this point, Grouchy responded to the role he was always intended for. Chasing hard with his cavalry corps (the heaviest of which was Exelmans' dragoons) and supported by Reille's infantry corps, he frequently got past the Prussians and, despite the skill the latter displayed in their withdrawal, managed to erode them by the constant ambushes and incursions along their line of retreat. Vandamme's and Gerard's corps, the two in best shape overall, were directed on Maastricht which forced the Prussians to change their route of march and try and cross the Maas river farther north. This delay allowed Grouchy to slip more troops around them though a short engagement at Hasselt let everyone know that the remnants of Blucher's army still had some fight in them.

Thielemann's corps had by this time already crossed the Maas and was retreating quickly for the Rhine where its commander intended to meet up with General Kleist near Coblenz and thus mass what was left of the Prussian army into one force; Kleist, like Thielemann, was in no mood to fight.

General Zieten, the commander of the shattered Prussian army by force of personality, was fast seeing his force disintegrate. Every minor engagement caused more desertions and the general lack of food and ammunition was weakening the soldiers that stayed with the colors; the Prussian train had been amongst the first things captured by Exelmans' dragoons. Grouchy's veteran troopers rarely pressed an attack but they did just enough for the Prussians to lose rearguards and flank guards almost with regularity. It was clear that Grouchy knew his business as the constant pressure was doing more to destroy Zieten's army than any pitched battle. Each morning he found the army to be a few hundred less and discipline was cracking as the troops starved. The villagers had taken flight in the area while others, tired of the depredations of Blucher's men, took up arms against them and made the nights unsafe. The engagement at Hasselt was probably the last uprising of Prussian arms, he thought, and from there, hoping to put the Maas in between him and Grouchy, he headed for Maastricht. Fortune finally smiled on him. A group of lost cavalry met up with his retreating troops and they told him that the French were in Tongres to the south and thus in striking distance of Maastricht. Based on this news he headed to another crossing point that provided protection and this was the city of Roermond, a place that had the added advantage of allowing him to cross one river and avoid another. Taking what was left of his troops towards there, he unfortunately ran into Grouchy again at the town of Dilsen where the latter, at last getting far enough ahead of the enemy, finally barred the way to Roermond with his cavalry. This was bad news. Worse news was that Reille's reinforced infantry corps was in pursuit behind them after having very quickly dealt with the demoralized garrison left in Hasselt with little artillery for its defense.

There was still one more hope. His scouts having discovered a workable bridge over the Maas only two miles from his current position, he boldly planned to make a dash for this bridge and blow it before the French could cross. In desperate times sometimes a very desperate plan is needed and the remaining troops, encouraged and ready, prepared for what many expected to be the run of their life. Playing for time, Zieten deployed all that was left of his guns against Grouchy's horse and then slipped his men eastwards towards the small bridge over the Maas available near Stokkem. To Grouchy's discredit, the ruse worked for a while and Zieten's men were able to get a good head start on the static French cavalry. However, though it was getting late in the day, the marshal, once he realized what was happening, acted with a very unexpected roar of energy and ordered the greater part of Exelmans' corps to attack the fleeing enemy columns and hold them onto the battlefield. Roder's cavalry, the only real force left intact from the battle of Ohain, reacted with desperate bravery but the hearts of the Prussians simply were no longer in the fight. Held at first, the French horse broke through and was able to cut off about half of Zieten's remaining soldiers before the others burned the bridge over the river and slipped away to safety. For the last remnants of Blucher's army on the west bank, the Maas was their last armed stop. The next morning, those that had not already surrendered did so and brought to a close the campaign in Belgium.

Napoleon was well pleased with Grouchy's display of the talent but the time was done for the French to be chasing the Prussians. Having arrived at Liege on the 24th, he issued orders for his corps to shift their operations south so that he could maneuver his army in the direction of Strasbourg and be placed centrally against any incursion that could be made by Schwarzenberg. The Emperor considered, correctly to be sure, that the Prussians were finished as a fighting force for the campaign and, without Blucher, not liable to rally any time soon. One army was out of the way.

Over the next few days, dispatches arrived from spies in Brussels and these informed him that Wellington and his broken army had retreated for Ostend and from there would be embarking for a return trip to England. It was noted that the Duke, riding ahead of his troops, had boarded the seventy four gun ship of the line, the Northumberland, with a heavy heart and had not said a word to anyone. The Dutch and Belgian units, realizing that their futures very much hung in the balance, retreated in separate directions and both countries sent emissaries asking for leniency on the part of Napoleon and for him to split their countries apart once more. Napoleon told Soult that he could only be impressed by countries that had so recently and gallantly fought him to be asking for favors already. Soult simply said that it was the way of the wind.

Napoleon had made another calculated risk by not pushing against the remnants of Wellington's army as he reasoned that, like Soult at Corunna against Sir John Moore's retreating army, he would be too late to change anything that was going to happen and that his presence was needed elsewhere in the country. Again, his decision was the right one. The Anglo-Dutch army split up in many directions and only the Duke's loyal troops followed him all the way to Ostend. Napoleon certainly would have liked to have taken this force but time and experience played both for and against him. With the biggest threat along the border in Alsace, he had to march there and forget about Wellington for the time being. On the other hand, his prediction that the war party in London would fall as a result of the disaster proved quite correct. Just as after Austerlitz when Pitt's map of Europe was ceremonially rolled up, the Belgian campaign caused an upheaval in British politics and a peace party, formerly known as the Opposition party, came on board to try and bring an end to a very costly and clearly losing effort. Like Pitt, Lord Castlereagh, the foreign minister, was broken at the thought of the disaster and, in a fit of self doubt, would commit suicide before the year was out.

The new British government reacted quickly. A bit of bad blood was flowing at the time which was due in part to the fact that Lord Castlereagh's government had intentionally misrepresented much about Napoleon's return and styled it as a military coup rather than what it really was. This form of trickery was not appreciated by a great many members of Parliament mostly because more than a few admired the mighty French emperor and they also felt that France should be left to its own devices. One minor point was that the Bourbons simply did not seem worth fighting over. About the only thing they did support and uphold was the protection of English commerce, an essential point, but with the strength and condition of the Royal Navy the potential French threat was minimized.

With the destruction of their field army fresh in mind, the new government passed changes relevant to the war raging on the continent. Subsidies for foreign powers were cut off, the cowardly and expensive Bourbons officially ignored and they voted to recognize Napoleon as the head of state in France. These were monumental steps and, realistically, the right ones to take. Napoleon had offered peace to the allies at Chatillon and had been rebuffed. Now, with the armies of Wellington and Blucher annihilated in Belgium, what possible gain could be made in prolonging the war? Indeed, Sir Samuel Burdett had put it best in March when he had asked if it was England's duty to continue the struggle for the Bourbon kings for another twenty years. That this reason was only a pale fiction is besides the point. The fact remained that Europe as a whole needed to take a deep breath and end the bloodshed before everyone went bankrupt.

These steps in the British Parliament led to feelers being extended across the channel to Napoleon's "government on horseback" marching along the countryside of France. The Emperor, having had a chance to recuperate during the campaign, was exhibiting his old energy again and his experienced and weathered eye noted a bit of truth written on the lines of the secret messages he had in front of him. England wanted peace, Prussia had no choice, Austria was wavering and the Russians were simply Russians. Perhaps this was the moment he had been waiting for after all of these years. Maybe now the monarchies of Europe, forced as they were to recognize him, would finally accept France for what it had become and leave the competitions to be made on more friendly terms much like the smuggling along the channel which had been going on for so many years despite peace or war.

As the Army of the North arrived in eastern France, the swell of replacements for the regiments to rebuild their strength along with supplies for the army, including many missing uniform items, began to arrive. Amongst the latter, interestingly, was a large shipment of shakos for the 1st Chasseurs who, because of the suddenness of the campaign, had suffered indignity in being forced to wear their Bourbon leather helmets during all of the fighting. It was relief that they received the new shakos and they all gave thanks to the Emperor except a distraught Colonel Simoneau who, right before the campaign, had sat for a portrait of himself in his leather helmet; his officers would remember his remarks with advantage.

The spirits of the soldiers was also on a mighty high. Eastern France, a traditionally good recruiting ground for the army, welcomed the heroes of Belgium to its cities and many were the peasants who came out to help the army move its wagons or give the thirsty soldiers something to drink. These people, having witnessed Bavarian looting first hand when Wrede's men marched through, were more than ready to help Napoleon in whatever he had in mind. At the very least, they could help to feed his ever hungry army. Many an officer would write in his memoirs the exuberant feelings given to them by these towns and villages and remember the time as a particularly fine one. Probably the best part about their writings was what happened just after the march. While the Army of the North met up with Rapp's corps in Alsace and commanded a central position against any invader, Napoleon agreed first to an armistice and, after quite a few break neck trips to the coast and back, a formal meeting to discuss a general peace. The campaign of 1815, barely a few weeks old, would now come to a close.

Inevitably, negotiations were a long and dragged out affair but in August of 1815 the government of France, embodied in Napoleon, was able to announce to the people of France what would become known as the Peace of Rouen. Czar Alexander removed his men from Germany, a tremendous relief for everyone involved, and Austria, suffering from cash flow problems, readily agreed to taking her men back home leaving the larger German states intact. France was ecstatic. The whole country, cautious at first when the Emperor had returned, then resigned when war became inevitable, was able to collectively exhale and thoroughly enjoy the news. Paris was once more allowed to bequeath wreaths of gold to be added to the eagles of the regiments that had served at Lasne and Mont St. Jean and, in spite of the price, the feelings were real enough. The Peace of Rouen had brought a sigh of relief throughout Europe and though costly, the peace was the proudest in French history and the troops could march back to their homes with pride and dignity to stack their muskets and spin their yarns. The active fighting of the Napoleonic Wars was over.

*   *   *

In late September of 1815, Napoleon traveled by coach to the port city of Rochefort to oversee the launching of a new two decked ship of the line, the Glorieux. Adorned with the usual garlands for good luck and proudly viewed by the men who constructed her, the event was one not to be missed in town, especially since the Emperor was in personal attendance. Escorted by the magnificently accoutered Chasseurs of the Guard, he was greeted with great enthusiasm and ceremoniously given the keys to the city. Being that the port was located within the heart of the Royalist Vendee district, Napoleon sensed that his welcome was one of resignation and relief which were certainly good first steps on the road to acceptance and reconciliation.

Aboard the seventy four gun ship of the line Allysicas, the Emperor met with Contre Amiral Crioux, one of the few successful naval officers of the nation, and spoke to him at length about the state of the French navy. With him was his usual entourage including the ever disparaging Soult, Amiral Decres and his new Minister of Police, General Savary; this commander had taken over from the recently executed Fouche who had played the game of treason one time too many.

"It is a pleasure having you here, sire," Crioux said as they walked along the spotless decks of the famous warship. "It has been a long time."

Napoleon took in a deep breath, the salt air was fresh and alive. It matched his mood. Ever since Emperor Francis of Austria had congratulated him and returned his son (the threat of exploiting Suchet's gains in Italy and attacking Schwarzenberg in Germany having paid off), he was in better spirits than he had been for a long time. He had not seen his wife, Marie Louise, in over a year and she had rebuffed every attempt to renew their relationship which angered him but, since he had his son, it was something he could live with. Another factor why he did not press the issue with her was that another lady had reentered his life. The Emperor's "Polish wife," Marie Walewska, took up residence in Paris with her son and Napoleon suddenly but happily had two offspring to care for. It was a wonderful time for an emperor and father.

"How many other ships are waiting to be launched, Crioux?" he asked.

"Three sire, the three decked Ville de Vienne, the Tonnant and the Venitien. We should have them constructed and ready to sail by summer of next year," Crioux replied quickly. He knew from previous conversations that the Emperor wanted fast and accurate answers.

Napoleon nodded as he scanned his ships in the harbor. "And how goes the training?"

Crioux smiled as the whole gamut of amusing mishaps swept past his eyes. "Better than expected sire, the crews learn a good deal faster without the threat of English cruisers always on the horizon."

"We gave them enough of our ships," the Emperor laughed. He returned to a serious tone. "But with Anvers again part of France and the alliance with Holland in place, we will be able to replace them."

"Indeed, sire. The peace will enable us to return the navy to a proper strength and ability." Crioux paused. "Will we face the English again?"

Napoleon took a step forward and placed his foot on the sliding carriage of a thirty six pound carronade. "It is not my wish but I will not sit idly by if they challenge our commerce on the sea or attempt to take our possessions. We have a peace treaty and I hope they keep to it. I would like to be able to raise my son without a war at my doorstep."

Crioux fell quiet and passed a glance at Decres who only shrugged. "We will be ready, sire."

"Good Crioux. Convince me and maybe I will not have you fight with the Spanish." He grinned. "Of course, they do not have much of a fleet left anyway. Did I tell you of the letter I received from Ferdinand?"

"No sire."

The Emperor paused and looked at Soult. The chief of staff actually broke out in a genuine smile and said, "Let us just say that they did not expect the letter to go to France."

Crioux nodded, an understanding expression on his face. "They did not have much faith, did they?"

A naval captain walked up and saluted to Crioux. "Sir, the Glorieux is ready to be launched."

As the admiral gestured to him, Napoleon stepped off the carronade. "Then let us watch the latest addition to the fleet, gentlemen."

THE ARMY OF THE NORTH AT THE BATTLE OF MONT ST. JEAN (WATERLOO)

Emperor Napoleon Bonaparte, Commander in Chief

Imperial Guard		18800

Grenadier Division	(4 Regt., 7 Battalions)	
Chasseur Division	(4 Regt., 8 Battalions)	
Young Guard Division	(4 Regt., 8 Battalions)	
Light Cavalry Division	(2 Regt., 10 Squadrons)	
Heavy Cavalry Division	(2 Regt., 8 Squadrons)	
Artillery	(14 Gun Co., 104 Cannon)	

I Army Corps		19800

1st Infantry Division	(4 Regt., 8 Battalions)	
2nd Infantry Division	(4 Regt., 9 Battalions)	
3rd Infantry Division	(4 Regt., 8 Battalions)	
4th Infantry Division	(4 Regt., 8 Battalions)	
1st Cavalry Division	(4 Regt., 11 Squadrons)	
Artillery	(6 Gun Co., 46 Cannon)	

II Army Corps   16500

5th Infantry Division	(4 Regt., 9 Battalions)
6th Infantry Division	(4 Regt., 13 Battalions)
9th Infantry Division	(4 Regt., 11 Battalions)
2nd Cavalry Division	(4 Regt., 15 Squadrons)
Artillery	(5 Gun Co., 38 Cannon)

VI Army Corps   10600

19th Infantry Division	(4 Regt., 9 Battalions)
20th Infantry Division	(3 Regt., 6 Battalions)
3rd Cavalry Division	(3 Regt., 9 Squadrons)
5th Cavalry Division	(3 Regt., 11 Squadrons)
Artillery	(6 Gun Co., 42 Cannon)

III Reserve Cavalry Corps   3800

11th Cavalry Division	(4 Regt., 13 Squadrons)
12th Cavalry Division	(4 Regt., 12 Squadrons)
Artillery	(2 Gun Co., 12 Cannon)

IV Reserve Cavalry Corps   3000

13th Cavalry Division	(4 Regt., 11 Squadrons)
14th Cavalry Division	(4 Regt., 13 Squadrons)
Artillery	(2 Gun Co., 12 Cannon)

Total French Troops   72500

THE ANGLO-DUTCH ARMY AT THE BATTLE OF MONT ST. JEAN (WATERLOO)

Field Marshal Arthur, Duke of Wellington, Commander in Chief

Army HQ   800

Support Troops

I Army Corps   27000

1st Infantry Division	(4 Battalions)
3rd Infantry Division	(13 Battalions)
2nd Dutch-Belgian Infantry Division	(10 Battalions)
3rd Dutch-Belgian Infantry Division	(12 Battalions)
Artillery	(8 Gun Btry., 56 Cannon)

II Army Corps   10400

2nd Infantry Division	(12 Battalions)
4th Infantry Division	(3 Battalions)
Artillery	(3 Gun Btry., 18 Cannon)

Army Reserve		21500
5th Infantry Division	(12 Battalions)	
6th Infantry Division	(7 Battalions)	
Brunswick Contingent	(8 Battalions, 5 Squadrons)	
Nassau Reserve Contingent	(3 Battalions)	
Artillery	(7 Gun Btry., 46 Cannon)	

Cavalry Corps		14500
1st Cavalry Brigade	(9 Squadrons)	
2nd Cavalry Brigade	(9 Squadrons)	
3rd Cavalry Brigade	(11 Squadrons)	
4th Cavalry Brigade	(9 Squadrons)	
5th Cavalry Brigade	(6 Squadrons)	
6th Cavalry Brigade	(10 Squadrons)	
7th Cavalry Brigade	(7 Squadrons)	
Hanoverian Cavalry Brigade	(4 Squadrons)	
Dutch-Belgian Cavalry Division	(23 Squadrons)	
Artillery	(7 Gun Btry., 43 Cannon)	

Total Anglo-Dutch Troops		74200

THE ARMY OF THE NORTH
AT THE
BATTLE OF OHAIN

Emperor Napoleon Bonaparte, Commander in Chief

Imperial Guard—General of Division Count Drouot

    Division of Grenadiers—General of Division Count Friant   3600
        1st Brigade
            1st Grenadiers (2 Bat.)
            2nd Grenadiers (2 Bat.)
            Brigade Artillery—8 Cannon
        2nd Brigade
            3rd Grenadiers (2 bat.)
            4th Grenadiers (1 bat.)
            Brigade Artillery—8 Cannon[1]

    Division of Chasseurs—General of Division Count Morand   3700
        1st Brigade
            1st Chasseurs (2 bat.)
            2nd Chasseurs (2 bat.)
            Brigade Artillery—8 Cannon
        2nd Brigade
            3rd Chasseurs (2 bat.)
            4th Chasseurs (2 bat.)
            Brigade Artillery—8 Cannon[2]

Young Guard Division—General of Division Count Duhesme 2900
    1st Brigade—General of Brigade Chevalier Chartrand
        1st Tirailleurs (2 bat.)
        1st Voltigeurs (2 bat.)
        Brigade Artillery—8 Cannon[3]
    2nd Brigade—General of Brigade Baron Guye
        3rd Tirailleurs (2 bat.)
        3rd Voltigeurs (2 bat.)
        Brigade Artillery—8 Cannon[4]

Light Cavalry Division—General of Division Count Lefebvre-Desnouettes 1900
    1st Brigade—General of Division Baron F. Lallemand
        Chasseurs a cheval (5 sqd.)
        Brigade Artillery—3 Cannon
    2nd Brigade—General of Division Baron de Colbert-Chabanais
        Lancers (5 sqd.)
        Brigade Artillery—6 Cannon

Heavy Cavalry Division—General of Division Count Guyot 1400
    1st Brigade—Colonel Venieres[5]
        Grenadiers a cheval (4 sqd.)
        Brigade Artillery—6 Cannon
    2nd Brigade—Colonel Hoffmayer[6]
        Dragoons (4 sqd.)
        Brigade Artillery—6 Cannon
    3rd Brigade—Captain Dyonnet
        Elite Gendarmes (One company)

Artillery Reserve—General of Brigade Baron H. Lallemand 800
    32 Cannon

Imperial Guard Engineers and Auxiliaries—General of Division Baron Haxo 900

Imperial Guard Totals—15,200 men and 101 cannon

I Army Corps—General of Division Drouet, Count d'Erlon

1st Infantry Division—General of Brigade Quiot du Passage[7] 3000
    1st Brigade—General of Brigade Quiot du Passage
        54th Ligne (2 bat.)
        55th Ligne (2 bat.)
    2nd Brigade—General of Brigade Baron Bourgeois
        28th Ligne (2 bat.)
        105th Ligne (2 bat.)
    Divisional Artillery—8 Cannon

2nd Infantry Division—General of Division Baron Donzelot   4000
 1st Brigade—General of Brigade Baron Schmitz
   13th Legere (3 bat.)
   17th Ligne (2 bat.)
 2nd Brigade—Colonel Trupel[8]
   19th Ligne (2 bat.)
   51st Ligne (2 bat.)
 Divisional Artillery—6 Cannon

3rd Infantry Division—General of Division Baron Marcognet 2800
 1st Brigade—General of Brigade Nogues
   21st Ligne (2 bat.)
   46th Ligne (2 bat.)
 2nd Brigade—General of Brigade Baron Grenier
   25th Ligne (2 bat.)
   45th Ligne (2 bat.)
 Divisional Artillery—5 Cannon

4th Infantry Division—General of Division Count Durutte   3000
 1st Brigade—General of Brigade Chevalier Pegot
   8th Ligne (2 bat.)
   29th Ligne (2 bat.)
 2nd Brigade—General of Brigade Brue
   85th Ligne (2 bat.)
   95th Ligne (2 bat.)
 Divisional Artillery—8 Cannon

1st Cavalry Division—General of Division Baron Jacquinot 1500
 1st Brigade - General of Brigade Baron Bruno
   7th Hussars (3 sqd.)
   3rd Chasseurs (3 sqd.)
 2nd Brigade—General of Brigade Baron Gobrecht
   3rd Lancers (3 sqd.)
   4th Lancers (2 sqd.)
 Divisional Artillery—6 Cannon

Corps Artillery Reserve—General of Brigade Desales   200
 7 Cannon

Corps Engineers—General of Brigade Baron Garbe   200

I Army Corps Totals—14,700 men and 40 Cannon

II Army Corps—General of Division Count Reille

    5th Infantry Division—General of Division Baron Bachelu[9]   2000
        1st Brigade—General of Brigade Baron Husson
            3rd Ligne (2 bat.)
            61st Ligne (2 bat.)
        2nd Brigade—General of Brigade Baron Campi
            72nd Ligne (2 bat.)
            108th Ligne (3 bat.)
        Divisional Artillery—8 Cannon

    6th Infantry Division—General of Division Prince Jerome Bonaparte[10]   4100
        1st Brigade—Colonel Despans-Cubieres[11]
            1st Legere (3 bat.)
            2nd Legere (4 bat.)
        2nd Brigade—General of Brigade Baron Soye
            1st Ligne (3 bat.)
            2nd Ligne (3 bat.)
        Divisional Artillery—8 Cannon

    9th Infantry Division—General of Division Count Foy   2800
        1st Brigade—General of Brigade Baron Gauthier
            92nd Ligne (2 bat.)
            93rd Ligne (3 bat.)
        2nd Brigade—General of Brigade Baron Jamin
            100th Ligne (3 bat.)
            4th Legere (3 bat.)
        Divisional Artillery—8 Cannon

    2nd Cavalry Division—General of Division Baron Pire   1700
        1st Brigade—General of Brigade Baron Huber
            1st Chasseurs (4 sqd.)
            6th Chasseurs (4 sqd.)
        2nd Brigade—General of Brigade Baron Wathiez
            5th Lancers (3 sqd.)
            6th Lancers (4 sqd.)
        Divisional Artillery—6 Cannon

    Corps Artillery Reserve—General of Brigade Baron le Pelletier   200
        7 Cannon

    Corps Engineers—General of Brigade Baron Richemont   400

II Army Corps Totals—11,200 men and 37 Cannon

VI Army Corps—General of Division Mouton, Count of Lobau

    19th Infantry Division—General of Division Baron Simmer   3600

1st Brigade—General of Brigade Baron de Bellair
    5th Ligne (2 bat.)
    11th Ligne (2 bat.)
2nd Brigade—General of Brigade Chevalier Thevenet
    27th Ligne (2 bat.)
    84th Ligne (2 bat.)
Divisional Artillery—8 Cannon

20th Infantry Division—General of Division Baron Jeanin   2500
  1st Brigade—General of Brigade Chevalier Bony
    5th Legere (2 bat.)
    10th Ligne (2 bat.)
  2nd Brigade—General of Brigade Count Tromelin
    107th Ligne (2 bat.)
  Divisional Artillery—7 Cannon

3rd Cavalry Division—General of Division Baron Domon[12]   1100
  1st Brigade—General of Brigade Baron Dommanget
    4th Chasseurs (3 sqd.)
    9th Chasseurs (3 sqd.)
  2nd Brigade—General of Brigade Baron Vinot
    12th Chasseurs (3 sqd.)
  Divisional Artillery—6 Cannon
  1st Brigade—General of Brigade Baron de Bellair
    5th Ligne (2 bat.)
    11th Ligne (2 bat.)
5th Cavalry Division—General of Division Baron Subervie[13]   1400
  1st Brigade—General of Brigade Count L. de Colbert
    1st Lancers (4 sqd.)
    2nd Lancers (4 sqd.)
  2nd Brigade—General of Brigade Chevalier Merlin
    11th Chasseurs (3 sqd.)
  Divisional Artillery—6 Cannon

Corps Artillery Reserve—General of Division Baron Noury   400
  14 Cannon

Corps Engineers—General of Brigade Sabatier   100

VI Army Corps Totals—9,100 men and 41 Cannon

III Reserve Cavalry Corps—General of Division Kellermann, Count of Valmy

11th Cavalry Division—General of Division Baron l'Heritier   1300
  1st Brigade—General of Brigade Baron Picquet
    2nd Dragoons (4 sqd.)
    7th Dragoons (4 sqd.)

2nd Brigade—General of Brigade Baron Guiton
    8th Cuirassiers (3 sqd.)
    11th Cuirassiers (2 sqd.)
Divisional Artillery—5 Cannon
12th Cavalry Division—General of Division Baron d'Hurbal   1100
  1st Brigade—General of Brigade Baron Blancard
    1st Carabiniers (3 sqd.)
    2nd Carabiniers (3 sqd.)
  2nd Brigade—Colonel Grandjean[15]
    2nd Cuirassiers (2 sqd.)
    3rd Cuirassiers (4 sqd.)
  Divisional Artillery—6 Cannon

III Reserve Cavalry Corps Totals—2,400 men and 11 cannon

IV Reserve Cavalry Corps—General of Division Count Milhaud

13th Cavalry Division—General of Division Watier, Count of Saint-Alphonse   900
  1st Brigade—General of Brigade Baron Dubios
    1st Cuirassiers (4 sqd.)
    4th Cuirassiers (3 sqd.)
  2nd Brigade—General of Brigade Travers, Baron of Jever
    7th Cuirassiers (2 sqd.)
    12th Cuirassiers (2 sqd.)
  Divisional Artillery—6 Cannon

14th Cavalry Division—General of Division Baron Delort   1000
  1st Brigade—General of Brigade Baron Farine du Creux
    5th Cuirassiers (3 sqd.)
    10th Cuirassiers (3 sqd.)
  2nd Brigade—General of Brigade Baron Vial
    6th Cuirassiers (3 sqd.)
    9th Cuirassiers (4 sqd.)
  Divisional Artillery—6 Cannon

IV Reserve Cavalry Corps Totals—1,900 men and 12 cannon

Army of the North Totals—54,500 men and 242 cannon

---

[1]   Line Artillery

[2]   Line Artillery

[3]   Line Artillery

[4]   Line Artillery

[5]   Brigade commander Jamin killed on June 18

[6]   Brigade commander Letort killed on June 15

[7]   Quiot took command in the absence of General Allix

[8]   Brigade commander Aulard killed on June 18

[9]   This division, due to its battered condition, was the army reserve and prisoner guards

[10] General Guilleminot took command of the division during the battle

[11] Brigade commander Bauduin killed on June 18

[12] This division attached from III Army Corps

[13] This division attached from I Reserve Cavalry Corps

[14] Includes 6 line horse guns from the Imperial Guard

[15] Brigade commander Donop missing on June 18

THE ROYAL PRUSSIAN ARMY
OF THE LOWER RHINE
AT THE BATTLE OF OHAIN

Field Marshall Prince Blucher von Wahlstadt, Commander in Chief

I Army Corps—Lieutenant General von Zieten II

    1st Infantry Brigade—Major General von Steinmetz   4000
        Infantry Regiment #12 (3 bat.)
        Infantry Regiment #24 (3 bat.)
        1st Westphalian Landwehr Infantry Regiment (3 bat.)

    2nd Infantry Brigade—Major General von Pirch II   4100
        Infantry Regiment #6 (3 bat.)
        Infantry Regiment #28 (3 bat.)
        2nd Westphalian Landwehr Infantry Regiment (3 bat.)

    3rd Infantry Brigade—Major General von Jagow   5200
        Infantry Regiment #7 (3 bat.)
        Infantry Regiment #29 (3 bat.)
        3rd Westphalian Landwehr Infantry Regiment (3 bat.)

    4th Infantry Brigade—Major General Count von Donnersmarck   700
        4th Westphalian Landwehr Infantry Regiment (1 bat.)

    I Army Corps Reserve Cavalry—Lieutenant General von Roeder

1st Cavalry Brigade—Major General von Treskow II   1900
     2nd Dragoon Regiment (3 sqd.)
     5th Dragoon Regiment (4 sqd.)
     4th Hussar Regiment (3 sqd.)
     3rd Uhlan Regiment (3 sqd.)

2nd Cavalry Brigade—Major von Folgersberg[1]   500
     1st Kurmark Landwehr Cavalry Regiment (3 sqd.)
     2nd Kurmark Landwehr Cavalry Regiment (4 sqd.)

I Army Corps Artillery—Lieutenant Colonel Lehmann   1600
     72 Cannon

I Army Corps Totals—18,000 men and 72 cannon

II Army Corps—Major General von Pirch I

5th Infantry Brigade—Major General Count von Tippelskirch   4600
     Infantry Regiment #2 (3 bat.)
     Infantry Regiment #25 (3 bat.)
     5th Westphalian Landwehr Infantry Regiment (3 bat.)

6th Infantry Brigade—Major General von Krafft   4200
     Infantry Regiment #9 (3 bat.)
     Infantry Regiment #26 (3 bat.)
     1st Elbe Landwehr Infantry Regiment (3 bat.)

8th Infantry Brigade—Major General von Bose   2500
     Infantry Regiment #21 (3 bat.)
     Infantry Regiment #23 (3 bat.)
     3rd Elbe Landwehr Infantry Regiment (3 bat.)

II Army Corps Reserve Cavalry—Major General von Wahlen-Jurgass

1st Cavalry Brigade—Colonel von Schmiedeberg2   1300
     1st Dragoon Regiment (4 sqd.)
     6th Dragoon Regiment (4 sqd.)
     2nd Uhlan Regiment (4 sqd.)

2nd Cavalry Brigade—Lieutenant Colonel von Sohr   1000
     3rd Hussar Regiment (4 sqd.)
     5th Hussar Regiment (4 sqd.)

3rd Cavalry Brigade—Colonel Count von Schulenberg   700
     4th Kurmark Landwehr Cavalry Regiment (6 sqd.)
     5th Kurmark Landwehr cavalry Regiment (4 sqd.)

Attached Cavalry[3]   800
    11th Hussar Regiment (3 sqd.)
    1st Elbe Landwehr Cavalry Regiment (4 sqd.)

II Army Corps Artillery—Lieutenant Colonel von Rohl   1400
    64 Cannon

II Army Corps Totals—16,500 men and 64 cannon

IV Army Corps—General of Infantry Count Bulow von Dennewitz

13th Infantry Brigade—Lieutenant General von Hake   6800
    Infantry Regiment #10 (3 bat.)
    2nd Neumark Landwehr Infantry Regiment (3 bat.)
    3rd Neumark Landwehr Infantry Regiment (3 bat.)

14th Infantry Brigade—Colonel von Funck[4]   6900
    Infantry Regiment #11 (3 bat.)
    1st Pommeranian Landwehr Infantry Regiment (3 bat.)
    2nd Pommeranian Landwehr Infantry Regiment (3 bat.)

15th Infantry Brigade—Major General von Losthin   4200
    Infantry Regiment #18 (3 bat.)
    3rd Silesian Landwehr Infantry Regiment (3 bat.)
    4th Silesian Landwehr Infantry Regiment (3 bat.)

16th Infantry Brigade—Colonel von Hiller   4400
    Infantry Regiment #15 (3 bat.)
    1st Silesian Landwehr Infantry Regiment (3 bat.)
    2nd Silesian Landwehr Infantry Regiment (3 bat.)

IV Army Corps Reserve Cavalry—General of Cavalry Prince Wilhelm of Prussia

1st Cavalry Brigade—Colonel von Eicke[5]   1200
    6th Hussar Regiment (4 sqd.)
    1st West Prussian Uhlan Regiment (4 sqd.)

2nd Cavalry Brigade—Major von Colomb[6]   400
    8th Hussar Regiment (3 sqd.)

3rd Cavalry Brigade—Major General von Sydow   1800
    1st Neumark Landwehr Cavalry Regiment (3 sqd.)
    2nd Neumark Landwehr Cavalry Regiment (3 sqd.)
    1st Pommeranian Landwehr Cavalry Regiment (3 sqd.)
    2nd Pommeranian Landwehr Cavalry Regiment (3 sqd.)
    1st Silesian Landwehr Cavalry Regiment (4 sqd.)

Attached Cavalry[7]
    2nd Silesian Landwehr Cavalry Regiment (4 sqd.)
    3rd Silesian Landwehr Cavalry Regiment (4 sqd.)

IV Army Corps Artillery—Major von Bardeleben   2200
    86 Cannon

IV Army Corps Totals – 27,900 men and 86 cannon

Royal Prussian Army of the Lower Rhine Totals—62,400 men and 222 cannon

---

[1]   Brigade commander Lutzow captured on June 16
[2]   Brigade commander Thumen killed on June 16
[3]   These units attached to infantry brigades by squadron pairs
[4]   Brigade commander Rijssel not present on June 19
[5]   Brigade commander Schwerin killed on June 18
[6]   Brigade commander Watzdorff killed on June 18
[7]   These units attached to infantry brigades in squadron pairs

BIBLIOGRAPHY

Becke, A. F., *Napoleon and Waterloo*, Greenhill Books, London, 1995.

Brett-James, Antony, *The Hundred Days*, St. Martin's, New York, 1964.

Bowden, Scott, *Armies at Waterloo*, Empire Press, Arlington, 1983.

De Chair, Somerset, *Napoleon on Napoleon*, Cassell, London, 1992.

Elting, John R., *Swords Around A Throne*, Free Press, New York, 1988.

Elting, John R., *Napoleonic Uniforms*, MacMillan, New York, 1993.

Esposito, Brigadier General Vincent J. and Elting, Colonel John R., *A Military History and Atlas of the Napoleonic Wars*, Praeger, New York, 1968.

Fosten, Bryan, *British Foot Guards At Waterloo June 1815*, Almark, Surrey.

Hibbert, Christopher, *Waterloo: Napoleon's Last Campaign*, The New American Library, New York, 1967.

Horsburgh, E.L.S., *Waterloo*, Methuen & Co., London, 1900.

Lachouque, Henry, *The Anatomy of Glory*, Brown University Press, Providence, 1961.

Lachouque, Henry, *Waterloo*, Arms and Armour Press, London, 1972.

Linck, Tony, *Napoleon's Generals*, The Emperor's Press, Chicago, 1994.

Manceron, Claude, *Napoleon Recaptures Paris*, George Allen & Unwin Ltd., London, 1968.

Mann, Michael, *And They Rode On*, Michael Russell (Publishing) Ltd., Salisbury, 1984.

Nash, David, *The Prussian Army*, Almark, London, 1972.

Rothenburg, Gunther E., *The Art of Warfare in the Age of Napoleon*, Indiana University Press, Bloomington, 1980.

Thompson, J.M., *Napoleon's Letters*, J.M. Dent & Sons Ltd., London, 1954.

Wooten, Geoffrey, *Waterloo 1815*, Osprey, London, 1992.

Young, Peter, *Blucher's Army 1813-1815*, Hippocrene Books, New York, 1973.

Made in the USA
Middletown, DE
05 July 2019